A Disorderly House

A Disorderly House

The Brown–Unruh Years
in Sacramento

James R. Mills

Heyday Books, Berkeley

Published by Heyday Books
Box 9145, Berkeley, California 94709

ISBN: 0-930588-34-7

Printed in the United States of America
10 9 8 7 6 5 4 3 2 1

This book is dedicated to the one woman
who will always be to me the most
beautiful thing in the world.

Contents

1

So Help Me God

My way is to begin with the beginning.

Lord Byron

$\mathcal{A}$t high noon on my first day as a member of the California Assembly, I stood with my right hand raised to take the oath of office. I knew I was under the eyes of dozens of powerful lobbyists in the gallery behind me, and what I was thinking about them was,"If you can't eat their food, drink their booze, screw their women, take their money, and then vote against them, you've got no business being up here."

I was being unwillingly reminded of those awful words by the massive form of Jesse Marvin Unruh, which loomed in the corner of my left eye. A few months before that he had so expressed himself when questioned about his letting lobbyists in Sacramento satisfy his allegedly epic appetites for such things.

Unruh, also known as Big Daddy, the obese and voracious chairman of the Assembly Ways and Means Committee, was magnificently arrayed in a powder-blue suit cut in the latest Italian style. It appeared to be made of silk, as did his pale pink shirt and lavender necktie. With his carnal features composed into an uncharacteristic sanctity and his heavy right hand raised, he looked like a dapper three-hundred-pound ogre taking a Boy Scout oath in order to get into a troop so he could eat all the other members.

On that first Monday of 1961, the opening day of my legislative career, it seemed a sacrilege to me that Big Daddy and his code of misconduct should fill my mind and distract me from the solemnity of the occasion. I had been spellbound with reverence at ten minutes to twelve, when I had passed with my wife, Joanna, into the Assembly chamber through the great, carved, black walnut

1

doors, which had been held open for us by two gray-haired sergeants-at-arms, one of whom had then escorted us to the loge chairs reserved for the guests of members. There were two boxes of them behind a curving colonnade of Doric pillars that supported a wide visitors' gallery overhead.

I had sat down for a few minutes, to worship with her in that temple of representative government. Together we'd raised our eyes to the tremendous marble columns that towered up to the ceiling on either side of the speaker's dais. Into their Corinthian capitols, and those of the great pilasters that framed sections of the pale green walls, had been sculpted imperial Roman eagles, to symbolize the sovereign authority of the Legislature of California. The classical splendor of that sanctuary had the same effect upon my spirit as the grandeur of a cathedral, that of inspiring reverence for the institution it houses.

At six minutes to twelve I had moved onto the floor, into the holy of holies, to wander about on the green carpeting among mahogany desks that had been there since the building first opened in 1874. I was roaming in search of the one that had been allocated to me. On the front of each desk was the name of a member printed upon a white card. When I found the one bearing my name, I had reverently lowered my hindquarters onto the green leather upholstery of the walnut swivel chair behind it. Having settled into my proper place, I'd turned to shake hands with my Republican seatmate, Captain Frank Luckel, who, like me, represented a part of the city of San Diego. The captain, a retired naval officer with white shoes and white hair, seemed as venerable as his desk and chair.

My spell of reverence was broken at three minutes to twelve when I saw Big Daddy come hulking into the chamber through a side door on my right. Behind him had trailed a company of retainers. Every person on the floor had turned to watch him moving ponderously across the front of the room to his desk. So overwhelming was his presence that the elected membership of the California Assembly had seemed reduced to a cast of supporting actors and extras.

As he had ebbed into his chair, I'd noticed Sheridan Hegland, the only Democratic assemblyman from San Diego County other than myself, come treading warily across the room toward his desk, the one in front of Captain Luckel's. Heg was one of the most conscientious and honest politicians in California. Unfortunately he was also one of the most nervous, which was why the more militant liberals in the Democratic Party called him Scared-Again Hegland.

It was one minute to twelve when Heg said, "Hi," to Captain Luckel and me and took his seat. He'd fumbled in one coat pocket to fish out a red pack of Pall Mall cigarettes and in another to extract a book of matches.

Arthur Ohnimus, a snowy-haired Yankee patriarch, who had been the chief clerk of the Assembly since before I was born, then mounted the rostrum. I turned to look at the electric clock on the front of the balcony in the chamber as its second hand swept up to show that the time was exactly twelve noon.

Heg fidgeted one of his Pall Malls from his pack to his lips, but he didn't get to light it before Arthur Ohnimus brought down the gravel decisively to begin the session and declared, "The hour of twelve o'clock having arrived, the Assembly will come to order and the clerk will call the roll."

After the reading clerk had called the roster of the members' names and all eighty of us had answered "Here," Arthur Ohnimus had announced, "A quorum is present. Will the members and their guests please rise for the pledge of allegiance to the flag and remain standing for the opening prayer."

After the pledge of allegiance, the chaplain for the previous session, a soft-spoken, elderly Methodist preacher, had prayed, "Almighty God, what canst Thou make of this new year, this new Assembly, this new opportunity to build a better way of life? We pray that an unlimited vision of the future may lead this Assembly to a high destiny of service, so that all of the people of this state will rise up and call its work good."

Arthur Ohnimus had then instructed us, "All of the duly elected members of the Assembly will present themselves at the bar of the Assembly to take the oath of office."

The eighty of us had risen from our ancient swivel chairs and trooped forward to the front of the chamber.

"Please form two ranks facing me," Ohnimus had directed us.

We all lined up, with Jesse Unruh to my left, his bulk again reminding me of his famous statement of principles, as I've reported, and Ohnimus said, "I should like to present to all who are here assembled the Honorable Roger Traynor, Associate Justice of the California Supreme Court, who will administer the oath of office."

A canonical figure in black robes, Justice Traynor elevated himself into our view from behind the podium where he had been sitting in a chair that was out of sight from the floor. He said, "Will you all please repeat after me. . . ."

On my immediate right stood a fellow freshman, Bill Bagley, a young Republican from Marin County with a face as round and red as a harvest moon. As we repeated the oath, I was distracted anew by the awareness that Bill Bagley was putting everything in reverse. As the rest of us were saying, "I do solemnly swear that I will support and defend the Constitution of the State of California against all enemies foreign and domestic," Bagley was saying, "I do solemnly swear that I will *not* support and defend the Constitution of the United States and the Constitution of the State of California against all enemies foreign and domestic," and so forth.

I was astonished. I turned my head enough to catch a glimpse of his face, which was as serenely dignified as Justice Traynor's. I wondered why he would do such a thing. (I was to spend a lot of time during my six years in the Assembly wondering about why Bill Bagley was doing one thing or another.)

Justice Traynor concluded the administration of the oath with "So help me, God," which we all repeated, including Bill Bagley— thereby adding the sin of impiety to that of impudence.

After I put my hand down I looked again at Unruh. Seeing him there sent a thrill of apprehension through me. Most of my supporters had labored to send me to Sacramento to beard that swollen monster in his den.

Well, I thought, *here I am, in his den.*

2

Big Daddy and the Hairshirts

*If those robber barons were somewhat grim and drunken
ogres, they had a certain grandeur of the wild beast in them.*

George Eliot

On that opening day of my first legislative session I
was an embodiment of liberal innocence, having been immacu-
lately conceived as a candidate for office by the holy spirits in the
California Democratic Council. Usually referred to only by its
initials as the C.D.C., it was a confederation of Democratic clubs
with a membership of sixty thousand volunteers fervently united by
their enthusiasm for liberal causes and their antipathy for Jesse
Marvin Unruh.

We, the selfless amateurs who made up the C.D.C., saw him as
three hundred pounds of cigar-smoking, booze-guzzling, Machi-
avellian rapacity. And God knows he looked it. His features were as
heavily sensual as a champion English bulldog's. His dun-colored
hair was always so perfectly arranged that he appeared at all times to
have just arisen from his stylist's chair. We held that against him,
too. In those days most Americans looked upon a man's having his
hair styled as a narcissistic excess. Real men had their hair cut by a
barber. Unruh's elephantine bulk was usually accoutered, as it was
on the first day of the session, in perfectly tailored suits, pastel shirts
and neckties, and calf-skin pumps, all in full accord with the latest
vagaries of Pucci or Gucci. In short, he looked like money—new
money.

By the time I arrived in the Capitol and stood at the bar of the
Assembly taking the oath of office, his credo relative to eating
lobbyists' food, drinking their booze, screwing their women, and
taking their money was being routinely cited as Unruh's first law of
politics. As such, I'd heard it repeated in Democratic club meetings

more often than the pledge of allegiance. It served as a reminder to all club members to be loyal to the C.D.C. in its war with the forces of evil, which he personified. And there were, in addition, any number of other frightful things that he said and we repeated.

Word wildfired around one C.D.C. convention in Fresno about an encounter between him and a sharp young man who worked for my state senator, Hugo Fisher. The young man, whose name was Lloyd Winburn, said he'd chanced to come upon California's modern Gargantua in a hotel suite, where he was carousing with a mixed company of both sexes after the adjournment of the floor session. Lloyd reported that he had confronted him and had said, "Tell me, Jesse, how does a guy with a big gut like yours get it on with all those lobbyists' women in Sacramento?" According to Lloyd, Unruh smiled condescendingly and replied, "You know, you're the third short-peckered son-of-a-bitch that's asked me that this month."

With that impiety he stirred us into a passion of righteousness.

I remember one time when he was invited to speak to a group made up mostly of C.D.C. liberals. The chairman of the meeting introduced him with a grudging recognition of his intelligence, his ability, and his accomplishments. He nodded in approval of each pained compliment. He rose before us huge and overbearing to rumble, "Thank you, Mr. Chairman, for saying all of those very true things about me." His voice was a basso profundo as deep as the lowest notes of a cathedral organ. When I heard him speak, I thought of how Kipling had described Disco Troop's voice in *Captains Courageous* as being the deepest Harvey Cheyne had ever heard, and I decided that I knew how the old Gloucesterman had sounded. "You might think I shouldn't be so quick to agree," he went on, "but modesty on the part of a man of great talents is pure hypocrisy."

A gargoylish grin revealed his strong, widely spaced, uneven teeth and his amusement at the way his audience froze into icy sculptures of disapproval.

Sheridan Hegland once said to me furtively over a cup of coffee at a Democratic club meeting, "Jess Unruh plays the role of chairman of the Ways and Means Committee like Charles Laughton played Henry VIII." (I shall spell Unruh's first name at times with the final *e* and at other times without it, depending upon whether or not it is to be pronounced. His legal name was Jesse, but more often than not he was called Jess by his friends.) After taking a quick nervous sip of his coffee, Heg quavered on, "If a bill gets twelve or thirteen aye votes in his committee and only two or three noes, he'll rule that the noes have it, if he's one of them."

I was already uncomfortably aware of that. Unruh had made headlines when one member of his committee had bawled in frustration, "This committee isn't being run democratically."

"This committee is being run democratically," Unruh had retorted, waving away the objection with a flourish of his cigar, "and it always will be, as long as the majority votes with the chairman."

We large *D* and small *d* democrats of the C.D.C. had shuddered as if he had walked across our graves when we read that line in our newspapers and saw it repeated by *Time* and *Newsweek* a few days later.

At a meeting of a C.D.C. club I attended in San Diego a short time later—it was the Point Loma Democratic Club—an arthritic petrification of an old lady struggled to an almost upright position and shrilled, "It is appalling to me that the most prominent Democratic leader in the State Legislature is tossing off the kind of remarks that went out with Louis XIV."

We all applauded till our hands stung. Clinging for support to the back of the steel folding chair in front of her, she peered about at us with grim satisfaction, and, when the applause subsided, she skirled on, "I am disgusted when I hear about how that big blowhard is raking in money. He threw that fund-raising dinner in L.A. and all of the Sacramento lobbyists showed up. You know he can't be taking in all of that mazuma from special interests without giving them something in return." She was shaking with rage and decrepitude and so was her voice. "Fat cats don't go around giving away thousands of dollars out of the goodness of their hearts. Big Daddy is selling out the people of this state for cash on the barrelhead. He claims that he's raising it to pass it along to other Democrats to get them elected to the Assembly. I guess he thinks that should make simple Democrats like us happy as larks, but he must be selling his own soul, if he has one, to the big money boys, and he must also be buying the souls of the schlemiels that he's passing his loot along to."

She was only saying what all the sixty thousand of us were thinking about his cold-cash approach to the electoral process.

We felt that in politics, as in sex and most other sports, money is the root of all evil because it turns enthusiastic amateurs into cold-eyed professionals.

When our cries of disapproval were quoted to him by the press, our enemy responded with Unruh's second law, "Money is the mother's milk of politics."

That gave us all hate headaches.

Club Democrats despised Jesse Unruh and what he stood for, the old business-as-usual, money-grubbing school of politics that had brought discredit upon both political parties in the United States. We hated him as Saint Paul told us to love God, with all of our hearts, with all of our minds, and with all of our souls, and we hallelujahed our feelings in all of our political prayer meetings.

He, in turn, summed up his opinion of us in Unruh's third law: "Winning isn't everything, but losing isn't anything."

That principle had already been expressed by Vince Lombardi not long before. It had amused us as a comment upon how the game of football should be played, but we thought it was a horrifying standard of conduct for political game players. And we were incensed by the inference that we weren't as concerned as we should be about electing Democrats.

The conflict between Jesse Unruh and the sixty thousand members of the Democratic club movement in California broke out in 1959, two years before I entered the legislature. It was in that year that the C.D.C. began having annual conventions to discuss the brightly burning issues of the day. Before that time the organization had met only in election years and for the purpose of endorsing candidates.

The annual conventions of the C.D.C. were customarily held in Fresno, and on various occasions the president, Joe Wyatt, was called upon to explain why.

"We go to Fresno every year," Joe used to say, "because it's halfway between Southern California and the San Francisco Bay Area. God knows there isn't any other reason to go to Fresno."

From 1959 on, every one of those annual conventions culminated in a multiple orgasm of resolutions. We always passed one calling for the abolition of the House Committee on Un-American Activities. We invariably approved one calling for the repeal of the Levering Act, a California law requiring that all public employees take an oath that they were not, and had not been at any time in the past, and promised never to become, members of any organization that advocates the overthrow of the government of the United States. In addition, the conventions routinely called for the recognition of Red China.

Heber McGinniss managed my first campaign in 1960. An old friend and classmate at San Diego State College, Heber was a saturnine, brilliant, sardonic, lean, hollow-cheeked failure in everything but politics.

His long thin face was engraved with lines of alcoholic disgruntlement; and because he worked as a parking lot attendant between campaigns, it had been burned to a mahogany color by the Southern California sun. For the same reason his narrow nose was scarred by the surgical removal of skin cancers. He smoked incessantly. His fingers were tobacco-stained, and so were his teeth, but he never smiled, so no one knew it. His hair was straight and black. He wore it combed straight back from a hairline that dipped into a deep widow's peak.

I took time off in the middle of my first campaign to attend the C.D.C. convention of 1960, during which Joanna and I got together with Heber and his schoolteacher wife Diane for breakfast Sunday morning in the art deco coffee shop of the headquarters hotel in downtown Fresno. After a late night of conventioneering, Heber looked unusually jaundiced; his eyes were bloodshot; he was soaking up coffee like a waitress's sponge and eyeing his bacon and eggs with loathing.

In a baritone roughened by years of heavy drinking, he groused, "Well, this afternoon we're going to pass some more of those God-awful resolutions."

Diane gave him the sort of disapproving look that she had fine-tuned over many years of teaching high school. "Heber McGinniss," she said, "you've told me a thousand times you think we should recognize Red China and abolish the House Un-American Activities Committee and the Levering Act."

"You're goddamned right I have. And the only way we'll ever get any of those things done is by electing Democrats who'll do them. But we won't be able to elect a goddamned dog catcher if we put our candidates on the line on those issues."

Joanna, who is as honest as George Washington was supposed to be, said, "Don't you think the people have a right to know where candidates stand?"

"Aw, come on, Joanna. What are we in this crazy business for?

We want to do what's best for the people, and you know as well as I do that nine times out of ten the dumb shits will be against it. Oh, don't look so goddamned shocked, girls. That's one thing, in fact it's damned near the only thing, that all political idealists agree on, no matter if they're liberals or conservatives. God, I wish I had a drink." He beckoned to a waitress who was passing with a pot of coffee. She refilled his empty cup.

He took a careful sip from it and went on. "Those resolutions we're going to pass this afternoon are going to be hung around the necks of our candidates like goddamned albatrosses. Most of the voters in this state think that people who go along with that kind of thinking are redder than Old MacDonald's skivvies. Jim's Republican opponent is going to spend the autumn calling on him to repudiate the support of the C.D.C., and if he doesn't, the voters are going to figure he's a goddamned Commie, and if he does, all of the red hots in the C.D.C. are going to stop helping in his campaign."

With long nervous fingers he pulled a cigarette out of a pack. He lighted it and puffed away without any evident satisfaction, while Joanna, Diane, and I silently tucked into our breakfasts.

He groused huskily, "Jesus H. Christ but I'm tired of all these woollies who think it's so goddamned virtuous to hang the party's nominees out to dry on every tough issue."

There were quite a few members of the C.D.C. who agreed with Heber, yet all sixty thousand of us resented it hotly when Jesse Unruh commented after the convention, "Those hairshirts don't have any right to commit ceremonial hara-kiri for the whole Democratic Party every year in Fresno."

At the next meeting of the Point Loma Democratic Club, the petrified little old lady struggled to her feet and shrilled again, "We don't need any fat political bosses to call us hairshirts and tell us what we can do and what we can't do."

The membership of the club broke into cheers. If the ceilings of the house where we were meeting had been higher, we would have carried her around on our shoulders. It's a good thing they weren't. If we had dropped her, she probably would have shattered like a china plate.

Things went from bad to worse. When one of Unruh's henchmen wisecracked, "The C.D.C. is the party's club foot," the press picked it up and gave it wide circulation. Most reporters wrote the story in such a way as to imply that he or she didn't believe the fellow was clever enough to have come up with the zinger himself and that he was probably just echoing a private remark of Jesse Unruh. The line certainly had that ring of indecency to it that was making the chairman of the Assembly Ways and Means Committee the most noted and quoted politician in the state.

Actually there was one other California officeholder who was as fat and as irreverent as Unruh, and that was Assemblyman Don Allen, a gruff, retired marine sergeant who represented Baldwin Hills and its oil-well-punctuated environs. Don was part Indian, and his ancestry was apparent in his red face and his full head of straight, jet-black hair. As for the rest of him, his proportions were as nobly grand as the soul of one of Rousseau's savages. His belly looked as if he had eaten a stuffed buffalo for dinner every day of his adult life. He it was who tagged Unruh with the nickname Big Daddy. The colossal megalomania of the character of Big Daddy in the play *Cat on a Hot Tin Roof* made calling him that a sublime outrage. Therefore Unruh laughed mountainously when he first heard it. Quite apparently he loved anything outrageous.

The purists in the C.D.C., whom he had grievously offended by calling them hairshirts, wanted to retaliate by calling him something equally offensive. They therefore approved highly when they heard that Don had called him Big Daddy, and they seldom used any other name for him from that time forward. They were terribly grim about it. They became even more so when they realized that he grinned impudently every time he heard one of them do it.

One day the featured cartoon on the editorial page of the *San Francisco Chronicle* was of an awful thing, *The Dread Unruh*, a bloated monster with huge jaws and teeth, an ogre that lay in wait in the noisome swamps of Sacramento for the innocent and the unwary. The sixty thousand Democratic club members happily mailed thermofaxed copies of the caricature to one another. However, the wine of jubilation turned to vinegar in their sixty thousand mouths when word circulated about how he reacted to the cartoon. He laughed even more hugely than when Don Allen called him Big Daddy. We heard that to please him, his staff got in touch with the editorial offices of the *Chronicle* and obtained the original ink drawing in order to have it framed and give it to him. From that time forward it hung on the wall of his office for all to see.

The antipathy in the breasts of the decent sixty thousand in the C.D.C. toward the highly indecent chairman of the Ways and Means Committee kept growing sharper and sharper into a chronic case of political heartburn. Yet, in spite of the terrible discomfort of it, we never lost heart. For we had a champion, a knight on a Democratic jackass, honorable, kindly, humble, decent Edmund G. "Pat" Brown, the Governor of California.

When I left my job as curator of the San Diego Historical Society's museum to run for the State Assembly, it was with the intention of becoming one of good old Pat's faithful spear carriers. I wanted to join him whenever he sallied forth on the field of dishonor to do battle with the Dread Unruh, which lurked in the political thickets, devouring lobbyists' food, guzzling their booze, raking in their money, screwing their women, and sneering at virtuous people like me and my friends.

3

Getting Acquainted
with Assemblyman X

It is not enough to do good; one must do it the right way.

John, Viscount Morley

In the heat of the August of 1960, when my first general election campaign was beginning to gather itself into existence like a summer storm, politicians were sweating about a nameless assemblyman from an unidentified state. In that month's issue of *Reader's Digest* an article had appeared about him under the title "This Is How Payola Works in Politics." The byline was "by Assemblyman X, as told to Lester Velie," who was one of the most respected muckrakers of that generation.

Through Velie, Assemblyman X told how he had come of age in politics. He said, "I first ran for the Legislature as an idealistic young man firmly set against taking any campaign contributions that might compromise me later."

He explained that he had won election to the Assembly by tramping from door to door and persuading a sufficient number of people to vote for him as I was then trying to do for myself. When he got to the state Capitol, he discovered, to his surprise, that he was ever so popular with all of the lobbyists who had contributed money to support the campaign of the incumbent whom he had just defeated. "I found that I need not pay for a single meal. A lobbyist was always ready to pick up my check. As a pure, and priggish, young freshman, I'd pass up the town's finest restaurant—where lobbyists took lawmakers—and grimly eat my bacon-and-tomato sandwich at a cafeteria. . . .

"Eight of us who used to spurn lobbyists' handouts to eat together at the cafeteria began to ask one another: 'How could we,

the lawmakers, regain control of the state's lawmaking machinery?'"

He said they agreed it could be done only through the election
of a new breed of young, independent men. "To accomplish this,"
he said, "we twisted and squirmed in search of the all-important
campaign money. In the end we found there was only one place
where it could be had readily—from the third house itself. So,
stilling our doubts and scruples, we began to play the dangerous
game of taking money from would-be corrupters—to elect men
who would fight corruption."

Assemblyman X said that he had taken the lead in raising
campaign funds by first deciding which side was in the right in
legislative battles where powerful interests were at odds with each
other. Then he would go to the lobbyists for that side and tell them
that he would help them with the members of his own party. He
mentioned having sided with the truckers against the railroads.
When election time came around, he had hit up the truckers, and
other interests he had assisted, for campaign contributions. By so
doing, he had helped to finance the campaigns of any number of
bright, honest, young candidates, he told Lester Velie.

"Within several years," he said, "we had built a solid bloc of
assemblymen who followed party leadership on basic issues. With
the support of the governor, I could now give our legislature the
direction that once came from the third house. The lobbies were
still strong. On matters of real importance to them, they often
prevailed. But we had broken the backbone of control from the
outside."

Assemblyman X was, as far as I could see, just another one
among many well-meaning officeholders who had begun by thinking they could use lobbyists' money for their own purposes only to
wind up hooked by their dependence upon it.

Assemblyman X wrapped up the problem himself in one con-
cluding paragraph.

"This is my dilemma: If I had stayed away from the lobbyists, I
would have been ineffective. If I take their money and do nothing
for it, I am a cheat. If I do their bidding, I could be cheating the
public. I find myself rationalizing what I have done. The tragedy is
that I may wind up serving the very elements I set out to beat—yet
not know that I have changed."

Pat Brown came to San Diego soon after the article appeared to
do a little socializing with the richest Democrats in town. He did

that in years when he wasn't running for office in order to be on good terms with them in years when he was.

That particular soiree was held in his honor in the hillside villa of a local manufacturer of war materials who found it expedient to be a Democrat for the time being. In the course of the conversation that night, one wealthy liberal said to Pat, "I hope that Assembly-man X, whoever he is, is trying to improve things in some other state and not in California."

"Oh, don't you know who that is?" Pat's smile betrayed his pleasure at being given the opportunity to provide an answer to that question. "Assemblyman X is Jesse Unruh," he said.

When I was in my swivel chair in the Assembly chamber, Big Daddy had a hypnotic fascination for me. His desk was the one in the front row on the end next to the north wall, which holds a classical rank of tall, round-topped Palladian windows that frame a formal set of views of downtown Sacramento. It's on the left side as members look to the front because the chamber faces, like a Catholic church or a Masonic lodge, toward the light of morning in the east.

One of the first things I noticed about him was that he seldom sat at his desk. Most of the time he stood up in the aisle between it and the north wall, turning his ponderous bulk this way and that way upon his expensively shod feet, surveying all the rest of us in our places levelly, like a straw boss overseeing a gang of hired hands. Occasionally, he would raise a thick hand up to his pastel shirt collar, and he would hook two of his big fingers over it and take two tugs at it. Obviously it was too tight. I thought there probably weren't any shirts made that didn't have collars that would be too tight for that neck. Sometimes he would raise his chin and thrust it forward at us in the manner of Benito Mussolini.

Being one of a crew of lesser men under the eye of a fat overseer who stuck out his chin at us from time to time didn't appeal to me. Not at all.

Furthermore, I found that whenever Jerry Waldie, the Democratic caucus chairman, called the Assembly Democrats together, Jesse Unruh was really as much in charge as he made himself appear to be when he looked out over us on the floor. As we met to consider the problems of the people of California and tried to compose legislative solutions to them, I saw that the overweight political boss, whom my friends had sent me to Sacramento to thwart in his evil designs, always took the lead. And, as his subterranean bass sang the melody, the rest of the members raised their smaller voices only to harmonize.

Samuel Johnson said, "No two men can be half an hour together but one shall acquire an evident superiority over the other."

I found that Jesse Unruh had long since acquired an evident superiority over all of the members of the caucus. He was, in fact, our leader, and that was all there was to it.

I soon became aware that most of the good liberal Democrats, who talked as I did when they were at C.D.C. meetings, accepted his opinions as the final word on almost all matters relating to state policy and the enactment of bills. I was at a loss to see such defiant C.D.C. convention orators performing like woolly lambs in his awful presence, allowing him to lead them about like a tremendous Judas goat.

I sat down with Tom Carrell, an old Texas populist who represented San Fernando, one morning, upon his invitation, when he was having breakfast with a professional-looking young man at the Senator Hotel. He introduced the young man as the president of one of the Democratic clubs in his district.

The young man said, "When is somebody going to do something about Big Daddy? He's a disgrace to the party."

Tom stifled a yawn and drawled sleepily, "Almost all of the good legislation we've put on the books since Pat was elected governor was pushed through the Senate and Assembly by old Jess."

"You've got to be kidding," the young man said.

Tom breathed on his coffee lazily. "Now I wouldn't kid about a thing like that."

"Tell me one really good thing Jesse Unruh has done."

"Well, you know most everybody gives Pat all the credit for getting the bill passed that set up the Fair Employment Practices Commission."

"He deserves it. He made it a major point in his legislative program."

"Pat's for all the right things." Tom felt the urge to yawn again and gave in to it. "But old Jess did a lot more to get it passed than Pat ever did."

Neither I nor the young man had heard anyone question the orthodox C.D.C. doctrine that Pat was the prime mover behind the progressive legislation that had been enacted into law since his inauguration. He might be just a little bit feather-brained—club members were constantly being told that by the leaders in the movement—but he knew enough to surround himself with bright, pure, young men who were synthesizing the most enlightened public policies ever seriously considered in California outside of a League of Women Voters meeting. And Pat would send his young Galahads forth to get their marvelous proposals enacted into law, overcoming in the process all of the political monsters in the Capitol, of which the Dread Unruh was the omnivorous archetype. It was, therefore, a cultural shock for the young man, and for me, when Tom Carrell said what he did that morning over breakfast.

Casually Tom also reminded him, "You know the two best liberal bills we've passed both have old Jess's name on them."

He was referring to the Unruh Civil Rights Act, which prohibited racial discrimination by any and all California businesses, and the Unruh Retail Credit Act, which limited the interest rates that stores and businesses could charge for money. His having carried those bills had mystified a lot of C.D.C. people.

Once Heber McGinniss, who liked to stir people up when he was feeling bored, said at a meeting of the Point Loma Democratic Club, "Why do you suppose Jess Unruh would carry such good liberal legislation?"

The little old arthritic lady hauled herself to her feet and cried out, "I'll tell you why. He does it to provide himself with a smoke screen he can hide behind while he shoots down all the bills that are really important to the lobbyists who supply him with his money, his food, his booze, and his women."

As usual, she had expressed the views of most of the sixty thousand members of the C.D.C.

In the Senator Hotel coffee shop Tom maundered on. "Pat's always going around telling folks that Jess made his reputation by latching onto Pat's legislative programs." Tom's eyelids were still drooping, even though he'd slowly sipped up all of his first cup of coffee, and he still sounded as if he might fall asleep in midsentence. "But it's really the other way around. Pat made his reputation by telling everybody he's for a lot of the same things that Jess is for and then by signing the bills when Jess puts them on his desk."

"But surely you can't justify the high-handed way he runs his committee," the young man said. "It's a public scandal. How can any committee chairman be defended who says, 'This committee is run democratically and always will be, as long as the majority votes with the chairman.'"

Tom said, "You know, there are lots of bad bills that most of the members will vote for, for one reason or another."

"That should be on their heads," the young man argued. "That's what democracy is all about."

"Maybe so," Tom said peaceably, "but you're going to find out that you're in agreement with old Jess on the issue about ten times out of ten when he uses his gavel to knock some bill on the head. You never hear any complaints from the liberals in the Assembly about how he runs his committee."

The winter of 1961 was dismal and overcast. The opening day of the session was, according to the newspapers, the coldest January second in the history of Sacramento. It must also have been the grayest. And every succeeding day was just as cheerless as week after week went by.

A month passed and we still had not seen the sun even once. Joanna had joined me in Sacramento for all of that session. She was pregnant with our first child and was depressed by morning sickness and the interminable overcast, and I was beginning to be a little mopish myself. So I suggested to her one Saturday morning in February that we go for a ride in our old Dodge far enough up into the Sierra Nevada Mountains to get above the wet blanket of fog that was chilling the Sacramento Valley. We came out from under the grayness abruptly in the middle of Placerville, which is also known as Old Hangtown because of the propensity of its citizens during the good old days to string up rascals from the nearest tree in order to keep lawyers from standing in the way of justice.

We wandered up and down the main street there, luxuriating in the cold brilliance of the winter sunshine, looking at the red-brick buildings, most of which were relics of Old Hangtown's gold-digging youth. The memory of our few hours in the sun there brightened our spirits during a number of clammy weeks that followed.

The only other brightness in our lives that winter was produced by the surprises Jesse Unruh had in store for us. Joanna had time on her hands, and she spent a good deal of it sitting in committee hearing rooms witnessing the proceedings. It was interesting, it was educational, and it was free. Joanna acted as my eyes and ears in various places where I couldn't be when duty called me somewhere else. Over supper in our one-bedroom apartment she would fill me in on what she had seen in the course of the day. She often told me about some position taken by the chairman of the Ways and Means Committee that she thought was much to his credit. At first she marveled at such behavior as curious, uncharacteristic, and incomprehensible. However, as she reported instances of that kind of thing after almost every meeting of his committee, we began to wonder if we had him figured out right.

She said to me one night in March, while we were polishing off a particularly distinguished meat loaf she had fixed for our dinner, "In spite of all the awful things Jesse Unruh says, he always seems to be on the side of the angels."

What puzzled me most in Sacramento during my first few months there was Governor Brown's coolness to me. I took pains to make it clear to him from the start that I wanted nothing more than to join the sanctified band that was gathered around him in his holy crusade against the Dread Unruh. He didn't respond. I couldn't understand it. I looked upon myself as a virtuous person. Why would the champion of virtue in Sacramento be unwilling to accept me as a friend? I knew that when Hugo Fisher, the Democratic state senator for San Diego County, had taken office two years before, Pat Brown had clasped him to his bosom and had showered all manner of gubernatorial blessings upon him.

Actually, the first time I was rebuffed by the Governor was even before I was elected. The caucus of Democrats in my congressional district had chosen me to be a member of his delegation to the Democratic National Convention in 1960. He ignored the caucus and didn't appoint me. That was distressing. I was well into my first campaign and was not helped by being publicly repudiated by the Governor. My Republican opponent talked a lot about how Pat didn't think I was even fit to go to the convention and, if the leader of my own party thought that, why should the voters think I was fit to become a member of the Legislature?

I couldn't imagine why Pat, whom I liked and admired, would do that to me, so I asked Heber McGinniss, who knew about such things, when he came into my campaign headquarters the morning after the Governor released the names of his delegates to the press.

Heber looked even more grumpy than he usually did in the morning. He said, "I guess you'll find out sooner or later, so I might as well tell you. As far as San Diego County was concerned, Hugo got to call the shots as to who was going to be on the delegation and who wasn't."

I was mystified. "Why wouldn't he want me on the delegation? The night he was elected he told me that I was responsible for him winning, and I think I was. This is a great way to thank me."

Heber looked uncomfortable. He was as close to Hugo Fisher as he was to me. He said, "Now, don't start acting like a goddamned prima donna."

"Why not? He's doing it. He must have given me the shaft because he doesn't want any competition. He wants to be the one and only star of the Democratic Party in this county. I don't think he wants me to win."

"Of course he wants you to win. Just keep your shirt on. The party can't afford to have any fights between you and Hugo, for Christ's sake. He's a funny guy sometimes, I have to admit, but everything will be okay between you two if you just don't go flying off the handle."

But since that time I had got nothing from Pat Brown, nothing at all. Hugo was close to him, and I came to the conclusion that Hugo must be at the bottom of it. I couldn't conceive of any other cause. I presumed that Hugo must have been peddling Pat the idea that I, as a member of the Assembly, would inevitably fall under the spell of the Fat and Evil One—if I hadn't done so already—and I knew that argument would be effective with Pat because there was bad blood between the Governor and Unruh.

Pat had recently been humiliated by Big Daddy, and Hugo had been the subject of the controversy.

Pat, knowing that Jack Kennedy would want a Californian in his cabinet, had urged him to appoint Hugo Fisher as postmaster general. I was at a political meeting with Hugo in San Diego when he received a phone call from Washington saying he had the job. But it turned out that he didn't. The same afternoon Kenny O'Donnell called Jesse Unruh to inform him of the decision to appoint Hugo, and Unruh asked O'Donnell, "Why him? He's a freshman state senator. What has he ever done to deserve consideration? I can think of a hundred Californians who would be better choices than he would." O'Donnell said, "Name one." At the time he received the phone call, Big Daddy was attending a symposium of Democratic businessmen. The president of it was a Los Angeles insurance executive named Edward Day. Unruh looked out of the phone booth at Day in the chair and he said, "How about Ed Day?"

O'Donnell liked the idea, so he passed it on to the President, who also liked it, and that is how Day came to be appointed Postmaster General.

The Governor was furious at being undercut on so important a matter. His press secretary, Hale Champion, said to Unruh's chief assistant, big Larry Margolis, "Just where does Jesse get off pulling a trick like that on the Governor?" Larry said, "Did you or any of the Governor's people ever talk to Jess about that appointment?" And Champion replied, "Why should the Governor have to clear his actions with that fat son-of-a-bitch?"

Before that time Brown and Unruh had both taken care to give the impression of cooperation, for the sake of the party, but after that all pretenses of civility were dropped.

As for what Hugo was doing to me, he had his reasons. He didn't want to share his influence over the Governor's actions in San Diego with me or anyone else.

Every judge appointed in the county during my first term was a friend of Hugo's. Not even one of them was anything to me. I was being damaged because each new appointment was a fresh reminder to the Democrats active in the party in San Diego that I was persona non grata with the Governor. Anyone who wanted anything from Pat soon got the message that he had better do all he could for Hugo and that he would be wasting his time and money if he did anything for me. That was creating problems for me in trying to line up the support I would need to get myself re-elected.

Time after time I went to the Governor's office to talk to him about it. I would say to him, "Governor, I'm not asking much. I'm not asking for you to listen to me when you appoint judges half of the time. I'm not asking you to listen to me a quarter of the time, or even an eighth of the time. All I'm asking is that you listen to me once in a while. You're making it look like you don't care at all about what I want or what I think."

He would listen to me owlishly in his big, beautiful, leather swivel chair in his big, beautiful, redwood-paneled office, and when I was done, he'd ask me how Joanna was. But perseverance is a virtue not even my enemies ever denied me. I kept on trying.

At last he decided he no longer wanted to put up with my pestering him about judgeships. During a Democratic caucus that had been convened in the Assembly lounge, at his request, to talk about problems in the relationships between the Assembly Democrats and himself, he disposed of me once and for all. Broaching the subject himself, he rasped, "Some problems with you fellows I can deal with. Some I can't. I know Jim Mills is unhappy with me because he doesn't have anything to say about the appointment of judges in his county."

I shrank into my chair, recoiling at his bringing the matter up before my colleagues.

His voice became even more gravelly than usual as he pressed on. "But Hugo Fisher is an attorney. He knows about attorneys. Jim Mills isn't; and he doesn't know about attorneys. And I'm going to have to keep on going along with Hugo when it comes to judgeships in San Diego County."

It was mortifying to have him announce to the caucus that my opinions and wishes relative to judgeship appointments were of no importance to him. Everyone present knew that his line about my not being an attorney—and therefore not to be listened to—was balderdash, to put it politely. There were other nonlawyers in the Legislature who were allowed to call the shots on all of the judgeship appointments in their counties.

I felt myself blushing from the slap. I said, "Governor, I have never asked you to appoint anyone to a judgeship on the basis of my opinion of his professional capacity. I wouldn't do that. I've never asked you to appoint anyone who wasn't rated as highly qualified to be a judge by the San Diego County Bar Association. But Hugo has, and you've appointed the guys. If you're interested in the opinions of attorneys, why listen to just one?"

He grated out the same line as before. "Hugo is an attorney. He knows about attorneys. And I'm going to keep going along with Hugo when it comes to judgeships in San Diego County. I'm sorry, but that's the way it is."

As I walked out of that caucus, under an overload of humiliation, Jesse Unruh gave me an avuncular slap on the shoulder and said, "That was pretty rough, but don't let it get you down."

But it did. Pat had accomplished his purpose. I never bothered him about a judgeship appointment again as long as Hugo was in the Senate.

Jefferson Peyser, the lobbyist for the California Wine Institute, was a small, urbane San Francisco attorney, a gentleman with impeccable tastes in everything from the conservative clothes he wore on his sparrowy frame to the liberal comforts he provided for us and for himself. I came to know him well because of his practice of inviting a dozen members at a time to his suite on the eighth floor of the Senator Hotel for dinner. Those occasions were the most pleasurable experiences connected with being a member of the Legislature. Somehow he prevailed upon the cooks in the hotel kitchen to prepare the most glorious feasts since Lucullus threw up his last entrée. And that was nothing short of amazing, in light of the crimes against humanity that were perpetrated by that gang of culinary cutthroats during every hour of every day's work. None of us ever understood what kind of a hold he had upon them.

Jeff put on his dinners to provide occasions to serve California's best wines to members of the Legislature. He wanted us to know about them, to appreciate them, to take an interest in them.

It was at those culinary extravaganzas on Wednesday nights that I got to know Jesse Unruh. It seemed that I was always invited to come on the same nights that he was. When our coats were off, our shirt collars unbuttoned, and our neckties loosened, and we were eating, drinking, and blowing cigar smoke around Jeff's table, I found that Big Daddy was the best of company. He engulfed good food and wine with as much zest as he embraced good causes. And when he had absorbed enough of the finer things in life that Jeff put before us, he became a natural fountain of good spirits, indecent jokes, bawdy songs, and witty remarks. It was impossible not to like him.

He volunteered fraternal advice to me and to all of the new members. As a freshman I had previously been counseled mostly by old foxes like Sam Geddes. Sam was a bluff, hearty, weather-beaten building contractor who represented the grape growers of the Napa Valley. Sam told me more than once, "Jim, if you want to stay here, just remember one rule. Always vote against every tax increase and for every appropriation, and if anybody ever asks you how you plan to finance the new programs you vote for, just tell them you're for cutting the fat out of government to do it."

I mentioned Sam's advice at one of Peyser's dinners one night, just as Jeff was pouring brandy for us.

Unruh chuckled like a mountain stream. He said, "The hypocritical old bastard does it, too, and he's right. He'll be here till he dies."

His heavy features settled into a more serious cast after he joined the rest of us in taking a first sip of brandy. He said, "Everybody who has thought about democracy since Plato has realized that its chief shortcoming is that the people always want more than they're willing to pay for. And as long as they keep on voting for phonies who tell them only what they want to hear, they'll be disillusioned with politicians."

I was surprised to find that Jesse Unruh's advice was a good deal more sound—and ethical—than most of what I got. One line that he repeated again and again was, "If you expect to stay around here any length of time, remember that you only have one thing to work with, your word. Never go back on it."

He was always entertaining, partly because he was as outrageously impious in private as he was in public.

Bob Crown, who, as I soon learned, idolized him, used to play the conversational role of James Boswell to his Samuel Johnson by feeding him questions to elicit responses. Bob's face was always expectant when he did it because Unruh's answers were no less memorable than Dr. Johnson's.

For example, Bob said to him one night at Peyser's, "Jess, have you ever gone to bed with an ugly woman?"

He replied in some amusement, "No, Bobby. I've never gone to bed with an ugly woman."

Bob persisted, "Not even once?"

"Not even once." He grinned and added, "Although I must admit I've gotten up in the morning with one or two."

As I got to know Jesse Unruh better, I began to make allowances for things that he did that had bothered me at first. I soon realized that the reason he stuck his chin out as he surveyed what was happening on the floor was that he wanted to move the skin on his neck enough to shift the discomfort of his collar to a new place. It was an alternative to reaching up continually to pull his collar down with two fingers. Unlike Mussolini, he was not sticking his chin out at decent people like me.

He seemed to want to be my friend, even if Pat Brown didn't. I realized that when Bob Crown told me that Jeff Peyser left it to Unruh to decide who should be invited on the nights he was to be present.

"He likes you," Bob said, "or he wouldn't be including you every time."

That comment gave me a lot to think about because it made me conscious that I was on the horns of a dilemma akin to the one described by Assemblyman X. In order to participate in the decision-making process in Sacramento, I would have to become involved with one of the decision makers. There were only two leaders a Democratic assemblyman could fall in behind. One of them was Pat Brown, who was beloved by all of my friends and supporters. The other was Big Daddy, the most infamous rascal in California politics, who was abominated by all of those same friends and supporters.

It was becoming quite clear to me that I had only one choice open if I wanted to take part in the making of state policy, but that exercising that option would entail turning my back upon all of the good people who had worked long and hard to put me in the Legislature.

4

How the Amiable Owl
Fell on His Tail

A man is the sum total of his misfortunes.

Richard Wilkins

*T*hat spring I spent a lot of time learning about how laws are made. My big bill of the session was one that required seat belts on all new cars sold in California. Carrying it made most people in Sacramento think me a pretty radical sort of fellow. That didn't trouble me, but my dilemma about whether to follow Pat Brown or Jess Unruh was costing Joanna and me a lot of sleep.

In the course of our bedtime agonizing, we took stock of the origins of the conflict between Pat Brown and Big Daddy, and, as we did so, we recalled how, during the first two years after his election as governor, Pat had been one of the most popular public officials in America, partly because, as far as the issues that affected Californians were concerned, he was an honest-to-God idealist, and partly because he was invariably as genial as an Irishman at an enemy's wake.

Stewart Alsop had taken into account Pat's round face, his beaked nose, his brown plumage, and his horn-rimmed glasses and had summed them all up in two well-chosen words. He said that Pat looked like an amiable owl. That was a masterpiece of an instant cliché, the kind of lustrous banality to be expected of so distinguished a journalist, one that newsmen and women could use every day. And use it they did. From that time forward they referred to Pat as owlish almost every time they put his name into print.

Unfortunately for him, Pat was further classified as a fluttery sort of hoot owl in 1960, two years after he was elected, when he fell off his high perch on his tail. That happened at the Democratic

26

National Convention in Los Angeles, when he fluttered his wings as a leader of the opposition to the nomination of John Kennedy.

In the primary election in the spring of 1960, in which I had gained the nomination of the Democratic Party for the Assembly in the Seventy-ninth District, Pat had won the support of the Democratic voters of California as a candidate for the office of president of the United States. He had run as a favorite son. The serious Democratic contenders, Kennedy, Humphrey, Symington, and Johnson, had all stayed out of the California primary. They did not want to challenge and, thereby, alienate Pat. All of them cherished the hope that they might win him over and persuade him to deliver his big delegation to them. As for Pat, he seemed to have it in mind to trade off the support of the California delegation in return for the nomination for the vice presidency. It appeared there was one man he didn't want to see win the party's presidential nomination and that was John Kennedy, presumably because he couldn't consider Pat as a running mate since they were both Catholics.

As soon as it became clear to everybody that Kennedy was going to get the votes he needed for the nomination, we heard that Pat had told him he would support him. Subsequent convention scuttlebutt reported that Kennedy expected, as a matter of course, that Pat would deliver the votes of his delegates to him. The press assumed the same thing.

At that juncture, Heber McGinniss said to me, "If that's what they're expecting, they're in for one hell of a shock."

The reason he said that was clear enough. In order to improve his relations with the party activists in the state, Pat had chosen his delegation in a manner that was novel in those days, when delegates' badges went to fat cats and labor leaders who had contributed big money to the candidates who had won the primary elections in their states. In the early part of the year Pat had issued an invitation to the tens of thousands of people who were active in party affairs to meet in caucuses all over the state. He asked them to select from among themselves individuals they would like to see him appoint as members of his delegation. In every caucus C.D.C. liberals outnumbered all of the other people put together. Therefore, most of the names recommended to Pat by the caucuses were of the prelates of local C.D.C. clubs.

As I have explained in the appendix to this book, the California Democratic Council had arisen like a phoenix out of the ashes of the Adlai Stevenson campaign organization of 1952. We club people revered Stevenson. We had bled and died with him twice in hopeless campaigns against the greatest national hero of the age, Dwight Eisenhower. Articulate, witty, and urbane, Stevenson represented all that we admired most in ourselves. We were sure that if he could be nominated again in 1960, he would defeat Richard Nixon in the fall and become president, and having a president as brilliant as we were, after eight olive-drab years of Eisenhower, was more exciting to daydream about than a night in a motel with Marilyn Monroe.

When I saw Heber and Diane McGinniss the day after Brown had come out for JFK, Heber said dourly, "If Pat tries to make that delegation vote for Kennedy, they'll tell him to kiss —."

Diane said, "Heber!"

And Heber said, "A pig. Those purity freaks despise Kennedy for being a big money, big city, machine politician, and they'll never forgive him for buying the West Virginia primary right out from under Minnesota Fats."

Diane shot another schoolteacherish look of disapproval at Heber for his irreverent reference to Hubert Humphrey, who rated almost with Adlai Stevenson in the hierarchy of C.D.C. saints, but she agreed with what he said. "C.D.C. people look upon the Kennedy campaign as an exercise in corrupting the democratic process with money."

I said, "The national press people all think Pat should get on the ball and line up his delegation for Kennedy, and if he does, he'll have a lot to gain, especially if Kennedy wins."

Heber snorted disdainfully. "He's got a lot more to lose, a hell of a lot more. Most of the delegation would absolutely defy him, and that would make him look like a jerk."

Pat apparently saw things the way Heber did because when he announced that he was releasing his delegates from their commitments to vote for him, he said, "They are free to vote in accordance with the dictates of their consciences." He lived up to his commitment to support Jack Kennedy only by casting his own individual vote for him, while a large part of his delegation went for Stevenson, who wasn't even a candidate.

The effect upon the Governor was disastrous. Jack Kennedy decided that Pat was a stumblebum. Both as presidential nominee and as president, he turned to Jesse Unruh as his man in California. Unruh had supported him aggressively and had done all he could to line up votes for him among the California delegates. By so doing,

Big Daddy had confirmed C.D.C. people in their ill opinion of him as a power broker with no convictions at all. They never doubted that he was supporting the front runner because he was interested only in being on the winning side for the personal advantages it would bring him.

The national press concurred with Kennedy's opinion of Pat Brown. *Time Magazine* said of him that at the convention he proved himself to be a literal tower of jelly.

Overnight our good governor became a national image of gutless, witless, feckless, aimless nincompoopery. And that wasn't fair. Pat had a lot of courage really. He never hesitated to speak out on issues. For example, he opposed capital punishment, even though most Californians supported it.

During the week after the convention, Heber McGinniss and I met in the coffee shop of the U.S. Grant Hotel in San Diego to lay out a flyer for the general election campaign. We were both fond of Pat, and we were commiserating with each other over what had happened to him.

"He didn't really bumble," I said, "and it's not fair of the press to say he did."

"Those fine-haired fakers," Heber croaked, "have never seen anything like the C.D.C. in New York or Connecticut." He sucked up a taste of his hot coffee and went on a little less hoarsely. "They didn't realize Pat had lost the support of a lot of the club people when he let Caryl Chessman go to the gas chamber and he got them all back at the convention and they're absolutely essential to him."

"I wonder if he had any idea that the press would make him out to be such a boob for what he did."

"It wouldn't have made any difference," Heber said, grumpily firing up a cigarette. "There wasn't anything else he could do. Not a goddamned thing."

The consequences of Pat's historic pratfall were historic. In the public eye he became established as a fluttery and feather-brained hoot owl, who was the leader of the Democratic Party in California in name only.

The party never recovered either, as long as he was governor. All during those years he did everything he could think of to show the world that he was more than just its titular head. Most particularly he was disposed to put down anyone who was mentioned by the press as a potential rival for party leadership.

There was only one person in that category, and that was Big Daddy.

For months Joanna and I had recognized that factor as one source of the conflicts between the Governor and Unruh, but it had made no difference to us. In wars between good and evil, the question of which side initiates hostilities at any given time is never important to adherents of either cause. But now Joanna's and my own understanding of the fight between our party's two leaders was no longer one of virtue opposing iniquity. Consequently, the propriety of Pat's disquieting the party's and, therefore, our minds and spirits began to be a subject in our nightly soul-searching about what I should do.

5

How Big Daddy Became Speaker

And the government shall be upon his shoulder.

Isaiah 9:6

"At Bill Pearl's health studio in Sacramento last week a grunting behemoth of a man did twelve push-ups, then collapsed in a sweat. 'God you're strong, Jesse,' gasped an admirer. California Assemblyman Jesse Marvin (Big Daddy) Unruh, 38, surveyed his 275-pound girth and rumbled happily: 'If I get any stronger, I'll be so goddamned strong I'll be deadly.'"

So began, in the May 5, 1961 issue of *Time Magazine,* an article entitled "Big Daddy."

It went on: "As a politician, Jesse Unruh already bids fair to become the most powerful Democrat in the nation's second most populous state. A resident of Los Angeles, he has made Southern California his undisputed Democratic barony. In the California Assembly, where he is chairman of the Ways and Means Committee, he has surrounded himself with a tough and loyal group of followers known as Unruh's Praetorian Guard. Last week, with a majority of the Assembly already pledged in writing to support him, Unruh seemed certain to become Sacramento's next speaker. All that remained was to remove incumbent speaker Ralph Brown, and Big Daddy felt sure he could arrange for Brown to be appointed shortly to a high state judgeship in Fresno."

Time did not mention that the judgeship had been created by legislation carried on the floor of the Assembly by Ralph Brown himself. At the time the bill was enacted, everyone had known that Ralph was slated to fill one of the two new seats on the appellate court bench that it created.

The *Time* article hailed Big Daddy as one of the rising stars on the national political horizon in these words: "When, sometime in early 1962, Unruh picks up the speaker's gavel, he will take over a post that by the nature of its duties stands second only to the governorship in importance. California's Democratic governor, Edmund G. (Pat) Brown, a political master of the hesitation waltz, should be no particular obstacle in the path of Unruh's drive for actual party power. Already Unruh is greeted more warmly in John Kennedy's White House than Brown."

When I mentioned that paragraph to Heber McGinniss the day after the magazine hit the newsstands, he frowned and muttered, "That's the kind of put-down that makes Pat Brown screech like a barn owl in a chicken-plucking machine."

"It won't make Hale Champion too happy either," I replied.

Hale Champion was the gray eminence behind the Governor. A pale, corpulent, clever newspaper reporter, he had gotten started with Brown as his press secretary. Soon he had wormed his way into the Governor's confidence and to the position of executive secretary, and by May 1962, when the article was published in *Time Magazine*, he was scheduled to take over the highest appointed post in the executive branch of government, that of Director of the Department of Finance. By then it was becoming apparent to me that Hale was nurturing in his bosom some arcane designs that made him want to see the mighty carcass of the Dread Unruh laid out stone cold dead in the political thicket.

The *Time Magazine* piece was a horror story for California Democrats. It piled worry upon worry paragraph by paragraph. It concluded with this: "Observing Unruh's rise to power, Pat Brown has begun to show signs of anxiety. Last week he nervously summoned members of the Praetorian Guard to his office to warn them that he would not necessarily go along with Unruh's drive to take over the speakership. But what Big Daddy wants Big Daddy usually gets — and what he wants is the speakership as a means of extending his political rule over the entire state."

I had already learned from Bob Crown about the meeting in the Governor's office. He had come back from it to the floor of the Assembly boiling over with astonishment.

To put it mildly, the Governor had been ill-advised to try to stand in the way of the election of Unruh as speaker after he had the forty-one votes he needed to win that election. Apparently Pat harbored a naïve hope that a simple word of disapproval from him would cause all good Democrats in the Assembly to change their minds about voting for the Dread Unruh. He didn't realize that a coalition to elect a speaker cannot be taken apart once it has been stuck together with the crazy glue of politics. The reason for that is simple enough. When a candidate accumulates forty-one votes, all of the pragmatists clamber onto his rolling bandwagon, and no politician with an instinct for self-preservation will desert a candidate for the speakership who has, say, fifty votes, as Unruh did almost as soon as he had forty-one. But Pat Brown never did understand the Legislature. Like most governors, he stood off at a distance and deplored it as an unfortunate mistake made by our founding fathers. He thought of it as an obstacle to the executive branch in carrying out its responsibilities and governing the people wisely and well. Most presidents feel the same way about Congress, of course.

In response to Pat's futile attempt to deny him the speakership, Big Daddy said nothing publicly. I heard from Bob Crown that privately he said, "Shit." Even though Unruh chose to refrain from public comment upon the Governor's faux pas, *Time*'s national coverage of it gave it a consequence for all California Democrats. The story made Pat appear to have once again played the part of an incompetent, hand-wringing nincompoop. And that inevitably served to prod him anew to show the world that he was the man in charge of the Democratic Party in California.

It was only natural that Pat Brown, while he was governor, should look upon himself as the leader of the party and feel that loyalty to the party consisted of unquestioning allegiance to him. He had, after all, grown up politically in San Francisco in a time when the head of the party was looked upon as the Democratic jackass himself, made flesh and dwelling amongst us.

Hale Champion, who was no dummy, encouraged him to think of himself in those terms. I always presumed that it was he who counseled Pat to tell the Praetorian Guard that he might not go along with the election of Unruh as speaker. Certainly the effects of that action, which were foreseeable by any clever person, fell in line with what seemed to be his policy of keeping the Governor at odds with Jesse Unruh.

Pat tried one last stratagem to keep Big Daddy from the speakership. It, too, appeared to me to be a ploy of Champion's, designed to succeed only to the extent that it exacerbated the ill feelings between Brown and Unruh. What Pat did was to delay the appointment of Ralph Brown as justice of the district court of appeals, apparently in the idle hope that the bloc of Democrats supporting

Unruh would crack under the pressures being brought to bear upon it by the sixty thousand members of the C.D.C., who hated Jesse M. Unruh even more than they hated Richard M. Nixon. However, as Pat Brown put off appointing Ralph, he began to make the whole Assembly unhappy. Our good gray speaker was the most beloved man in the Capitol.

Of course, Big Daddy was infuriated by the Governor's actions, and that made Democrats like me worry. The situation was terribly serious and was getting to be more so with every day that passed because of the ill will that was building up between the Governor and the Speaker-to-be.

The end of the session came in June. On the last day we passed a resolution commending Ralph Brown for his many services to the state and wishing him well, even though he did not yet have his appointment as justice of the appellate court.

Pat Brown finally decided that he had better deliver on his promise to appoint Ralph, before a bad situation got worse. With an air of ungracious resignation, he at last announced the appointment of Ralph Brown as justice of the Fifth District Court of Appeals.

On September 30, 1961, the California Assembly seated itself in its stately chamber for the purpose of electing a new speaker. As it was the fall of the year, the regular session of the Legislature had long since been adjourned and the members' time was being taken up with attending hearings of committees and with listening to constituents' complaints. Consequently, it would have required all of us to cancel a lot of appointments to come to Sacramento on a weekday. That was one of the two reasons we met on September 30, a Saturday. The other was that the day was Jesse Unruh's thirty-ninth birthday, and Tom Bane thought it would be nice for him to get the speakership as a birthday present. That was a little schmaltzy for my tastes, but nobody asked for my opinion.

The speaker pro tempore, Carlos Bee, acting in the absence of a speaker, called the Assembly to order. Jesse Unruh stood by his desk on the floor, turning his huge bulk this way and that on his feet, counting the house. I knew he was concerned about the possibility that those members who were against him would not put themselves to the trouble of flying in from the four corners of the state to be spectators at an event they didn't want to see take place. He knew that some newspaper reporters would make the most of it if many assemblymen boycotted his moment of triumph. His muzzle relaxed when all but eight members answered the roll call at the beginning of the session.

There was no doubt in anyone's mind as to the outcome of the election. After Carlos Bee, his only serious rival, had dropped out, all of the Democrats in the Assembly had fallen in behind Unruh, with the sole exception of Gordon Winton, a battle-scarred veteran in the never-ending war against windmills. Gordon had decided to save the Assembly from dishonor by offering himself as a candidate for speaker to whose banner all good Democrats could flock, but none of them did.

As soon as the roll had been called and we had saluted the flag and heard the chaplain's prayer for us, Jerry Waldie rose to nominate Jesse Unruh. There were seconding speeches from three others: Gus Hawkins, at that time the senior member of the Assembly; Carley Porter, whose main goal in life was to secure an adequate supply of water for Southern California, as long as he didn't have to drink any of it; and Gus Garrigus, a homespun philosopher-poet from Reedley, a jerkwater cow town in Fresno County. (It seems to me it would be more appropriate to refer to such places as jerkmilk cow towns, but who am I to challenge so established a usage?)

In perusing the newspaper accounts of the event recently to refresh my memory of it, I read that the three speakers said Unruh was "strong, honest, honorable . . . motivated by the highest principles . . . with great ability, personal integrity, firmness, fairness, and the will and courage to act for the good of the Assembly and the state of California."

I noticed a few C.D.C. Democrats in the visitors' gallery. As they listened to the speeches, they looked as if they'd all had toadstool omelets for breakfast.

The dramatic climax of the scene came when Carlos Bee ordered the reading clerk to call the roll. Most of the members sang out "Unruh" with varying degrees of enthusiasm when their names were called. A corporal's guard of Republicans, who wanted to make it clear to the world that they disapproved of Big Daddy, yelled "Winton" defiantly, as did Gordon Winton himself. Charlie Chapel, a retired marine officer, who was wearing his uniform military look, bawled out the name of Harold Levering, a grumpy old red-baiter whom Charlie didn't like very much. It got a few laughs, so Harold Levering hollered "Charlie Chapel" and got a few more.

Carlos announced the result. "Fifty-three votes for Unruh,

twelve for Winton, one for Chapel, and one for Levering. Mr. Unruh has been elected speaker of the Assembly. Will the Speaker please come to the rostrum to be sworn in by Justice Ralph M. Brown of the Fifth District Court of Appeals."

Ralph Brown rose from one of the high-backed, carved, spindly thrones that have stood in back of the podium since the building was first occupied in 1874. It was the first time he had ever put on his black judicial robe, and swearing in Jesse Unruh was his first act as a justice of the appellate court. He did it with half a smile, giving us the impression that he found it a droll piece of stage business and difficult to get through with a straight face.

When Unruh had repeated after Ralph Brown the words of the oath through to the final "So help me, God," Tom Bane, Bob Crown, Nick Petris, and Tommy Rees marched in through a door just behind the rostrum bearing an ice floe of a birthday cake on their shoulders. A huge gavel made of blue and white icing rested on the top, as if it had just been used to strike the cake to bring the Assembly to order. On each end of a snowfield of frosting a clump of candles blazed away like a tiny torchlight parade in winter.

"Come on, fellows," Tom Bane said into the microphone, "Let's sing 'Happy Birthday' to the Speaker."

We did, with the birthday boy beaming down upon us. The staff at the Assembly desk and the lobbyists in the balcony all joined in, helping to make the pillars, pilasters, friezes, and cornices ring. After a minute of orderly applause, there ensued a silence punctuated by the popping of news photographers' flashbulbs as the new Speaker turned to the cake and blew out the two files of candles with two mighty whooshes. In a display of prudent enthusiasm we cheered, members, staff, lobbyists, and everyone else who would benefit by being in the good graces of the speaker of the Assembly. When he bellied up to the lectern to make his acceptance speech, his basso profundo was as soft as the rumbling of a three-hundred-pound turtledove.

He said, "Anything I might say at this point would be anti-climactic, except to thank all of you who voted for me for your support and all of those who didn't for being here. You have all contributed to one of the happiest days of my life. There is no thrill quite like being elected by your peers—those who know your strengths and weaknesses. I hope I can be half as good a speaker as my predecessor, Ralph Brown." Here he nodded respectfully toward

Ralph in his black robe, and Ralph nodded back at him with amused judicial detachment.

The Speaker concluded, "I thank you all from the bottom of my heart. If you're ever dissatisfied with any of my actions as speaker, I hope you'll let me be the first to know."

From behind me Don Allen said, "You bet your sweet ass we will, Jesse."

Unruh relinquished the gavel to Carlos Bee and lumbered grandly among congregations of back-slapping handshakers toward his desk on the floor.

A few procedural motions were disposed of. Then Carlos Bee announced, "Mr. Unruh, the desk is clear."

The Speaker said, "I move that this special session adjourn."

The motion was adopted by a unanimous voice vote. We all got up from our desks and congratulated the new speaker, including those members who hadn't voted for him. We all ate a piece of the birthday cake, and then we went to the basement and got into cars and were driven by sergeants-at-arms to the Sacramento Municipal Airport, where we scattered to the winds.

Any number of theses, dissertations, articles, and books have been written about the age of Unruh in the California Legislature, mostly by political science professors who preferred publishing to perishing and by journalists who wanted to earn a few extra dollars after hours by pounding a typewriter instead of their ears. They have explained to all who cared to read that Jesse Marvin Unruh became the speaker of the California Assembly by persuading his predecessor, Ralph Brown, to appoint his friend Bob Crown as chairman of the Elections and Reapportionment Committee to preside over the gerrymandering of the Assembly after the decennial census of 1960. As work on the reapportionment bill progressed, Bob Crown and Jesse Unruh could—and did—trade off comfortable districts to members in return for their votes for Unruh as speaker. However, that explanation of how Big Daddy rose to power is only the beginning of the truth. While he did in fact amass a solid bloc of support that way, it did not amount to enough votes to win him the speakership. In fact, it didn't even bring him within striking distance of it.

He was actually mounted upon the speaker's rostrum by a cabal of nine liberal Democrats, of which I was one. I had become a member of it during the third week of the legislative session. John Williamson, a lean, gray Bakersfield service station operator who represented half of Kern County, had stopped by my desk on the floor to have a few words with me. John was the sort of man anyone would instinctively trust. Born and bred in Kansas, he looked the part of an honest cattle rancher all dressed up in his good suit to go to church on Sunday. He had steady gray eyes that were surrounded by crinkles and crow's-feet etched there by the sun and wind. Everyone agreed he was one of the best members of the Assembly, no matter what measurement was applied to the eighty of us.

John settled his lanky frame into Captain Luckel's swivel chair, the one next to mine. He crinkled his eyes at me and said, "Jim, there are a few of us who meet on Tuesday mornings for breakfast in a little room upstairs at the back of the Chukker on J Street, to exchange scuttlebutt we've picked up in the course of the week. We are all Democrats who haven't been around here very long, so nobody thinks we're important enough to tell us what is going on. We try to find out what we can and tell each other what we've learned when we get together on Tuesday morning.

"We also meet to lay our problems on the table, in order to pool our inexperience to try to deal with them." He paused to let that thought sink in. "Tom Carrell is a member, so is Joe Kennick and Gus Garrigus and Jack Casey." He was naming people he knew I liked and respected. "This morning at breakfast the other members asked me to invite you to become a member of the group."

"Thank you," I said. "I'd like to."

I attended my first meeting the following Tuesday. Among the subjects discussed was the bill that created a judgeship for Ralph Brown. The entire breakfast club agreed that it would sail through to final passage without opposition and that there would then be an election to choose a new speaker, before the year was out probably.

By that time two members of the Assembly had let it be known that they wished to be considered as candidates for the speakership. They were Jesse Unruh and Carlos Bee. Carlos was the speaker pro tempore, which is the official title of the member who stands in for the speaker at the podium when he has to take up a bill on the floor himself or go to the men's room.

Carlos Bee and Jesse Unruh had each managed to round up twenty-eight votes of the forty-one required to elect a speaker in the eighty-member Assembly, but neither one of them seemed to be able to break through that barrier. All of the uncommitted members were holding out to see which of the two bandwagons was going to roll. They wanted to be *on* it, not *under* its wheels. We discussed that problem at every meeting of the breakfast club throughout January and February.

One morning over our bacon and eggs at the Chukker, Tom Carrell, my skinny old populist friend from east Texas, drawled sleepily, "You know, most of us are uncommitted in the speakership fight. We hadn't ought to let ourselves get picked off one by one by Jess or Carlos. We ought to agree among ourselves that we're all going to go together as a group."

All of us stopped chewing as if we had simultaneously bitten down on bits of something surprisingly delicious.

Tom took a long sip of black coffee, apparently in the hope that it might wake him up. "You know," he rambled on, "if we can agree to that, we'll be the ones who'll decide who the next speaker will be, and I can't think of anybody I'd rather have do it."

We all nodded in chorus except for Gus Garrigus, the philosopher-poet from the fleshpots (and milk pots) of Reedley, and Jack Casey of Bakersfield.

Gus Garrigus was as big and folksy as Burl Ives. He wiped his mouth with a napkin, smiled charitably, and said, "I love Carlos Bee like a brother, and I've already committed myself to him."

"So have I," Jack Casey chipped in.

Jack was a short, stocky Irishman with a red face and a flannel mouth, a fine barroom tenor who, in another life, had taught history at the community college in Bakersfield. He was one of these happy-go-lucky sons of Erin who could never say no to anybody. Jesse Unruh used to say of him, "If Jack Casey were a woman, he'd be pregnant all the time."

"If you can commit yourselves, I guess you can uncommit yourselves." Tom rubbed his wrinkled face with his bony hand as if to wipe away the sleepiness. "Naturally you're going to have to tell him why. Now he won't like losing two votes much, but you should point out to him that you'll be trying to get nine votes for him out of it."

All of us backed Tom up. Gus and Jack resisted because both of them loved Carlos, who was an easy man to love, but by the time we had finished our third cup of coffee, we had worn them down, and they agreed.

The following Tuesday at breakfast, Tom lazily made another proposal. "I'd like to have you all come for a confab some weekend at my place in San Fernando. You can bring your wives, and they can all chew the fat while we decide who's going to be the speaker."

Everyone liked the idea of settling down for a long discussion before we reached any conclusions, so a date was agreed upon.

On the appointed weekend all of us drove to Tom and Dolly Carrell's house, arriving just after lunchtime on a sunny Saturday afternoon. The Carrells' home was a pink, tile-roofed, two-story stucco palace that architecturally recalled Southern California's Spanish heritage. From its appearance I judged that it had been built in the early 1930's when that gracious style of home building reached its climax. Standing alone among wildflowers and chaparral on the south slope of a hill, it overlooked the subdivided sweep of the San Fernando Valley through close-set ranks of large windows. On our arrival, Joanna and I drove up a long asphalt driveway and parked our car in front of the Carrells' Spanish-style garage. We walked up a flight of red concrete steps onto a wide verandah of a front porch. There we said hello to the Carrells and those others who had already arrived, and we joined them in standing around and vocally admiring the view.

A fugitive from the poverty of eastern Texas and its hardscrabble farming, Tom was a self-made man; and he had done a good job of it while he was at it. He had migrated to Los Angeles from Cooper, Texas, to teach school but had soon decided to sell cars instead and had become a Chevrolet dealer in due time. As a result he was as rich as if he'd stayed home and had oil found on his south forty.

He was always somnolent and rational. No matter how other members might lose their heads in times of crisis, his weatherbeaten, mostly bald old noggin remained securely attached to his well-wrinkled neck. He lived mostly on rare beefsteaks and whiskey, as a good Texan is supposed to do. He liked a few sliced tomatoes on the side. As for whiskey, his choice was Old Rarity.

After the last couple, the Caseys, had arrived and joined us for a few minutes of commentary upon the view, Tom put an end to the socializing.

The sitting room, which was in back of the house, was the sort of parlor any old Texan would feel right at home in. The walls were knotty pine planking, and the floor was oak; the whole room was finished in clear varnish. In the southwest corner a regular round-up fire crackled and blazed in a chimney corner of round river stones. The fire and the fireplace were big enough to roast a steer in. On the floor were spread two large, oval, braided rag rugs that Dolly told us had been made in Texas by her mother many years before. The furniture was traditional American, maple chairs and the like, and it included a round dinner table under a set of mullioned sash windows that looked out on a green springtime hillside.

"Let's pull up some chairs and sit around the fire," Tom suggested.

We arranged nine chairs in a semicircle around the hearth. A middle-aged black maid in a black uniform trimmed with white lace made an unobtrusive entrance, and Tom said, "Any of you fellows care to wet your whistles?"

We all said we would. She took our orders, and we made small talk and watched the elemental magic of the flames until she returned and distributed a trayful of drinks.

After his first leisurely sip of Old Rarity, Tom said, "Well, boys, I guess it's about time we got on with choosing a speaker."

With a big Irish smile Jack Casey replied, "How can we go against Carlos? We all love him dearly, and he's almost as funny as Ralph Brown and that's important. We need a speaker who has a good sense of humor to keep us from going for each other's throats."

Joe Kennick, a solid ex-juvenile officer, who looked very British with his neatly trimmed white hair and mustache, said, "It's funny about Carlos. He's always so red in the face that he looks like he's mad enough to have a stroke, but he's probably the sweetest-tempered man in the Assembly."

"True, true," Gus Garrigus said, shaking his head and smiling in wonder at Carlos's good nature.

Carlos was, in fact, one of the nicest men in the world. He was kindly, gentle, friendly, cheerful, and witty. Usually his wife Jean Bee, the Queen Bee, stayed home in the district with their children, and Carlos circulated at night in Sacramento, eating, drinking, playing cards, and making friends wherever he went.

Carlos came from an aristocratic South Carolina family. He was the great-grandson of Hamilton Bee, a Confederate general. He was also the great-grandnephew of another Confederate general, Barnard Bee, the one who said, at the First Battle of Bull Run, "There stands Jackson like a stone wall," thereby tagging General Thomas J. Jackson with one of the most famous nicknames in history.

Still smiling expansively, Gus Garrigus went on. "Carlos's great-grandfather the general served as speaker of the Texas Assembly after the war. The idea of following in the old gentleman's footsteps means a lot to our friend."

The hottest club liberal among us was a passionate young attorney whom I shall call Terry. He is the only politician in this book to whom I have not referred by his right name. In appearance he was smoothly dark and handsome. He looked like a youthful Bela Lugosi made up to play a romantic role.

Impatient with us because we had any doubts in our minds as to what we should do, he cried, "Good grief! Can you imagine what our club people would say if we voted for Big Daddy? They'd be outraged. And don't forget that they're the people who put all of us in the Assembly."

However, John Williamson took a different tack. He said, "Carlos Bee is a sweetheart, and if this speakership election is going to be decided on the basis of the personal popularity of the two candidates, he'll win it going away. And I don't want to upset any of my club people any more than you do, Terry, but we all know that Carlos is not what anyone would call a leader of men. We all ran for the Assembly because we wanted to try to solve the problems of the people of the state, and that should be our first concern." John always spoke as matter-of-factly as if he were selling you an oil filter at his filling station in Bakersfield. He was always so reasonable in everything he said that he was sometimes tiresome to have around. He went on, "We all know that Jess is the one who's been providing the leadership in every fight for every cause that we believe in. He did more than anybody else to get the bill passed that set up the Fair Employment Practices Commission. He carried the bills outlawing racial discrimination by businesses. He led the fight to keep the loan sharks from grinding the faces of the poor. He . . ."

"He still can," Terry broke in. "He doesn't have to be speaker to do that. He wasn't in the past when he did all of that."

"He could do it better if he was the speaker," John replied calmly.

For a moment we pondered the truth of that statement in a silence broken only by the crackling of the fire. By its flickering light I saw Tom Carrell wipe the shadow of a smile off his face with his right hand. He seemed to be pleased with the turn the discussion had taken.

He took a little sip of Old Rarity and mused, "I bet old Jess would sure love to know what we're talking about."

The conversation continued in the same vein, with the logic of

John Williamson beginning to prevail, in my mind at least, over the passion of Terry. Every fifteen minutes or so Tom would arise, as if he were getting out of bed, to toss a few more logs onto the fire from a woodbox that was replenished from time to time by the silent black maid's silent black husband. With the thwack of each log on the fire a shower of sparks swirled up the cavernous chimney. As the afternoon passed away, more of the members of the group were won over by the patient logic of John Williamson. At last Tom roused himself from the edge of slumber to make a sleepy little speech.

"It seems to me that most of us are for old Jess, and we ought to find out if there's anybody here who doesn't think he can go along. Jess knows about our meeting, and he told me he'd stick around his house, just in case we ever decide we'd like to talk to him."

As I listened to Tom, I had no doubt in my mind as to who had let old Jess in on the secret of our meeting so he'd keep himself available in case we wanted to talk to him.

Tom drawled on. "Why don't I just call him up and ask him to come on over?"

Terry protested, "I'm not at all sure I'm willing to go along. Big Daddy can be pretty heavy-handed, you know, even now. Can you imagine what he'd be like if he was the speaker?"

Tom yawned during the silence that followed that comment and then said, "Oh, I've got a hunch old Jess'll settle down if we make him speaker. It's a big responsibility, and he'll sure want to do it right."

We all looked at Terry, awaiting his response.

He said grudgingly, "If the majority of you have decided you want to vote for Big Daddy and the rest are willing to go along, I'm not going to be the only holdout. I'll go along too, but only if he promises to give all of us chairmanships."

"Well, why don't we get him over here," Tom said, "and offer him that as a deal?"

Terry agreed to that glumly. Tom got up from his maple chair by the fire and went to the far side of the room to a maple side table with a telephone on it. He called Unruh at his home in Inglewood and said, "Jess, you reckon you could come on over and talk with the boys here?" After a pause he said, "That'll be fine. We'll see you in about an hour then."

He went into the kitchen to consult with the maid, who was also the cook. He came back and said, "I'm going to go ask the girls to come in and join us for a drink. Soup'll be on in a few minutes."

We had one drink each and some conversation about our families, and then sat down to eat at the round table. The maid put before us a piping-hot supper of fried chicken, yams, black-eyed peas, corn bread, and all the trimmings. After an hour of marvelous Texas-style chomping, during which the shades of dusk fell upon the springtime hillside outside the window, we heard Jesse Unruh growling up the steep driveway in his sporty gray Borg-Ward.

Tom wiped his mouth with his napkin. He looked around at us and said, "I guess I ought to go and show him in."

On entering the house, Jesse Unruh filled it with his mighty presence. We men at the table looked at each other uncomfortably, thinking about the self-serving demand we were going to put to him. When he loomed through the doorway into our sight, we had just finished our dinners and were waiting for our desserts. He lowered himself into a chair that Tom had pulled up to the table for him. It was next to Mrs. Casey, a very proper and refined lady. He said, "Hello," and everyone said, "Hello" back to him. The dinner plates had not yet been cleared away. He gazed at the one in front of Mrs. Casey. There was still some food on it.

He boomed, "BLACK-EYED PEAS!"

He seized the nearest fork and cleaned the leftover peas off Mrs. Casey's plate in five seconds.

The maid cleared away our dishes and served us apple pie and cheese, which we disposed of in a few minutes of amiable chin-wagging. When we had finished both pie and our last cups of coffee, Tom took a sip of water, swished it around his mouth to wash his teeth, and swallowed it. Then he drawled, "Why don't you girls go back to the living room while we get things sorted out with Jess."

As the women talked their way out of the room, we picked up our chairs and arranged them once again around the fire. The maid's husband had been appearing at intervals during supper to feed the flame a few logs, and it was still big enough to roast a steer. Tom must have burned half an acre of forest that afternoon and evening.

As soon as we had taken our places with our faces toward the fire, Tom said, "Jess, we just wanted to tell you we've decided we're going to support you, but . . ."

Terry broke in, "But we have to have a commitment from you that you'll give all of us chairmanships—good ones—ones that we want."

Our huge visitor responded with all the sincerity and cordiality of a college football coach recruiting on a high school campus.

"Everything's open. I haven't made any commitments to anyone. I think you all know Bobby Crown can have anything from me
that he wants, but he hasn't asked me for anything yet. Let me . . ."

Terry, his eyes narrowing with suspicion, interrupted again,
"You're not willing to promise us that you'll give all of us chairmanships?"

"That's right. I haven't promised any chairmanships to anybody else, so it wouldn't be fair to make that kind of commitment to
any of you. I can't start handing out chairmanships till I see how the
Assembly should be organized."

Terry carried on in the same vein for another ten minutes,
continually asking the same question and getting the same answer,
while we all squirmed, except for Tom Carrell, who looked content
enough to take a nice nap.

As far as everyone but Terry was concerned, it was a friendly
discussion. None of us felt too comfortable with the thought of
selling our votes for a stated price. It had been Terry's idea and no
one else's. We were all calling Unruh Jess, as his friends did, rather
than Jesse.

Terry seemed to be afraid that we all were going to desert him.
He had it figured out that if any of us didn't get a chairmanship from
Unruh, it would be he. He had rubbed Jess the wrong way more
than once, and he was doing it again that night in the flickering
light of the great fire.

He said finally and defiantly, "You know the condition for our
support. Take it or leave it."

Unruh was unperturbed. "I can only tell you that if you go
along, none of you will regret it."

Tom Carrell slipped drowsily into that opening. "That's good
enough for me. How about you, John?"

John Williamson said, "That's fine with me."

Tom looked at Gus Garrigus, who wanted to be everybody's
friend. "How about it, Gus?"

Gus smiled expansively and said, "Everybody knows Jess's
word is good. I'll go along."

"Me too," said Joe Kennick.

And so it went, until all had concurred, one by one.

Terry was the last. With disgruntlement curdling his voice he
said, "Okay, if you fellows have decided to go along, I guess I will."

When we all escorted Jess Unruh out of the Carrells' house
that night and saw him slip into his little Borg-Ward as if it were a

tight shoe, we knew we were saying good night to the next speaker of the Assembly. With our nine votes to add to the twenty-eight he already had, he only needed to pick up four more, which would be child's play for him.

The following week in Sacramento he gathered four Republican realists into the fold. He invited them to dinner at a restaurant on the east side of Sacramento, where he fed them lobsters that had been flown in live from Maine, plied them with a good California chablis, and explained to them how close he was to getting the forty-one votes he needed and how he would always remember with appreciation those who helped him get up to that magic number. They already knew about the decision of the breakfast club, of course. They had come prepared to commit themselves to vote for him, and they did it as soon as he asked them.

On April 21 Jess Unruh announced to the world that he had forty-one votes. In a few days after that the figure had risen to fifty-three, as stragglers scrambled onto his bandwagon. And that is how the die was cast and Jess Unruh crossed the Rubicon, causing Pat Brown, like Pompey, to look to his defenses.

A week later, Tom and I were having a drink together before lunch amid the ferment of lawmakers and lobbyists at the bar at Bedell's restaurant a half a block away from the Capitol. He drawled in my ear, "I knew how things would go if I could get the group together and get them to agree to let old Jess come over and talk to us, and I didn't think that'd be too hard to do."

Sometimes I am a little slow. It hadn't dawned on me till then that Tom had decided right at the start that Jess should be speaker and that he had conducted the performance of our little ensemble like a rustic Arturo Toscanini.

6

The Chubbiest Chubb Fellow

He was a scholar, and a ripe and good one.

William Shakespeare

I hope God will forgive me for having introduced, in 1966, an amendment to the constitution of California that raised the salaries of members of the Legislature to $16,000 a year and provided for annual general sessions. The Legislature put it on the ballot in the November election of that year, and the voters approved it. Prior to the adoption of that measure, the Legislature had messed with the laws of California only during the odd-numbered years. In the even-numbered years, we assembled briefly in what were called budget sessions to adopt a spending program for the ensuing fiscal year. We would convene early in February and, after a week of drinking at lobbyists' expense, recess for a month while the Assembly Ways and Means Committee and the Senate Finance Committee scrutinized the budget line by line. When they were done, the two houses would reconvene and vote on the budget bill they had formulated, and then we would adjourn and go home to campaign for re-election.

In February of 1962, when the Legislature convened for its week of budget session revelry and Jess Unruh was getting settled into the spacious office of the speaker of the Assembly for the first time, he invited me to come there and sit in on a meeting of his Praetorian Guard, which then consisted of Bob Crown, Tom Bane, Jerry Waldie, and Jess himself. I presumed I had been included that one time because they were going to be considering some subject of special interest to me, like election reform. However, the discussion was a general one about how much we could increase state spending for welfare and education.

I was surprised when Jess spoke to me on the floor the following day and asked me to sit in on the next meeting. He invited me to the one after that, too, and I realized that I was being called into all of the conferences of the Speaker's inner circle and that I had apparently become a member of it. I would have had qualms about finding myself so intimately involved with Big Daddy only a few months before, but he and Pat Brown had opened my mind for me. Therefore, I accepted my new position of influence with heartfelt surprise and gratification.

At the close of most working days we would congregate in Unruh's office to settle into the big, cool, brown leather easy chairs there, though the Speaker would remain in his high-backed, tan leather swivel chair behind his seven-foot-wide walnut desk, which had recently been made to order for his office in the furniture shop at San Quentin prison. It was symbolic of that era of California history, being aerospace modern in its design. The top of it had a uniformly curved leading edge like that of a flying wing. In the middle, where a blotter might have been, there was let into it a leather rectangle, upon which the Speaker customarily rested his massive forearms.

The office was a twenty-by-twenty-foot cubicle, the four walls of which were paneled with walnut the same tan color as the desk. The ceiling was framed into oblongs of translucent white plastic that glowed with the ghostly light of the fluorescent tubes above them. The red flush of the dying day normally burned behind the Speaker's high-backed chair, where the only window in the room framed a rectangle of California sky and the midsections of three redwood trees just outside in Capitol Park. On either side of that window, flanking the Speaker's chair, were an American flag on an eight-foot, varnished, pine pole, which ended in a brass eagle, and a flag of California on a like staff that was armed with a brass spearhead on its tip.

As we gathered in that office, we would contemplate the semi-abstract paintings on the walnut walls. Betty Coffey, the Speaker's secretary, would serve us drinks from a little closet that contained a white porcelain washbowl, a medicine cabinet full of glasses, a refrigerator full of mixers, and a shelf full of liquor bottles. We would then discuss legislative tactics and political strategies, economic theories and governmental philosophies, sports, moving pictures, books, and women.

With the passage of the next few months I began to realize that behind the Gargantuan front of Big Daddy there beat the heart of an academician. I also became aware that I was not alone in discerning that, because at about that time he was appointed resident politician at the Eagleton Institute for the Study of Politics at Rutgers and elected a trustee of the Institute of American Universities. In 1963 he was chosen to be a Chubb Fellow. That fellowship was named for Hendon Chubb, a New York insurance tycoon who had endowed a program of bringing notable public figures to Yale to deliver lectures on politics and government. Among Jess's predecessors as Chubb Fellows had been Harry Truman, Adlai Stevenson, Barry Goldwater, and C. P. Snow. Illustrious as they were, none of those worthies attracted the attention of the national news media while at Yale in the way Jess Unruh did.

Look Magazine ran a feature entitled "Big Daddy Goes to Yale." It was illustrated by a gallery of photographs of his colossal form in the lecture hall, about the campus, and at a table down at Mory's. In every picture he was surrounded by a coterie of admiring students. He was obviously captivating them, even though, as Look observed, "he seemed like a bulldozer about to cultivate a bed of petunias."

I liked that figure of speech. I had never before thought of Yalies as petunias.

Newsweek entitled its story of the Speaker's sojourn at old Eli, "Big Daddy on Campus." The president of the senior honors group expressed the student view of the visiting heavyweight in this Newsweek quote: "He looks like Tammany Hall, but he sounds like the New Frontier."

In the Newsweek article there was a blinky-kinky sidelight. A twenty-four-year-old law student, one Edmund G. Brown, Jr., otherwise known as Jerry, Pat's only son, was among those who sat in on a lecture Jess gave on the subject of the 1962 gubernatorial campaign, in which Pat, running for re-election, had defeated Richard Nixon. Newsweek reported that during the time allowed for questions at the end of the hour, Jerry had asked, "How did my mother contribute to my father's victory?" It was a smart-aleck question, and I was surprised when I read it, even though I had always thought that Jerry was a little odd. Although there are lots of young men and boys who feel hostility toward their mothers, with and without cause, there aren't many who make such a public display of that feeling, especially not when their mothers would read about it in print, along with everybody else.

A dozen years later, during Jerry's own first term as governor, I was reminded of that gaucherie of his. Pat had come by my office to visit and talk about old times. Just before going out the door, he said, "Say, Jim, the next time you see Jerry would you ask him to call his mother? She hasn't had a word from him for months. She feels very bad about it."

I love Bernice Brown, as does everyone else who knows her except, perhaps, for Jerry, so I said, "I'd be glad to, Pat, but why don't you do it yourself?"

With a specter of a smile, Pat said, "I can never get to see him."

Quite apparently Jerry Brown was still in the throes of his adolescent rebellion. I was surprised that becoming governor hadn't snapped him out of it, and I have wondered since if having succeeded in either of his campaigns for the presidency would have done it.

Jess Unruh wisecracked about the distinction Yale had conferred upon him. The magazine stories said that at the beginning of his first lecture he had commented, "I guess I must be the chubbiest Chubb Fellow of all."

He repeated the line when he got back to California, but I thought he only joked about the fellowship because it meant a great deal to him and he couldn't speak seriously about it without feeling uncomfortable, and that would not have been in character for the Dread Unruh.

His public image did not suggest the complexity of his character, and in that, of course, he was like all other public figures. He was much more of a political philosopher than anyone else in either house of the California Legislature. When I mentioned to him that Sam Geddes had told me that the way to stay in the Legislature was to vote for every appropriation and against every tax increase, he had surprised me by quoting Plato to the effect that the greatest danger to a democracy is that the people will always want more than they will be willing to pay for. When we discussed politics and government and legislation in his office, he often cited Plato or Seneca or Montesquieu or Locke or de Tocqueville relative to the principles at issue. No matter how others might urge upon him short-term political considerations when we were reaching a decision, he was always concerned about the ultimate implications. I had never suspected that of him before I got to know him.

Because he agreed with Polybius that the past is the best prompter of governmental actions, he was a student of history. And since I was the only professional historian among the leadership of the house, he enjoyed getting one up on me from time to time. He scored a point in that game just after Lyndon Johnson swamped Barry Goldwater in the presidential election in November 1964. In that same election the Democrats lost three seats in the State Assembly.

In an interview on election night, at the office of the Registrar of Voters, I was asked by Harold Keen, the dean of San Diego's television commentators, "Do you have anything you'd like to say about the Democratic landslide?"

"A few more Democratic landslides like this one," I replied, "and the Republicans will do the next reapportionment."

That comment was picked up and quoted by the news media throughout the state. Jess referred to it in a speech he made to members of the Democratic State Central Committee at the Ambassador Hotel in Los Angeles a few weeks later. I was sitting in the back with Heber McGinniss. Jess grinned at me across the audience and said, "Jim Mills summed up the results of the last election better than anyone else when he paraphrased what King Pyrrhus said after the Battle of Asculum. When one of his aides told him that he'd won a great victory, he answered him, 'Yes, and another victory like that one and I'll be ruined.'"

Heber McGinniss said to me, "Is that where you got that line from?"

I nodded.

He said, "Well, I'll be dipped in shit."

An old lady behind us said, "Ssssh."

I was talking to Heber in the back of the room as the meeting began to disintegrate. When Jess came by on his way out, he rumbled happily at me, "You didn't expect me to know where you lifted that line from, did you?"

"I can't say that I did," I replied, "and neither did Heber."

He walked away looking as triumphant as Lucius Cornelius Lentulus after he defeated Pyrrhus (with the assistance of Manius Curius Dentatus, of course) at the Battle of Beneventum.

7

An Unmatched Pair

No man is unimportant who has a friend.

> Variously attributed to
> Bert Lance,
> G. Gordon Liddy,
> and Tonto

*J*ust a few feet down the green back hall from the Assembly chamber, there was, in an aluminum doorway frame, a pale birchwood slab door. On the wall to one side of that portal was affixed a black formica sign with these words in white Roman letters graven into it, *MEN, Reserved for the Use of Members.* It was beyond that door that I met Charlie Meyers on the day I was sworn in, just after the adjournment of the session.

Conscious of a modest pride that I was entitled to pass into that sanctuary of movers and shakers, I had stepped up to a shining white porcelain urinal. Already facing up to the adjacent fixture and the green ceramic tile wall upon which it was mounted stood a well-rounded fellow of middle height. He turned upon me with a smile that wreathed a face as soft, as fresh, and as pink as a tea rose. His expression was that of a happy baby in a television commercial for diapers. His chestnut hair had a high sheen and perfectly regular Brylcream wave.

Quickly he changed hands, in order to take in his left that which he ordinarily held in his right at such times. As he did so, words tumbled out of him in a freshet of good will. "I'm Charlie Meyers and you must be Jim Mills from San Diego." He extended to me the right hand of fellowship and carried on brightly, "Welcome to the Assembly. Is everything all right?"

I stared at his extended hand. Not being quick-witted enough to think of anything else to do, I followed his example. I shifted over from the right-handed stance to the left and shook hands. His grip was warm and hearty.

Still with his right hand he reached into a jacket pocket and withdrew something wrapped in silver foil. He said, "Would you care for a mint?"

I took it, put it in one of my pockets, and said, "Thanks." That was the first of hundreds of mints he would give me during my six years in the Assembly.

It really hadn't been necessary for him to introduce himself to me. I knew who he was. For years I had been reading in the newspapers about his wonderful bills. There had been one that would have made it a misdemeanor to jump off the Golden Gate Bridge. Inasmuch as nobody survives that plunge, it wasn't a bill that would have affected anybody if it had been enacted, which it wasn't; yet it was the subject of a great deal of press coverage and commentary. It was presented by the news media to the public as an illustration of the shimmering brilliance of the statesmen in the California Assembly.

Charlie's most famous crusade was one to overthrow the cruel tyranny of the plutocrats who had imposed pay toilets upon the long-suffering public. He surfaced with a bill that would have made it the law of California that no more than two-thirds of the johnny doors in any public restroom could be coin-operated.

Newspapers carried Charlie's clarion call throughout the state:

ONE IN THREE
MUST BE FREE!

It was a good bill, but no one noticed because Charlie was carrying it, and everyone found it hard to take him seriously. However, as soon as he retired, another legislative original, a lady who rejoiced in the euphonious name of March Fong, introduced a similar bill. She declared that the passage of the bill would represent an important victory in the battle for equal treatment of women because men didn't have to come up with a dime when they only wanted to tinkle and women did.

Charlie had said the same thing, and the newspapers had played it as high humor, except for those who played it as low humor. However, when March Fong voiced the very same call for equal rights and smashed a toilet bowl into glistening shards on the steps of the Capitol with a claw hammer, the journalists of California clasped her to their inky hearts. She got her bill passed, and the publicity the press gave her smash-hit performance convinced their readers that she was qualified for higher office. As a result, she rode into the office of secretary of state of California in 1974, figuratively astride a toilet bowl as a metaphorical white horse. And she is there still.

Charlie was one of an unlikely pair of friends. The other was Robert W. Crown of Alameda. They were living proof that opposites attract, whenever birds of a feather aren't flocking together. When Bob wasn't spending time in the company of his other best friend, Jess Unruh, he would pal around with Charlie, who was as unlike him as anyone could be.

There is a youthful innocence about Charlie Meyers even today, twenty-four years after I first reluctantly shook his outstretched hand in the men's room. There is no one so far beyond the reach of the clawing fingernails of time in all history and literature as he, with the sole exception of Dorian Gray. Jess Unruh once said, in that connection, "The difference between Charlie and Dorian Gray is that if Charlie had in his attic a painting of himself like the one Dorian Gray had, it would look as bright-eyed and bushy-tailed as the squirrels in Capitol Park."

Bob Crown, on the other hand, was sophisticated, brilliant, debonair, graceful, and scintillating. From the first Monday in January 1957 when he was first sworn in, he had been charming everyone in the Capitol out of his or her socks, although with reference to the secretaries in the building, I suppose it would be more apropos to say that he had been charming them out of their panty hose.

Despite the acquisitive designs of any number of young women about the Capitol, Bob had never married. He told me once, "I agree with Plato when he said, 'It is better if men who rule do not take wives unto themselves'—unless the wives are someone else's, of course."

His Brooks Brothers suits concealed a physique like Clark Kent's. Every day he took time to work out or to run. He did push-ups and sit-ups before sundown with as much dedication as he did nip-ups for his lady friends after night had fallen.

It was always a joy to see Bobby come cake-walking down the hall respendent in the burnished armor of his vitality. He was full of friendship and useless information. He and I always played the trivia game when we passed each other on our daily rounds.

"In what round did Jim Jeffries knock out Bob Fitzsimmons in their second fight?" I called to him when our paths crossed one day in the main hall on the third floor of the annex in front of the stainless steel bank of elevators.

"The eighth," he replied. "Name the captains of the *Monitor* and the *Merrimack* when they fought at Hampton Roads."

"Worden and Buchanan. Who was the only man to hold the powers of the president of the United States for less than twenty-four hours?"

"David Atchison," he called back to me as he disappeared around the corner into another hallway and I went off in the other direction, leaving the people who were waiting for elevators to wonder if we really knew what we were talking about or if we were only putting them on.

Because being a member of the Assembly gave him the opportunity to promote such things for his district as the filling of a good deal of San Francisco Bay to provide land for all kinds of facilities for the port of Oakland, Bob said he enjoyed being a member of the Legislature more than anything else he could have done to earn a living. He even told Pat Brown that once, but Pat didn't understand when we said things like that. Bob had gone to see the Governor to ask him to appoint one of his friends to a judgeship. Of course Pat never wanted to do any of Jess's friends any favors that might enhance their reputations for political influence or effectiveness. Therefore, he evaded Bob's question.

Lifting a line from Longfellow, he said, "Why don't you speak for yourself, Bob? You'd be a great judge."

Pat was offering Bob the judgeship as a way out of an awkward situation. He owed Bob a lot because Bob was always pulling his chestnuts out of the fire in the Assembly Ways and Means Committee by killing appropriations that Pat would otherwise have to veto, to his political disadvantage. (The chairmanship of that committee was what Bob had asked Jess Unruh for after the speakership fight was over.) Pat's offer of a judgeship was undoubtedly made in good faith; Bob would indeed have made a great judge. As a lawmaker he concerned himself more about the integrity of the judiciary than any other subject, and he fought for it so well that even his most outspoken opponents respected him highly.

Bob brushed the offer aside with, "No, thanks, Governor. I've found a home here."

Pat rasped jovially, "Oh, really. I didn't know you'd bought a house in Sacramento."

That became Bob's favorite Pat Brown story. It was the kind of answer we expected only from Charlie Meyers and the Governor. Like Charlie, Pat was a curious mixture of guile and simplicity. The two of them were both old-fashioned San Francisco politicians, and that is a breed made charming by its cynical innocence.

Bob Crown and Charlie Meyers were two of the friendliest men in the Assembly, and that was all that they had in common. Bobby spent his off-hours in pursuit of sex. Charlie was a devoted husband and father. Bobby was an agnostic. Charlie was a good Catholic. Even before Bobby became the chairman of the Ways and Means Committee, he had been one of the most influential members of the Assembly. Charlie never was and never could have been. Bobby had a splendid elegance about him. Charlie changed hands in the men's room to glad-hand anyone who stood next to him. Yet they got along like Peter Pan and Wendy. They went to dinner together; they went to the movies together; they sat for hours in quiet places together, all wrapped up in private conversations.

Seeing them head to head at Frank Fat's Chinese restaurant one night, Jerry Waldie, the Democratic caucus chairman, said to me, "I wonder what they have to talk about."

That started me to wondering too, and I haven't stopped yet.

Nowadays Charlie is remembered in the Legislature mostly for lugging a stack of folders around under his arm wherever he went. It was never less than ten inches thick. I once asked Carlos Bee, "Do you know what Charlie has in those folders?"

Carlos told me, "He has everything relating to a lot of bills he carried in past sessions. And he has all of the literature and flyers and mailing pieces from all of his past campaigns and all of his opponents' campaigns, too. He totes all of it around with him in case anyone he meets asks him about any of those things, but nobody ever does."

Charlie was the hero of many a Sacramento folktale. Most of them had to do with his practice of making phone calls in the middle of the night. Any time he thought of something he'd like to say to someone, he would call. Sometimes it was from a phone booth on the way home from dinners, meetings, dances, or other gatherings where he could press the flesh with his constituents. Sometimes he would be lying awake in his bed when he thought of something he wanted to say to somebody. Not uncommonly he just wanted to say, "Hello. Is everything all right?"

He called Bob Crown every night or two. Bob loved him and didn't like to say anything that would make people laugh at him, but there were times when he was so amused by something Charlie did that he couldn't keep it to himself.

Bob came home from a vacation spent chasing golden women in Hawaii, and the day after his return, at a meeting in Jess's office, he said gaily, "Can you guess who called me up in the middle of the night while I was in Hawaii?"

"Charlie," everyone chorused.

"I was sound asleep after a busy day and the phone rang. I picked it up and what did I hear?"

"Bobby, this is Charlie," we sang out. "Is everything all right?"

"I squinted at my watch and said, 'My god, Charlie! It's a quarter after three in the morning! Couldn't you have waited to talk to me tomorrow?'"

"And do you know what Charlie said?" Bobby was bursting with glee. "He said, 'Gee, Bobby, I'm sorry, but I didn't think you'd mind talking to me because you'd have to wake up to answer the phone anyway.'"

That was a typical Charlie Meyers phone call story. Invariably the person he called complained about the hour, and Charlie offered a lame-brained apology and went on with whatever it was he wanted to say. It was clear that he felt he was complying with the rules of etiquette by offering any excuse, no matter what it was, and by expressing his regrets. Like the rest of us, Charlie knew that social usages are, in large part, empty forms and that courtesy has become mostly a matter of custom in this ungraceful age, but Charlie, unlike the rest of us, governed his conduct accordingly. To him it seemed perfectly appropriate to go ahead and carry on a friendly conversation after he had observed the usual formalities as formalities. Every few weeks someone would report Charlie's latest apology for a nocturnal phone call, and the story would sweep through the Capitol like a merry little breeze. He couldn't have come up with better lines if he had employed a professional gag writer. In fact, he couldn't have done half so well. It was Charlie's invincible innocence that made the stories bewitching.

Once he called up a prominent Democrat in San Francisco, an

Italian druggist named Al, upon whom Charlie counted for support in every campaign. Most politicians spend a lot time on the phone massaging the egos of people who have helped them in the past; it is done in the hope that it will inspire them to do it again in the future. The only difference about what Charlie did was that he did it in the middle of the night.

It was Al who told the world the story of Charlie's call, of course. He said that when he answered the phone, he heard Charlie's cry of, "Al, this is Charlie. Is everything all right?"

He said he replied, "Charlie, for God's sake, it's past midnight and I'm making love to my wife."

"Oh, gee, Al, I'm sorry," Charlie said. "Go right ahead. I'll hold the phone."

One day in 1966, my last year in the Assembly, I dropped by Charlie's office to talk to him about some legislation that was coming up for a vote. Charlie wasn't in, so I asked his secretary to tell him I wanted to talk with him.

When Charlie heard from his secretary that I wanted words with him, he was disquieted. He wanted to know what I'd come to see him about before he met with me. Therefore, while I was attending a Ways and Means Committee meeting, he dropped by to pump my secretary, Madeline Haskins.

First he offered her a mint, of course. Then he asked her why I wanted to see him. I hadn't told her, so she said she didn't know. He asked her if she could guess.

She said she told him, "Maybe he just dropped by to pay a friendly call."

She told me, "He shook his head and said, 'Oh, no. Oh, no. Jim Mills doesn't just drop by to pay a friendly call.'"

"What happened then?" I asked her.

"He went away worrying."

"I guess he'll keep on worrying till he comes in to see me," I said and went on to deal with the mail on my desk.

At that time my chief aide was Phil Schott, an apprentice master of men of German-American ancestry. Phil was a hefty fellow with a Teutonic head of short, dun-colored hair and a full beard, which he kept trimmed short. It made him look like the commander of a German zeppelin in an old motion picture about World War I. Since then Phil has gone on to better things; he has become a lobbyist. When he achieved that distinction, he cut off his beard because it is not considered good form for lobbyists to look like zeppelin commanders. It is thought to be more seemly for them to look like the pilots of Messerschmitts.

Charlie must have been lying awake all night after the day I went by his office, worrying about what it might be that I wanted to discuss with him, because at four in the morning he decided to call Phil to try to find out.

Phil marched into my office looking militarily light-hearted to tell me about it the following day. He said, "The phone beside my bed rang in the middle of the night, and when I mumbled 'Unh?' into it, I heard, 'Phil, this is Charlie. Is everything all right?'

"'It was, till you called me,' I told him. 'I was asleep. Charlie, have you any idea what time it is?'

"'Yes, Phil,' he said, as chipper as hell, 'It's three minutes after four.'" Here Phil began to grin.

"'Why in the hell are you waking me up at three minutes after four?' I said, and he said, 'Gee, I'm sorry, Phil, I wouldn't have called you if I'd known you were home.'"

"I love it," I said to Phil.

"So did I," he said. "It made me laugh for about five minutes. When I finally got over the giggles I said, 'Okay, Charlie. What do you want to talk to me about?' and Charlie said, 'Jim Mills came by my office today and told my secretary he wants to talk to me. Naturally if one of the members of the Democratic leadership wants to talk to me I'd like to know what it's about.'"

"What did you tell him?" I asked Phil.

"I said, 'Charlie, if Jim Mills says he wants to talk to you, you should let him, but I wouldn't call him up at this hour, if I were you, because he might be at home, too.'"

Charlie Meyers was first elected to the Assembly in 1948, when the salary of the members was $100 a month. It had been set at that figure by a vote of the people, who never want to spend much on their lawmakers and who generally get just about what they pay for. Charlie served a total of twenty years, during which time the salary of members was raised three times and better-paid newcomers upgraded the operation until the California Legislature was generally conceded to be the best in the nation. Every election year Charlie would turn back the challenges of the brightest young men the Republicans could recruit to run against him.

The secret of his success was that he never missed a baptism, a *bris*, a bar mitzvah, a wedding, a funeral, or a wake within the city of

San Francisco. Jess Unruh used to say of him, "Whenever two or three people are gathered together in San Francisco, one of them will be Charlie Meyers."

He was never known to arrive anywhere on time, but, on the other hand, he never showed up too late to say good-bye to every-body. His constituents all knew him and appreciated him for what he was, a warm-hearted friend.

However, in the spring of 1966 he got into trouble. He had working for him at that time an intense Serb named Bob Visnick. Bob was the administrative assistant who ran his district office in San Francisco. One morning in February I saw in the *San Francisco Chronicle*, to my surprise, that Bob had taken out papers to file as a candidate for the Assembly in the Nineteenth District, which was Charlie's district. Members of the Legislature consider it bad form for any of their office staffs to run against them, so Charlie fired Bob. Shortly thereafter Bob announced that he would not be a candidate after all. Then he seemed to disappear from the face of California till August, when, after having nurtured the sacred fire of his wrath in seclusion for six months, he let it blaze forth. He called a press conference in San Francisco and made all kinds of charges against Charlie, some of which may have been justified.

The two San Francisco daily papers made a journalistic circus of the story. They both had been trying to get rid of Charlie for years. They didn't think he was a fit representative for the city for some reason.

Because Charlie was thought to be unbeatable until Visnick tossed his bombshells to the press in August of 1966, the Republi-cans had only fielded a token candidate against him. However, in anticipation of the 1968 elections, they began to put together a blizzard of a campaign to snow him under. Jess Unruh conferred at length with his inner circle about Charlie's plight. The conclusion was that all of those terrible newspaper stories had destroyed him politically. Everyone present agreed that poor Charlie could not be re-elected and that he should retire for the sake of the party, so Democrats wouldn't lose the seat.

Naturally it was Bobby Crown who drew the assignment of prevailing upon Charlie not to be a candidate for re-election. We all knew he would believe Bob when he told him it would be better for him if he didn't run, whereas he might not believe anyone else.

Bob spent a long evening with him and convinced him not to

file for re-election. He told me afterwards, "God! That was the toughest thing I ever had to do."

Charlie announced his retirement in due time. A few days later a cool young Irishman from New Zealand named Leo McCarthy declared that he would be a candidate for Charlie's seat. He put together an effective campaign, and the Republicans lost the Nineteenth Assembly District again.

Just six years later Leo McCarthy was the speaker of the Assembly and the second most powerful man in the government of California. And another six years after that he was elected lieutenant governor of California, and now he's running for United States senator, and that shows how the ripples from every political splash spread for ever and ever.

8

Wine, Women, and Politicians

The nakedness of woman is the work of God.

William Blake

There were journalists who gave the people of California to believe that, as far as their lawmakers were concerned, every night in Sacramento was an orgy of wine, women, and song. That was not entirely true. Only when Jess Unruh had a skinful and raised a basso profundo like rolling thunder in some melodic old favorite like "Cats on the Rooftops" did song become anything of a problem.

There were other ways in which the impression those journalists gave to the public, with regard to nightlife in Sacramento, was inaccurate. It was not at all just to charge the Legislature as a whole with drunkenness and philandering; for example, such a blanket accusation did not allow for the disparities between the two houses. In general the Senate was guilty of drunkenness but, unlike the Assembly, was innocent of philandering. Its members were, in large part, old goats who did not engage in the pursuit of women because it conflicted with their favorite pastime, drinking. The only women whom they ever tried to attract were cocktail waitresses.

Jess Unruh once expressed that difference between the two houses in these words: "When an assemblyman starts telling you about somebody he'd like to screw, he'll be talking about a secretary; but when a senator does, he'll be talking about a colleague."

There were also some other tribal customs that distinguished Republicans from Democrats with regard to sexual behavior. Jess delivered himself of Unruh's maxim on partisan sexual peculiarities in the course of a dinner he threw for—or perhaps I should say at—a young Republican newspaper publisher. It was an intimate affair staged in the subterranean gloaming of the wine cellar of the

Firehouse, one of Sacramento's more pretentious steak and chop houses. (It was the only one where the waiters wore tuxedoes.) The room really was an honest-to-goodness wine cellar; one end of it was cross-hatched into bins filled with wine bottles.

The company that night was exclusive. Aside from the young publisher, the only ones seated around the long, dark, polished mahogany table in the light of dozens of tall, white, tapered candles in two branching silver candelabra were Jess Unruh, Carlos Bee, Jerry Waldie, Bob Crown, myself, and a few other members whom the Speaker thought would make a favorable impression upon the honored guest. We were all ensconced in dark, antique chairs with high backs carved into open scrollwork. The rounded tops of the backs of the chairs were visible behind our heads like old haloes that had gone out as a result of our misbehavior.

The dinner, the wines, and the conversation had as high a finish as our guest, who was the scion of a dynasty of newspaper owners. Though he was a New Yorker born and bred, he affected a wonderfully fruity upper-class English accent.

At one point our guest said, "I say, Unruh, there really isn't all that much difference between Republicans and Democrats in the State Legislature, now is there?"

"Yes, there really is," Jess replied, nodding at a waiter who held out a box of expensive cigars for him to look at. The waiter unwrapped one for him, lighted a match, and applied the flame to one end after Unruh put the other in his mouth.

The young man followed up on his question.

"Really? Could you express it for me in a few words?" He gave the impression that he was bearing up manfully under an Oxonian burden of ennui.

Jess smiled fraternally upon him through the redolent murk of his cigar and rumbled, "If a Democratic member of the Assembly is having an affair with one of the secretaries in the Capitol, you'll see the two of them from time to time having dinner together at Frank Fat's or at the Firehouse. But if a Republican gets involved with a woman, the only thing she'll get from him is the key to the back door of his motel."

We all laughed.

Bob Crown said, "That's absolutely true, and it explains why men like Thomas Jefferson, Franklin Roosevelt, and Jack Kennedy were Democrats, and Calvin Coolidge and Herbert Hoover could never have been."

"I say, Unruh, am I to assume from what you just said that a lot of the members bed their secretaries?" the young publisher drawled.

"No," Jess was admiring his cigar, "they don't. They do it with other members' secretaries. As George Miller says, 'You take your secretary to bed with you and you might as well tie the key to your office safe around your cock with a blue ribbon.'"

"You're referring to Senator George Miller?"

"I am."

"It sounds more like what a businessman would say than it does like what a politician would."

"George was in business before he got into politics, but the principle applies to politics as much as it does to business."

"So you pursue each other's female help?"

Jess sucked in a double lungful of cigar smoke and exhaled it gently toward a candelabrum. "You have to remember that a considerable percentage of the women around the Capitol are unattached and working in a building where a lot of the men are also footloose because their wives are hundreds of miles away taking care of the kids."

"Doesn't that result in a lot of divorces?"

"Divorce is one of the occupational hazards for members. The other two are alcoholism and heart failure. The alcoholism is the consequence of having a lobbyist at your elbow all the time ordering another drink whenever a cocktail waitress comes by. The heart failures are caused mostly by political pressures and by wives who find out about the secretarial services their husbands are receiving in Sacramento after hours. Of course some heart attacks are caused by secretaries. You know the old saying, 'If you're concerned about your heart, don't go to bed with anybody but your wife. That way you won't get too excited.'"

The rich young publisher said, "All those lurid stories about Jack Kennedy and Lyndon Johnson, and you, for that matter, are they true? Are you politicians really all that concupiscent?"

After another appreciative draw at his cigar, Unruh said, "It takes more drive to succeed in politics than in any other field I can think of. It takes a hell of a set of gonads to get to the top. I don't think it's surprising if successful politicians also manifest their sex drives in normal ways."

Carlos Bee said, "While we're on the subject, have you all heard about the end of Terry's last affair?" (Terry was, you will recall, the member of the breakfast club who had been so adamantly opposed to our supporting Jess Unruh for speaker.) Every head shook in a unanimous display of negative anticipation.

"You all know who he's been hitting the sack with?" Carlos looked all around the table. From the silent smile on each of our faces, it was obvious that everyone did know, except for the young publisher, who didn't know any Capitol secretaries at all, so he also kept quiet and smiled.

The secretary in question was a young, fine-featured, raven-haired damozel, of the sort you might expect to see leaning over the bar of heaven in the direction of Dante Gabriel Rossetti.

Physically and spiritually she and Terry were ideally matched, being just the right height, color, and luster for each other. For some time they had been making their entrances into the night spots of ungay old Sacramento with the grace of a pair of ballroom dancers. They were both highly charged emotionally and tended to overflow like charm school graduates. They appeared to go together perfectly, whether drunk or sober.

"Well," Carlos went on, "he was taking her home after one of their usual evenings of steady drinking before, during, and after dinner, and he was going like a bat out of hell like he always does, when a policeman in a patrol car saw him and took out after him with red lights flashing and siren going. Naturally he didn't want the cop to pull him over when he had a woman in the car, especially not one who had been drinking."

Carlos said to the young publisher, "Being intoxicated in an automobile is a crime in California, you know, even if you're not driving, and you can be arrested for it. So he was worried that, if he and his lady friend were both booked, the report the cop submitted might be picked up off the blotter at the station by one of the reporters who cover the police beat; and that would result in a lot of black ink in the newspapers. So he stepped on the gas and tore around Sacramento with the cop after him. Since he was drunk, he was willing to take chances the cop wouldn't take. In the eastern part of town, after he had opened a good lead on the cop, he slammed his brakes on and brought his car to a screeching stop.

"He shouted at his girlfriend to hide behind a billboard in a vacant lot a few feet away. She jumped out of the car and hotfooted it over to the sign, and she was crouched in the weeds behind it by the time the policeman skidded to a stop.

"When the cop saw the legislative license plates and looked at Terry's driver's license and realized what he had caught, he was very respectful." Carlos again addressed the young publisher. "The police officers' associations are always asking the Legislature for something they shouldn't have; so most policemen try not to antagonize members.

"He told Terry he'd been driving pretty fast, and Terry agreed with him."

I could picture the scene because I had been present as a passenger in Terry's car on a couple of occasions when he was pulled over for speeding. Whenever he had three drinks in him, which was any time after five-thirty in the evening on any day, he drove like a movie bank robber fleeing the scene of the crime.

Carlos went on, "The cop said, 'I should give you a ticket, but I won't if you'll go straight home.'

"'That's very good of you, officer,' Terry said.

"'I'll follow you to make sure you get home all right,' the cop said. What he meant was, of course, to make sure Terry went straight home and didn't stop someplace for another drink.

"So Terry started his car and drove away, leaving his lady friend hunkered down behind the sign. He didn't have much choice, after all. And once the policeman had escorted him home and had watched him go into his house, where his wife was waiting for him, there wasn't much he could do. He couldn't very well tell her that he had to go out again to pick up a girl who was waiting for him behind a sign. So he went to bed.

"For a while his girlfriend stayed there squatting in the weeds behind the signboard, waiting in the dark for young Lochinvar to come riding out of the West to rescue her. At last she realized that she was going to have to walk home, and while she was doing that, she decided that he wasn't quite what she was looking for in a man."

"Women are like that," Bob Crown observed.

At that point the young publisher peered at his watch and said, "This has all been frightfully pleasant, but I'm afraid it's time for me to be getting out onto the highway, if I want to get home before the witching hour."

He said, "Toodle oo" to us all and left, and those of us who didn't have our wives in Sacramento went off looking for each other's secretaries.

9

The Reformer

A Democrat may be honest in his convictions.

Ellery Channing

*J*erry Waldie, who represented the eastern half of Contra Costa County, held the chairmanship of the Democratic caucus when I arrived in Sacramento. A sharp young suburban attorney then in his second term in the Assembly, he was looked upon by the members of all three houses as the most impressive political intelligence on the floor, with the sole exception of the Speaker. And some thought Jerry's dark, crew-cut head to be, if anything, even cooler and more calculating than Jess's. His appearance, however, was deceptive. He had an adolescent look about him and a bashful smile that conveyed an impression of winsome innocence.

I liked him very much from the first time I met him, as did everyone, including even his political enemies, and he had no others. Above all, I was captivated by his rare ability to turn an unnerving compliment. When I met him in the halls of the Capitol or on the floor of the Assembly, he would usually say something like, "Gee, Jim, I really like your necktie. I was sorry when those wide ones went out of style."

During the first meeting in the Speaker's office after the opening of the general session of 1963, Jess Unruh proposed that I should be the new chairman of the Democratic caucus, to replace Jerry, since he had become majority floor leader upon the departure of the old one, Billy Munnell, who had been appointed by the Governor to the superior court bench in Los Angeles County.

By the way, that judgeship had not come easily to Billy. Pat Brown had promised it to him early in 1961 but had kept him waiting for over a year. Pat's idea was to use the pending appointment as both carrot and stick to get Billy to go along with the

Governor's position on every issue, bill, and question that came before the Assembly. After twelve months Billy decided that he'd had enough of that. The Old Man was famous for keeping lawmakers he had pledged himself to appoint to judgeships in suspense, cooling their heels indefinitely as he strung them along from day to day. Other legislators waited for years for their promised judgeships and were shaken down for their votes in the meanwhile, over and over and over again.

However, Billy Munnell was a tough little rooster. He noised it about that he was thinking about running for governor against Pat in the Democratic primary election in 1962. He began to range up and down the state, meeting with Democrats and telling them that poor old Pat Brown was simply too wishy-washy ever to be re-elected and that he, Billy Munnell, would be willing to run for the sake of the party, if enough Democrats thought he should, and he reported gravely that he was finding ever so many who did. As soon as the Governor got word of what Billy was doing, he lived up to his commitment and put him on the bench.

Bob Crown, Tom Bane, and Jerry Waldie agreed when Jess said I should be the new caucus chairman. Jerry called a caucus, Jess nominated me to be the chairman, Tom Bane moved that the nominations be closed, the motion was adopted unanimously, and I was elected. By that time Jess had already put me on the Ways and Means Committee, the one committee every member wanted to serve on because it passed on all proposals to expend money. During the month I became caucus chairman, the Speaker also appointed me to be the chairman of the Finance and Insurance Committee, the most potent committee in the Assembly insofar as political fundraising was concerned. That was the panel that had jurisdiction over legislation relating to banks, insurance companies, savings and loans, and such other financial mammoths, mastodons, and saber-toothed tigers. At the beginning of my second term in the Assembly, I was wearing more hats than anyone else in the Legislature.

I learned a great deal about Jess Unruh as the Democratic caucus chairman and as a member of his Praetorian Guard, but I found out even more as the chairman of the Finance and Insurance Committee. In that position I knew that if he really was selling bills for money to the special interests, as his critics alleged he was, I would soon know more than I wanted to about it.

But I discovered that he was as pure as Pope John XXIII, at least in that respect. While it is true that he was raising a lot of money from the third house to be used to support Democratic candidates, he was only following the procedures he had described in the person of Assemblyman X, in the article Lester Velie wrote for *Reader's Digest*, and there was nothing very reprehensible in that, as long as he limited himself to that. The general feeling among members of the C.D.C. clubs, that he was allowing acceptance of contributions from various special interests to warp his decisions affecting them, was without foundation.

He never once asked me to do anything I didn't want to do. He would often tell me what he thought about a bill that was coming before my committee, and he would do his best to convince me that he was right. If he succeeded, well and good, but if he didn't he would say, "Jimmy, I made you chairman of that committee because I thought you have good judgment. I'm not going to ask you not to exercise it."

It was ironic that he should have then had the reputation for being an agent of special interests, voluntarily used by them to corrupt the legislative process. That public misapprehension was a consequence of his inability to resist the temptation to give an outrageous answer to anyone who asked him an offensive question.

I doubt that any student of the California Legislature today would dispute the fact that he was the most beneficial influence upon it in its entire history. He had an agenda in mind for cleaning up the operation of the Assembly when he ran for speaker. Almost twenty years later, in an interview published in the April 1980 issue of the *California Journal*, he said, "What I could see in those early days . . . was that things could be done, that things needed to be done.

"In 1959, when I was chairman of the Ways and Means Committee, my staff consisted of one secretary. Then the committee chairman was appointed by the governor, and so his appointee had to turn to his Finance Department. Eventually I talked Ralph Brown into giving me $400 a month to hire a staff person; he gave it to me reluctantly, too."

Jess was accurately, although not technically, describing the situation when he said that the governor used to appoint the chairman of the Assembly Ways and Means Committee. Formally and legally, the speaker made all committee appointments, but it had become the custom for the speaker to defer to the wishes of the governor when it came to the selection of the chairman of the Ways and Means Committee, who was expected to introduce the governor's budget and to shepherd it through the Legislature to the governor's desk to be signed into law. Jess first ran afoul of Pat Brown at the very start of the Governor's first term by getting the newly elected speaker of the Assembly, Ralph Brown, to agree to appoint him to chair the Ways and Means Committee in return for having helped Ralph get elected speaker. The Governor had decided that Tom MacBride of Sacramento should have the committee. When Pat called Ralph to let him know of his decision, the Speaker broke the news to him that he had committed himself to appoint Unruh. Pat highly resented having been diddled out of an important prerogative.

Pat felt that salt was being rubbed into the wound where Jess had pinked him when Unruh asked Ralph Brown for, and got his approval to hire, a committee consultant. That $400-a-month position was an indication that the new chairman of the Ways and Means Committee did not intend to follow meekly wherever the Governor's people chose to lead him. The consultant could only be useful to the chairman if he was not planning to rely on the Governor's right-hand man, the director of the Department of Finance, as his source of information on all fiscal matters. By hiring that staff man, Unruh was declaring his independence of the Governor and the third house at the same time. To the press he expressed as a general principle that every legislative committee should have competent staff in order that all proposed legislation might be objectively analyzed as to its effects before any action to dispose of it was taken. He did not accept as a divinely revealed truth the often-quoted comment of one drunken lobbyist, "The Legislature is dependent on lobbyists for information, as God intended it to be."

Unlike others who had wrung their hands about that ancient evil but had accepted it as the natural state of affairs in a wicked world, Jess Unruh proceeded to mitigate it. When he became speaker, he moved not only to develop adequate staffing for all of the Assembly committees, he even proposed to provide the Republicans with staff. In that connection he said to the press, "An informed opposition is essential to the proper functioning of the system."

All politicians look gift horses in the mouth as a matter of course, to see if there are any Greeks inside. In considering whether or not to accept the staff positions the Speaker had offered them,

Republicans couldn't believe that he would give them anything unless he had an ulterior motive, and, as a matter of fact, he did have one, although it was not so important in his mind as the one he had given to the press. It didn't take them long to figure out what it was; he wanted them to have more staff so they couldn't complain if the Democrats did. They finally decided that the benefits to them and to the people were worth that price, so they took him up on his offer.

The most outspoken critic of the legislative staff buildup was the Governor. He was in the same houseboat with the special interests in many respects. The Governor's people lobbied us on bills and, like other third-house operations, they supplied us with information, but only that which supported whatever position it was that they were taking. Since they provided us with more intelligence on more bills than anyone else, they had more opportunities to shape our decisions that way than anybody else did.

Pat Brown put on his righteous act when he told the press, in response to Unruh's hiring that consultant for the Ways and Means Committee, "This is a public declaration on the part of Jess Unruh that he doubts my integrity and the integrity of the people who work for me. The executive branch of government in California has always provided all necessary information to the Legislature relative to the finances of the state. This expansion of staff in the Assembly is an unwarranted additional burden upon the taxpayers."

The hiring of that consultant was regarded by Pat as a personal attack. He represented it to the leading Democrats of the state as evidence of Jess's lust for power, and I am sure that is just how he perceived it.

After Jess became speaker and proceeded with his plans to staff all of the committees, Pat made noises like a screech owl about the whole program. He knew that the development of analytical capabilities on the part of Assembly committees would reduce the power of the administration to influence the lawmaking process; and he resented it highly because he understood it only as part of an offensive against him.

The news media played up this escalation of hostilities between the state's two most powerful Democrats. They sided with Pat editorially, saying that Big Daddy should not be so free with the taxpayers' hard-earned dollars as to use them to finance a new offensive of his personal war against the Governor.

The conflict was put into a proper perspective a few years later, after Pat and Jess were both relegated by the voters to political oblivion. The Citizens' Conference on State Governments made an official finding in 1971 that the California Legislature was the best in the nation, mostly because it possessed an independent staff capacity to analyze legislation and its potential effects.

Another of Unruh's reforms enraged the Governor more than any of the rest of them. For many years lobbyists had been prohibited by law from coming onto the floor of either house of the Legislature, a policy manifestly desirable in every way. Yet in those days there was one category of legislative advocates not covered by that ban. The people who represented the Governor and all of his departments were free to come into the chambers and twist the arms of lawmakers without let or hindrance. Jess put an end to that by getting the Assembly to include the Governor's minions with all other legislative advocates under the rules of the house.

When that was done, Pat was almost incoherent with rage. He took it as the most egregious of provocations. It greatly curtailed his power to sway legislative decisions, and he submitted the change to Democrats as a further act of disloyalty on Jess's part, both to himself and to the party, because his influence was often employed to promote Democratic policies as legislation. He told party leaders the rule change was just one more case of the Speaker's putting his pursuit of power ahead of the interests of the people. The press, naturally, made the most of the discord.

Jess had anticipated the Governor's reaction. He brought it up to his inner circle in the first discussion of the proposed rule change. However, he told us he thought we should go ahead with it anyway because it was such a major reform in the legislative process and an essential step toward making the Legislature independent of outside influences, whatever they might be. Those of us around him agreed that it was highly undesirable to treat one set of lobbyists differently from all the rest.

Today it would be hard to find anyone in the Legislature or out of it who would question the propriety of the rule change. A return to the practice of letting the governor's enforcers work over the members of the legislature on the floor would be viewed as deplorable by everyone.

By the time that change was made, my perspective of the Governor had altered so much that I was glad he had not accepted me as one of his adherents. I was satisfied that providence and Jess

Unruh had aligned me with the right side in the not very civil war among the Democrats of California.

I attended some sessions of the National Conference of State Legislatures, and I discovered that its members, who represented both houses of all of the fifty states, looked upon Unruh as the outstanding lawmaker in the nation. But to the press in California he was still just Big Daddy, the power-mad bully boy of the Capitol cloakrooms, whose program of promoting the independence of the Legislature was seen as aggressive and arrogant behavior toward the inoffensive Governor who was the leader of his party.

Once at a dinner in the wine cellar at the Firehouse, when Jess was feeling morose about how the newspapers were caricaturing him, Bob Crown said to him, "Remember what Jesus said when a delegation of his friends and neighbors tried to push him off a cliff on the outskirts of Nazareth: 'A prophet is not without honor, save in his own country.'"

Jess grimaced like Bacchus with a bellyache and rumbled, "I couldn't have said it better myself."

10

Tippecanoe and Unruh, Too

'Before virtue the immortal gods put the sweat of man's brow.

Hesiod

*T*hose who were close to the Speaker called him Jess most of the time, as I have mentioned elsewhere, although when we were feeling playful, we sometimes hailed him as Jesse Marvin or simply as Marvin. We started doing that one night in the white-painted dining room of Jeff Peyser's suite in the Senator Hotel, when we found out how much he liked his middle name.

As our dinner-jacketed waiter was clearing away our cherries jubilee dishes after one of Jeff's seven-course dinners, our conversation had been turning in its own wind.

Bob Crown said, "God, but Marvin is an awful name. How did you get tagged with it, Jess?"

Jess looked amused. "Why don't you like Marvin, Bobby? It's a nice Jewish name."

Although he looked like an Aryan superman, Bob was one of only three Jews in the Assembly at that time. In response to the Speaker's comment he made a face as if he had smelled something unpleasant. "I like the biblical Jewish names, like Abraham, David, Joseph, and Samuel, but I can't stand the schmaltzy modern ones, like Melvin, Irving, and Marvin. Anyway your parents weren't Jewish, Jess; how did you wind up with an awful name like Marvin?"

Jess was sniffing the brandy in his glass like a genteel bulldog addressing himself to a beef bone.

Without looking up from his brandy, he rumbled amiably, "I've always liked the name."

"Liked it?" Bob was radiant with disbelief.

Jess sipped a little brandy, savored it, swallowed it, and explained. "My old man was a Texas sharecropper, and his hero was

Jesse James. Like most Texas sharecroppers he thought Jesse James was the greatest man in American history because he held up the railroads and the banks. The life of a poor dirt farmer in our part of the country was a losing struggle to get enough money together to pay off the banks and the railroads. People like my dad figured that the banks and railroads had been holding up the farmers all along, and they idolized Jesse James because he was one farmer who turned the tables on them."

He paused for another contemplative snort of brandy.

Bob said, "What has that got to do with your having the name Marvin?"

"My old man told my mother when she was carrying me that, if the baby turned out to be a boy, he wanted to name him Jesse James Unruh, but she said it might give the kid the wrong idea. She told Dad she'd like to give a son a nice name, like Marvin. They finally compromised, and that's how I came to be named Jesse Marvin."

His face broadened into a smile. "And that's why I like having Marvin for a middle name. If I hadn't been named Jesse Marvin Unruh, I'd have been named Jesse James Unruh, and how far do you think I'd have gone in politics with a name like that?"

Bob Crown turned to me with a look that would have quickened the pulse of any secretary in the Capitol, and he said, "In what year did Jesse James die?"

"1882," I replied. "And under what circumstances?"

"Bob Ford shot him in the back of the head while he was hanging up a picture."

Jess nodded approvingly. "Just like it says in the song."

"Did you learn that song when you were little?" Bob asked.

"All poor farmers' kids did."

"How poor were you?" Bob was once again slipping into the conversational role of James Boswell, as he so often did, to get his illustrious friend to hold forth on some subject of interest.

"We were dirt poor." Unruh's face showed no flicker of emotion. "Neither my mother nor my dad ever had a chance to learn how to read or write. Their parents could never spare them from the farm work while they were growing up. They never got to go to school at all, and they wanted to see to it that their kids got a better start in life, so they made sure I went to school. When I was just a little kid, my mom would drop me off at the schoolhouse on her way to work in our old Star touring car. For a while she had a job candling eggs in town, and she had to be there by eight o'clock, but school didn't begin until nine, so she had to leave me standing there for an hour on the schoolhouse steps every morning, barefooted in the dead of winter, all alone and crying, with the tears freezing on my cheeks, waiting for the teacher to come and open the door and start a fire in the pot-bellied stove."

He seemed as detached from the memory of that sad little boy as a history professor delivering a lecture upon the childhood of some famous personage.

"How poor were we?" he repeated Bob's question, "We were so poor I didn't know that other people took baths on Saturday night until I was ten. After I found out, I always took one every Saturday night in our horse trough, if the weather wasn't too bad."

In the hope that he would go on reminiscing, Bob Crown surreptitiously held a forefinger to his lips to keep us from breaking the silence while Jess bit off the end of one of Jeff Peyser's excellent cigars. He touched a match to the other end and took in a breath of the expensive air pollution it produced.

He gently exhaled the smoke over the table and, since no one was saying anything, he continued. "We were so poor I never wore underwear until I went in the navy. My folks figured it was just something to waste money on, and we didn't have money to waste."

He paused and surveyed his cigar with appreciation; and again our collective reply was an expectant silence, so he rumbled on.

"Like any other poor farm kid, I had to do my share of the chores around the place. They included drawing the water from the well for the animals and the family. We didn't have enough money to buy a pump, so the water had to be hoisted up out of the well, which was a deep one, a bucket at a time. That was the most tedious work I've ever done in my life, and I had to do it rain, snow, hail, sleet, or shine. The weather could never be so bad that the animals and the family didn't have to have water."

At the point Jess decided he had talked about himself as much as he cared to. He said, "Have you all heard about the Indian chief who was so near-sighted he couldn't tell heads from tails?"

"No," Bob said.

"He had the goddamnedest collection of scalps hanging from his belt that you ever saw."

After we laughed at that, Bob looked at his watch and said, "I've got to be getting along."

Jess commented with a wry cheerfulness, "New friends for old."

Bob grinned. "If you could see the new friend, you'd understand."

"Why couldn't I have been born a woman?" Jess sighed.

Bob grinned again and said, "Good night, Jesse Marvin."

Jess chuckled at being called Jesse Marvin, and, since it gave him such apparent pleasure, we all started doing it, and those of us who are left haven't stopped to this day.

At various times since then I have read accounts of Jess's early life in books and in magazine and newspaper articles. In them people who had known him in his childhood were quoted as saying that they weren't surprised at his rise to prominence. They recalled that, in spite of having to spend long hours drawing water every day, he always found sufficient time to study to be the outstanding student in his class. He was the valedictorian at his high school graduation, like Lyndon Johnson, and that was a clear indication that he, like Johnson, decided early in his life that he was one Texas farm boy who was going to make something of himself.

After dinner at Jeff Peyser's another night, Bob asked Jess how he happened to come to California. I'm sure Bob already knew, but he wanted us to know, too.

"I hitchhiked," he said, "at the beginning of World War II. I was eighteen years old, and I wanted to get a job in a defense plant."

"And did you?" Bob asked him.

"I did."

"And where did you live?"

"I slept on a mattress stuffed with wadded papers on the floor of a chicken coop in the backyard behind my brother Ervin's house in Hawthorne, but I wasn't there long; after Pearl Harbor I joined the navy, which shipped me off to shiver out the war in the Aleutian Islands."

In a speech I once heard him say, "I believe in education because the GI Bill of Rights was the gateway to opportunity for me, as it was for so many others. I used it to get a degree in economics at the University of Southern California. While I was a student there, some of the campus liberals got me involved in school politics. Subsequently, some of the same people pulled me into Democratic Party affairs.

"They were also the ones who encouraged me to become a candidate for the Legislature. They also provided a good deal of the manpower for my early campaigns. They stuck with me even though I lost my first race for the Assembly, and my second, and my third; but once I got it into my mind that I wanted to be a member of the California Legislature, I kept on running until I got myself elected."

Hearing him say that made me think American politics hasn't changed very much since those homespun times when Andrew Jackson, William Henry Harrison, and Abraham Lincoln were elected president. The same frontier qualities of unwavering determination, shrewd brilliance, and durable integrity that carried Old Hickory and Tippecanoe and Honest Abe from log cabins to the White House so long ago were what took Jess Unruh from the twentieth-century equivalent of a log cabin to the speakership of the California State Assembly, and might have taken him much further if fate, in the wispy form of Victor Veysey, hadn't cut him off early.

11

How We Buried the Hatchet
and Dug It Up Again

> *'Every man should have the right to say what he thinks,*
> *and every other man should have the right to knock him*
> *down for it.*

Samuel Johnson

*I*n the year 1962 the most talked about political stage
production in North America was the comeback appearance of
Richard Nixon, who was trying to return to stardom in the role of
governor of California. Two years earlier he had, of course, lost out
in his bid to nail down the part of the top banana in the Washington
follies. In the meanwhile he had decided that the best place to try to
get a new start in show business would be back home where he had
first risen from a most becoming obscurity.

As everyone knows, he originally became a hit in the role of a
dauntless crusader against the Commies. In 1962, he fell back upon
that characterization since it had so captivated the cosmopolitan
multitudes of Southern California in times past. As the campaign
warmed up, Nixon promised the voters that, when he became
governor, he would devote himself body and soul to contending
with what he called "the grave danger of Communism in California." In order to minimize that peril, he pledged himself to stage
a hard-hitting offensive against the Reds in the state on three
fronts: through legislation, investigation, and education. He gave
his word that as governor he would set up "a public school program
of indoctrination which would provide California with the best
Communist control of any state in the United States."

Naturally that promise appealed to the good people of Anaheim, Azusa, and Cucamonga—and all of the other subdivisions of Greater Disneyland.

In his speeches Nixon linked Communism with big government, and big government with the administration of Pat Brown. In an ostentatious display of good taste, he refrained from completing the syllogism, leaving it to his listeners to conclude that Pat was a part of the international Communist conspiracy.

Haunted by memories of earlier Democratic opponents like Jerry Voorhis and Helen Douglas, whom Nixon had daubed into a red oblivion, Pat Brown decided that he would have to pull the Democratic Party together if he was to survive; and that meant making up with Jess Unruh. So it was that when his prospects appeared bleakest, Pat asked the Speaker to come to the old governor's mansion to meet with him. When he went to that meeting, Jess took Bob Crown along. They spent the early part of the evening conferring with Pat while the politicians, lobbyists, secretaries, and other professionals at Frank Fat's bar were speculating upon how the discussion was going.

The following morning in the Assembly coffee room, Bob gave me a report of the meeting. With a mixture of amusement, concern, and excitement lighting his clear blue eyes, he said, "Pat's really afraid he's going to lose, so he asked for Jess's help. He wants it so much that he held up his right hand like he was taking an oath and said, 'Jess, I give you my word of honor that I won't run for reelection in 1966. The only thing I really want out of this is maybe you'll appoint me to the Supreme Court when you get to be governor.' I guess he thought that that would be the incentive Jess would need to really want Pat to win."

Jess confirmed the story later in the day when I went to his office to talk with him about a bill I was carrying.

He said to me, with relief partially clearing some of the usual Churchillian lines from his face, "I think Pat and I have finally buried the hatchet."

In a few days the Governor announced that Jess Unruh was going to be the chairman of his re-election campaign in Southern California. I heard it one morning from Charlie Meyers, who was very pleased, as was I—as were all of the Speaker's friends.

John F. Kennedy had come out of the 1960 presidential campaign nurturing feelings in his heart for Richard Nixon that most Irishmen reserve for Oliver Cromwell. What is more, the President believed that if Nixon were to be elected governor of California, he would use the office as a launching pad for another shot at the presidency in 1964. It is true that Nixon had already protested that he wouldn't seek the Republican presidential nomination in two years, but Kennedy thought he would probably arrange to get himself drafted to run. Everyone I talked to thought the same thing.

The President and Jess Unruh were remarkably fond of each other. Bob Crown once told me, "With Jack Kennedy and Jess, it was love at first sight. That was why Jess went all out for him in 1960. All those stories about him doing it as a way to get at Pat were pure bull."

That special friendship was the reason that Jess got a call one day from Kenny O'Donnell, telling him the President wanted him to do everything he could to defeat Nixon. A few days later he got another call, this one from Bob Kennedy, saying the same thing and advising him that the President wanted him to come to the White House as soon as possible to talk about it. Jess caught the next plane to Washington. When he arrived at the White House, the President, the Attorney General, as well as Kenny O'Donnell and Larry O'Brien, met with him.

At that meeting Jess set forth a plan he had worked out. Since the greatest problem for Democratic candidates is always one of getting registered Democrats to the polls, Jess proposed to recruit 10,000 precinct workers to turn out the vote in the heavily Democratic black and brown neighborhoods in Los Angeles County. He said that could be done by paying the workers ten dollars each to badger their families, friends, and neighbors into going to the polling places, and it should be possible by that means to produce a margin of 100,000 votes in Los Angeles County for Pat Brown for $100,000; and that should be enough to sweep Richard Nixon onto the dust heap of history. The President bought the plan, with the understanding that Unruh would scare up as much money in California as he could to pay for the program and that the White House would cover the remaining deficit, if there was one. The project was undertaken, and it worked. It produced the expected margin for Pat Brown in Los Angeles in the November election; Pat defeated Richard Nixon; and there was rejoicing in the White House.

Everyone thought that Nixon was through in politics, including Nixon himself. The day after the election he called his most famous press conference and made his never-to-be-forgotten farewell speech to the reporters who had covered him during the campaign. I felt a pang of sympathy for the man when he said, "You won't have Dick Nixon to kick around anymore." All politicians have that thought when they retire, though few express it publicly.

On the night of the election, the Los Angeles Democrats held a result-watching vigil in the Hollywood Palladium. Manny Post, a Volkswagen dealer and Democratic sachem, arranged for a trailer to be located in the parking lot for the big wheels of the party to roll into and turn about in sync with each other before trundling together into the Palladium to rotate with a myriad of lesser wheels, the precinct workers and other Democratic commoners. I was not there. Election nights I always spent at the Registrar of Voters Office in San Diego in order to be available to hometown reporters in case they wanted to interview me.

Manny later told me about what happened in the trailer in Los Angeles. "When it became clear that Pat was going to win, he shook Jess's hand and said, 'I never could have done it without you, Jess. The next time is your time.'"

Word of that conversation cheered the hearts of Unruh's friends. We hoped the peace between the Governor and the Speaker would survive and continue to bless our daily lives. It didn't.

The trouble started with a story that appeared in the January 1963 issue of *Harper's Magazine*. It began, "The newest and probably the most powerful of America's political bosses is Jesse Unruh."

Bob Crown mentioned the article to me on the floor in a voice clouded with disgust. He said, "Why do they always use catch phrases like 'political boss'? What is a political boss anyway? Why is it that Jess Unruh is a boss and Jack Kennedy isn't?"

We both knew that Kennedy was ten times as ready as Jess to apply torque to the tender parts of lesser politicians. The conduct of the whole Kennedy clan was expressed by their favorite maxim, "If you can grab a man by the balls, his mind will follow."

Actually, we both were well enough aware why Jess was called a boss. In politics appearances are the only reality. Unlike the President, the Speaker physically fitted the part of a boss, and he amused himself by playing it too whenever anyone pestered him with hostile questions; and those were the reasons he became known as Boss Unruh.

In the *Harper's* article Boss Unruh was said to be responsible for Pat Brown's victory over Richard Nixon, which wasn't fair to the Governor. Pat had carried on a fighting campaign and had convinced the majority of the people of California that he really wasn't a Commie. When all the returns finally came in, it turned out that Pat had won by a quarter of a million votes, more than twice as many as Jess Unruh's paid fieldhands had reaped on election day, and Pat understandably thought that he should be given a little credit for the victory himself.

The writer then probed the wound he had just inflicted on Pat. He pointed out that the President had called Jess and asked him to fly to Washington to discuss what should be done to save Pat Brown from defeat, and that he hadn't called Pat himself. The writer suggested that the President thought the Governor was too much of a schlemiel to be worth talking to.

The purport of the article was that the Governor was a chump who had to be rescued from the consequences of his ineptitude by Boss Unruh. The writer dashed the flagon of the red wine of victory from the lips of Pat Brown and spilled it all over him, so that it appeared more like his heart's blood.

Even more destructive to harmony within the Democratic Party in California was a *Time Magazine* article that appeared at about the same time. It described the growing conflict between the Speaker and the California Democratic Council.

The C.D.C. had gone berserk over Unruh's big get-out-the-vote campaign in Los Angeles, and for good reason. The only precinct work done among Democratic voters in California in the recent past had been that carried on by the Democratic clubs. Although voluntary, it had been effective—as far as it went. It was one of the two foundations upon which the power of the C.D.C. was based. The other was the pre-primary endorsement, which was presented to the voters as if it were the official seal of approval of the party itself. After a few years of existence as the only effective wing of the party, the club movement had come to think that it *was* the Democratic Party. The development of any other corps of precinct workers would make it clear to the public that it was not. For that reason, the use of cash to raise an army of paid workers was bound to kindle rage in the simoniously pure hearts of the amateurs in the

C.D.C., who felt that politics would always be corrupted by money in a direct ratio to the extent to which money is used to decide elections.

The article in *Time Magazine* was entitled "Big Daddy's Ten Dollar Bills."

Paul Ziffren, a silver-haired, thin-featured, political ascetic, who acted at that time as the high priest of the club movement, was the central figure in the story. The *Time* anonyms who composed it conferred upon Paul the highest praise that they knew how to bestow upon a Democrat; that is to say, they identified him as a limousine liberal. They did it directly, by referring to him as a Beverly Hills tax attorney who drove a silver Rolls-Royce. That meant something in those days, when every Tom, Dick, and Harry in Beverly Hills wasn't driving a Rolls-Royce, the way they are now.

Paul opened fire on Big Daddy and his ten dollar bills with: "We are going to have a power struggle for the governorship, that's inevitable. Therefore, let it be on a worthwhile issue; payroll politics versus citizen participation."

That bombilating salvo left no doubt that Paul Ziffren was among those who believed Pat had committed himself to Jess and others not to run for re-election in 1966, because, if the Governor did run again, no good Democrat would challenge him for the nomination. Such a power struggle for the governorship as Paul Ziffren declared to be inevitable would instead be unthinkable.

After explaining how Big Daddy had used $100,000 to pay precinct workers in Los Angeles, the *Time* writers followed the lead of the *Harper's* author in suggesting that the program probably accounted for Pat Brown's victory over Nixon. The inference that the paid workers had re-elected Pat was as much of an offense to Ziffren as it was to the Governor.

Paul naturally avoided making any mention of the White House sanction of the payment of the workers as he blitzed Jess Unruh. In a statement released to the press and quoted by *Time*, Paul said: "I don't like the picture of an armored truck driving up to Democratic headquarters with more than $100,000 in ten dollar bills. That's not the symbol of the party that many of us who have worked for it for many years had in mind. If we condone the hiring of 10,000 in this election, what's to prevent the hiring of 100,000 in the next? At what point do you draw the line at hiring a worker whose only job is to deliver the votes of his wife, sister, or brother?"

Paul Ziffren was then, and is still, one of the good guys in

American politics. The country would be a lot better off if there were more like him in the ranks of the political movers and shakers. I always knew that his concerns were sincere and his motives above reproach, even when I disagreed with him, as I did in this instance, because I thought that President Kennedy was quite right in thinking that the defeat of Richard Nixon was the most important priority for Democrats that year.

In declaring to the press that a state of war existed between the C.D.C. and the Speaker, Paul Ziffren had also announced the organization's choice of a battle ground. He said the war would be fought over Unruh's ambition to be the Democratic nominee for governor in 1966.

Jess moved quickly to defuse the most effective weapon the C.D.C. could use against him. He and Tom Bane got an inoffensive freshman named Harvey Johnson to put in a bill that provided that any unofficial organization that uses the title of a political party in its own name must identify itself in any materials it distributes as an unofficial body. The measure was presented as a simple truth-in-packaging bill, but it was a political bloc buster.

The candidates endorsed by the C.D.C. had been winning the Democratic primary elections consistently because the endorsements were represented to the Democratic voters as the recommendations of the official party (which was, of course, forbidden by law to make any such recommendations).

The opposition to the measure was rallied by Alan Cranston, the founder of the C.D.C. In his sermons upon the bill to the liberal Democrats in the Legislature, he said it represented a power grab by Big Daddy, who wanted to destroy the influence of the pure, bright, selfless volunteers in politics in order that the operators of machines that run on money, like Jess Unruh, would not have any virtuous people in a position to challenge them in the execution of any of their nefarious designs. Cranston made sure that all of the Democrats in both houses received telegrams, letters, and phone calls from every person in a C.D.C. club who ever had been involved in any of their campaigns. But Jess kept making the irrefutable argument that the public was entitled to know the true charcter of any political organization that presented endorsements to it.

At the time of the introduction of the bill, spokesmen for the C.D.C. wildly denounced Unruh as a power-mad bully and a fascist dictator, and they became shriller and shriller as the bill cleared one legislative hurdle after another on its way to final passage. Initially, the leaders of the club movement had been confident that all of their liberal friends in the two houses of the Legislature would defend them.

Even those few who thought Big Daddy might force it through an unwilling Legislature were confident that the bill would never become law; they were perfectly sure that their friend and champion, Pat Brown, would veto it. It didn't occur to them at first that Pat was too much of a politician to take the heat for vetoing a bill that the major newspapers were supporting as a commendable piece of election reform. So the Governor signed the bill into law, and the C.D.C. was required to put the word *Unofficial* on all of its slate mailers from that time forward.

Transformed by the magic power of fury, the club people howled like a chorus of sixty thousand Greek tragedians.

Although Brown signed the bill that had emasculated the C.D.C. because the press had editorially applauded it, he still looked upon the club people as his chief source of support in the party, so he decided to end the armistice with Jess. He did it mostly, I think, as a way to renew his credentials as a good guy with the club people, perhaps at the instigation of Hale Champion, who seemed to have his reasons to want the Governor and the Speaker to be at each other's throats.

Pat resumed hostilities rather casually, with some offhand remarks. In the middle of a conversation with a few of us in his office one day, he smiled owlishly and said, "Did you know that *Unruh* is the German word for unrest? It's where the English word *unruly* comes from. Appropriate, isn't it?"

He said that to us, knowing that someone present would pass it on to Jess. When I mentioned it to him, the Speaker looked very unruly indeed.

On one occasion Pat said in a news conference, "On the whole, I think Jess Unruh has probably done more good than he has harm."

When Jess heard that, his face looked like the death mask of Grendel.

As the internecine war broke out again, the Governor reminded us that he had learned to play political hardball on the turf of that old master, San Francisco's boss Tom Finn.

Pat called Tom Carrell, who was one of Jess's staunchest allies, into his office one day. Solemnly he rasped, "You'd better start to go along, or you could be in trouble. You're a car dealer, and you're licensed by the state to do business."

That was an unveiled threat that the Governor would set the Department of Motor Vehicles to investigating Tom's Chevrolet dealership and business practices if he didn't do as he was told.

Tom smiled peaceably as he told the Tuesday morning breakfast club the story in his sleepy drawl.

Jack Casey said, "What did you say to him?"

"I told him, 'You do whatever you think is right, Pat.'"

It was a good thing for Tom that he was an honest old country boy because the department did go through his business records for weeks with a fine-toothed comb. At one Tuesday morning breakfast after another, Tom told us that it was still going on and tying up his employees with answering questions and providing information.

"It's a nuisance," he said evenly, "but I'm not going to change my opinions just because they pester me."

The harassment was a waste of the taxpayers' money. The investigators found nothing wrong, and Tom just became more and more quietly determined that Pat wasn't going to push him around.

"Isn't it funny," Tom commented over coffee one Tuesday morning, "how the press has everybody thinking that Jess is such a big bully and Pat is such a soft-hearted pushover."

When warfare becomes bitter and the leaders lose their self-control, the troops who follow them lose their minds. It is not, therefore, surprising that Democratic club people came to be consumed by hatred like any other partisans in a long, hard, guerrilla war.

One of the ayatollahs of the true faith in the C.D.C., a reporter for liberal publications named Gene Marine, wrote a tongue-in-cheek hymn of hate for the organization. It was sung at Democratic club meetings and was printed in various newspapers, including the *People's World*, the official organ of the Communist Party in California.

The new Marine hymn was supposed to be the theme song of assemblymen like me who had become friends of Jess Unruh's after being elected with C.D.C. help. None of us thought it was funny. Neither did he.

Here is how it went:

My Heart Belongs to Daddy

I used to be in CDC
I dined on hamburger patty;
But I had no strain
In my last campaign
Now my heart belongs to Daddy.
I used to fare
Like any square
Integrity drove my friends batty;
But now I'm hip
With my chairmanship
And my heart belongs to Daddy;

Yes, my heart belongs to Daddy
And the halt are leading the lame;
All my votes belong to Daddy,
What a shame, what a shame, what a shame!

Sorry, Alan, Glenn, and Paddy, *
Though you know that I love all,
Still my heart belongs to Daddy,
And I come when I hear him call.

Now I'm a Sac-
Ramento hack,
I ride in a lobbyists' Caddy;
I'm never far
From the Mirador Bar
And my heart belongs to Daddy.
I operate 'til very late,
I eat well and keep my clothes natty;
I sold my heart
To Howard and Bart, **
And that heart belongs to Daddy.

Yes, my heart belongs to Daddy
At Frank Fat's his banner unfurls,
And my calls are all from Daddy,
Calls for votes, calls for booze, calls for girls.

Now I'd like to tell you, laddy,
Stand on principle all you please,
Still my heart belongs to Daddy
And when Jesse has a cold, I sneeze.

So go ahead,
Pretend he's dead,
Keep sneering and calling him fatty;
I'll get my kicks in '66
'Cause my heart belongs to Daddy.

* Alan Cranston, Glenn Anderson, and Pat Brown.
**California Savings and Loan tycoons Howard Ahmanson and Bart Lytton.

12

It Was Just One of Those Nights

*Then I commended mirth, because a man hath no better
thing than to eat, drink, and be merry.*

Ecclesiastes

$\mathcal{M}$ost California state senators and assemblymen
have maintained a household in Sacramento ever since membership in the Legislature became a reasonably well-paid, full-time job,
as the result of that constitutional amendment I carried through to
passage by the Legislature, which was approved by the voters in
November of 1966. Nowadays they stay in Sacramento most of the
year. After putting in a day of lawmaking at the Capitol, they drive
home and spend their evenings with their wives and children, like
other middle-class Americans, staring at the boob tube and going to
bed when their eyes give out.

Twenty years ago that was not the case. There were not many
members then who bought houses or condominiums in Sacramento.
We lived most of our lives in our districts because the general
sessions of the Legislature were much shorter and took place only
every other year. And on our salary of five hundred dollars a month,
we couldn't afford two mortgages anyway. In those days, whenever
our wives weren't with us in Sacramento, our night life was just
what might have been expected of a fraternity of extroverts on
furlough from domestic duties.

I remember well one night that began slowly, as most of our
nights did, in Jess Unruh's big, leather-upholstered, walnut-
paneled office. I had run into Jerry Waldie in the terrazzoed hall just
outside the double walnut doors, and he had said to me, "Gee, Jim,
I think you look very nice in that hair cut. You really ought to get
one more often."

"Why, thank you. I always like yours. Where do you get them done, at Fort Ord?"

When we had gone in, said hello to Jess and Bob Crown, who were already there, and sat down on a leather couch, the Speaker's secretary, Betty Coffey, served each of us a glass of whatever we preferred from the little closet that held booze, mixers, glasses, and a little ice-making refrigerator. Over our drinks we analyzed the events of the day and laid our plans for the morrow. We were mostly concerned with how we were going to engineer the passage of Jess's major bill of the session, which proposed to increase state support for public schools in California by $173 million, a part of which was in the form of incentives to smaller school districts to unify. That was a much-needed reform; there were 1,700 school districts in the state in those days, and most of them were wasting money in all directions on duplication of administrative functions.

After we were done with discussing that, Jerry Waldie took a few minutes to tell us about his big bill of that session. He described it as one that would set up a program of special education for the neurologically handicapped and emotionally disturbed children of California. Jerry had made himself a champion in the cause of the mentally retarded, and this bill was one of a series that he carried to improve their lives. He explained it as reasonably and as persuasively as he explained everything, and he convinced us all to do everything we could to help him get it passed.

When we were done with conferring on legislative business, no one moved to leave. We each went to the liquor closet and made ourselves another drink, except for Bob Crown, who never drank anything stronger than milk, and we talked for a while about politics, sex, and baseball. After twenty minutes Bob, who used to get bored watching the rest of us drink, broke into our communal cerebrations with, "Why don't we all go down to the Español for dinner?"

"Great idea!" Jess boomed. "Who's free for dinner?"

Bob reached for the telephone on the Speaker's swept-wing desk, saying, "I've got to call Charlie Meyers. I promised to have dinner with him, so I'll have to see if he'd like to come with us." He dialed Charlie's number, and after a five-second wait, he said, "Charlie, this is Bob . . . Everything's fine, Charlie. Jess and some of the guys are going to the Español for dinner. How would you like to go along?" After he hung up, he reported, "Charlie says he'll meet us there as soon as he's made some phone calls."

By the time we rode the elevators down to the basement and started to pile into automobiles, we had picked up a number of other people. We had come upon John Francis Foran in the hall on the third floor, waiting for an elevator. He joined us, as did George Zenovich, who was on the elevator we had all gotten into. George, a freshman from Fresno, was a laid-back jazz musician, a lackadaisical master of the art of thumping a bull fiddle. He was usually ready to take off in any direction, and he was always as charming as an unemployed gigolo. We recruited Dick Donovan in the basement garage. Dick was a young Republican from Chula Vista. We all liked him. He wasn't as uptight as most young Republicans.

Full of good spirits, though not so full as we would be later in the evening, a dozen of us in four cars roared away in the direction of the Español.

The Español was an ancient, ruinous, two-story brick building, a mouldering relic of Sacramento's halcyon years as the most famous gold town in the world. It stood brooding over the corner of Third and I Streets, just across the way from the Southern Pacific station. The site now is overlaid by a concrete ramp that siphons cars and trucks up onto Interstate Highway Five. Along with all of the other architectural specters of the past in that neighborhood, it was exorcised in recent years when the city council of Sacramento invoked the mystic spirit of urban renewal.

The Español was quite special. The eroding brick walls were framed with weathered woodwork, which, on the level of the second story, had been fashioned by forgotten carpenters into a Gothic rampart of bay windows topped by cupolas. All of those Victorian trimmings had been painted green long ago, but that color coat had been fading and flaking away for a hundred years or more, exposing wood smooth and white with antiquity. Across the front wall, over the window of the barroom, there was a streak of planking, its green paint all alligatored with age, and out of it projected what appeared to be a green muzzle-loading cannon. Actually it was a six-by-six timber that had been turned on a lathe to look like a frigate's broadside gun. It had been mounted there once upon a time by the owner of the place as a mock defense against the Southern Pacific Railroad and its trains after a boxcar had crashed through the front window into the dark, lead-green painted, wooden barroom. That intrusion had resulted from the bartender's refusing to serve any more drinks to an off-duty locomotive engineer who had already had enough. The engineer raged out of the bar swearing vengeance. He stumbled into the railroad yards where he'd left his steam locomotive, and he used it to shove a train of freight cars right off the end of the yard track, clear across the street and through the plate glass window of the Español.

The furrows left by the steel wheels of the boxcar were still to be seen as linear scars that slashed across the floor of the gloomy old saloon from the window to the bar, parallel ruts that had been filled with concrete to become gray stripes across a vitreous white surface of small hexagonal tiles of the kind that all American houses once had on their bathroom floors. There was a dent in the front of the bar where the coupler of the car had punched it. An ancient newspaper photograph in a wooden frame on the wall showed the boxcar filling the old barroom, with its steel fist of a coupler lodged in the dent it had made in the front of the bar. The room hadn't been painted since that picture was taken, by all appearances. The interior had once been avocado green, but it had been dulled and darkened by age and grime and tobacco smoke into a gangrenous gloom. It was the sort of an antique saloon that today would fill up every night with single yuppies, but in those days it was just another dilapidated old joint that was not making enough money to pay the upkeep.

We had no trouble finding parking. Very few people who are on skid row go there in automobiles. We all trooped through the front door and along the entire length of the old bar, past winos slumping on bar stools in dirty old overcoats, cherishing their glasses of golden muscatel. At the end of the bar we filed through another door into the back room, where meals were served at reasonable prices. A great loft of a dining room it was, with plaster walls and a tongue-and-groove ceiling, both of which had been painted beige, probably only twenty years before. The impression was of freshness, as opposed to the decrepitude of the rest of the place. Unlike the bar, the restaurant attracted a respectable clientele. It was well lighted by a dozen bare bulbs that hung down from the ceiling at the ends of long wires. The tables were square and were covered with red and white checkered tablecloths. They were all surrounded by bow-backed, cane-seated chairs.

Our waitress was Mary, an energetic little familiar spirit from Spain. She started to bustle about pushing four of the square tables together to make one long one that would accommodate us. We helped her with the job and placed enough of the bow-backed chairs around the table to seat us all.

Mary was a delight. She was short, friendly, and lively, with hands quick enough to play castanets. At that time, I'd heard she had worked at the Español for twenty years. She started there when it was the restaurant of a little hotel that catered to Basque sheepherders who used to come into town from time to time to enjoy some two-legged company.

On that night she soon began to fetch us our food. It was all Italian style. A fellow named Luigi had bought the place some years before and had changed the menu but not the name. It was and is still probably the only Italian dining room in the world called "The Spanish Restaurant"—and in Spanish, at that.

Mary brought us big tureens of tomato and rice soup. When we finished that, she supplied us with spaghetti and ravioli. The main course that night was fried chicken, which she carried in on big platters. With it came French fried potatoes and green beans. The food was very good and very hot. The house wine was a good Dago red, and it was cold. We ate and drank hugely.

We were happy. We told jokes. We sang songs. By the time we were halfway through with our dinner, the other people in the dining room had paid their checks and gone. In the book of Job it says that it is God who sends us songs in the night, but I'm sure God didn't send us all of the ones we sang that night, because when Jess had put away a heroic ration of chicken and French fried potatoes and had washed them down with a gallon or so of wine, he broke into "Cats on the Rooftops," perhaps the most indecent song ever written, and all of us joined him in the chorus after each verse. He conducted his little choir, using a fork for a baton, with the fervor of Leonard Bernstein. Then he led us in another of his favorites, the one about the dirty little coward who shot Mr. Howard and laid Jesse James in his grave.

Just as we finished that one, Mary scurried in to announce, "There's somebody on the phone for Mr. Crown."

Bob went to the telephone, which hung on one of the dark green walls of the barroom. When he returned, we were warbling about the sinking of the *Titanic*. After we sang for the last time, "It was sad when that great ship went down," Bob told us, "That was Charlie Meyers. He wanted to know if we were still here at the Español. He's coming down to join us." With the sober half-smile to be expected of a milk drinker on such occasions, he added, "You know Charlie. He'll be late for his own funeral."

"Why not?" said John Francis Foran. "He's been late to every other funeral that's been held in San Francisco in the last twenty years." Joy suffused John's round face and eyes. "Let's teach him a lesson. Let's pay the bill now, and when he gets here, we'll all take off. Everybody should think of a good excuse for going, one he'll believe. We can leave him here all by himself with his supper in front of him, and we can have Mary give him a duplicate of the check for all of our dinners. It ought to be at least fifty dollars. I bet he'll go right out the window." John turned in his bow-backed chair with a Shakespearean gesture toward the tall, narrow sash windows that enfiladed the beige-painted brick wall on the I Street side of the room. "We can watch him from the sidewalk. He won't be able to see us through those gauze curtains, but we'll be able to see him."

Amid cries of glee, we explained John's plan to Mary when she came in with a coffee pot to refill the cups for the few who had been drinking coffee. She wrote up our check; we took up a collection and paid it and gave her a handsome tip. Then she brought in our ice cream. As we were diving into it, Charlie arrived, with a cheerful, "Hi! Is everything all right?"

"Everything's fantastic," John Francis replied, "but I've got to get back to the Capitol. Connie's expecting me to call her tonight." He shoveled his ice cream into his mouth and left. I finished mine a moment later, announced that I had some things on my desk that I had to go through before morning, and became the second to go.

By the time Mary put Charlie's soup in front of him, we were all gathered out on the sidewalk in the light from the dining room windows, watching him through the white gauze curtains as he sat alone spooning up his soup at a long table that was heaped with dirty dishes and platters full of chicken bones.

Finally the moment of truth came. Mary discreetly laid the duplicate check for all of our dinners on the table by Charlie, who put down his soup spoon to pick it up and look at it very seriously.

"He'll never pay it," John Francis exulted in a very small voice. "Not in a thousand years."

We held our breaths, waiting for Mary to leave the room. Charlie continued to study the check pensively. When Mary tripped out into the kitchen with a tray of dirty dishes, he bolted out of his chair toward us. He raised the ancient sash of one of the windows and vaulted through it and into the midst of what must have seemed to him, blinded as he was by the darkness, a corral of jackasses all suddenly aroused and hee-hawing.

Bewildered and at bay, he blinked this way and that at the braying circle around him. It took a few seconds to make out who we were and a few seconds more to figure out what in the hell was going on. When he did, he grinned. "You fellows were playing a joke on me," he said. And he joined in the mad laughter. Then he dashed suddenly at George Zenovich. He tossed him over his shoulder and ran off with him around the corner.

The approach to the I Street bridge started to rise right alongside the Español. That is a museum piece of an old swing bridge across the Sacramento River, an angular black iron relic of the days when bridges were built by men with hammers and forges. It carries the Southern Pacific tracks on the lower level and a narrow two-lane roadway on the upper.

We ran after Charlie, cheering him on as he scampered off into the darkness across the long bridge with Zeno, as limp as a wet zoot suit, draped over his shoulder.

We walked back to where we'd been standing on the sidewalk on I Street, in the light from the dining room windows, hee-hawing joyfully until Zeno strolled back around the corner and into the light, as casual as ever.

"Man," he marveled, "that cat is really strong. He didn't put me down till we were all the way across the river in Yolo County."

"He carried you all the way across the river?" Jess rumbled joyously.

"That's right, Jesse baby. All the way across."

From around the corner of the building Charlie appeared out of the darkness chortling.

When he was twenty feet from us on the sidewalk, approaching slowly, tentatively, Jess crooned to him, "Come here, Charlie."

"Oh, no," Charlies answered, between a chuckle and a giggle.

Jess advanced upon him with his arms spread, like a sumo wrestler.

"Stay away from me, Jess," Charlie said, his laugh suddenly nervous. "You're too strong."

"Come here, Charlie," Jess crooned again. "Turnabout's fair play, Charlie."

Then he charged. Charlie took off around the corner like a champion Olympic sprinter. Jess was astonishingly fast for a man of his size, but dread propelled Charlie like a jet engine.

Five minutes later Jess reappeared blowing some. He told us gleefully, "I chased Charlie across the river and lost him in the bushes over there."

Taking off his shoes, like any Texas country boy, to run faster, he vowed, "Next time I'll catch him."

In his stocking feet he backed up a sloping green cellar door that was under one of the windows of the dining room of the Español. "Up here," he rumbled, "I'll get a faster start than Charlie."

"Atta baby, Jesse," Zeno sang.

"Damn!" Jess exclaimed, "I'm getting slivers in my feet." He had been moving them a little to back up to the very top of the door. He stopped. Poised at the head of the splintery old board door, silhouetted against the white gauze curtains behind him, he loomed, a tremendous dark fate awaiting Charlie.

When Charlie at last reappeared out of the night from around the corner, they went through the same routine again.

"Come here, Charlie," Jess crooned.

Again Charlie laughed nervously. "Oh, no. You're too strong, Jess."

Then Jess rocketed from his launching ramp, and Charlie shot off again around the corner and across the old bridge with Jess only a few feet behind him. Jess didn't catch him that time either, despite his fast start and a noisy cheering section.

"Go, Marvin, go!" we were shouting. The regular customers in the barroom, huddled on their barstools in their old overcoats, must have thought it was a hell of a note when a man couldn't enjoy a glass of muscatel in peace.

After ten minutes Jess returned, blowing a little harder. "I'll get him," he swore, as he backed up the cellar door again, taking short steps.

He almost did. After Charlie showed up again and they went through the same dialogue as before, Jess sprang from his perch and nearly caught him. As they tore around the corner of the building, Jess came within inches of gathering Charlie into his mighty arms.

After that run Jess returned again and took up his station at the top of the ancient cellar door, but Charlie never came back. That had been too close a call. Not caring to run the risk of being squeezed all out of shape like a tube of toothpaste, Charlie stayed in Yolo County. We didn't see him again that night.

Standing at the granite curbstone that edged the time-worn

sidewalk—glimmering in the light that shone through the gauze window curtains, resplendent in the gloom of that decaying neighborhood—reposed Bobby Crown's new car, a beautiful cream-colored Chevrolet Impala with black decorator stripes drawn along the sides.

Jess looked down at it from his vantage point at the top of the cellar door. "That certainly is a beautiful car, Bobby," he cooed.

"It's the nicest car I ever had," Bob replied.

"A car like that should have good springs," Jess mused, as he descended noiselessly down the cellar door in his stocking feet to the sidewalk.

"It has great springs," Bobby answered, as care began to compress his noble brow.

"I think we ought to try them out." Jess was looking crafty as his enemies said he was. "We ought to see if they're as good as they should be."

"No, Jess, don't do it," Bob cried, as Jess heaved himself heavily onto the top of the car and started to bounce up and down on it on his Herculean behind.

In two more seconds Jerry Waldie was out of his shoes and onto the hood, bounding up and down on his backside in unison with Jess. Before long the Impala was surging like a waterbed under a pair of overweight newlyweds.

The merry band on the sidewalk was shouting, "Great springs, Bobby! Great springs!"

Bob was wailing, "Stop it. Stop it. Stop it," appealing to Jess and Jerry frantically from the sidewalk. "It's the nicest car I ever had."

None of us had ever seen him so excited.

"You're going to put big dents in it," he ululated.

When the two bounders rested and slid off at last, Bobby dashed around to the driver's door. He flung it open, and a carton of milk fell off the seat into the street. He must have opened it to take a before-dinner drink prior to coming into the Español, because it lay on its side spilling white milk onto the black asphalt. He ignored it in his desperate haste to get his car away from us before we checked it out any further. He jumped in, slammed the door, started the motor, and tried to get the car out of the parking place, but he was too hysterical to do it. He kept making the wrong moves as we cheered him on and shouted bad advice. After six or seven passes at it, he finally got the nose of his Impala clear and roared away from the scene. Like Charlie, he disappeared out of the evening.

We stood contemplating each other for a minute after Bob left, breaking into maniacal laughter every minute or so. Jess sat down on the lower end of the cellar door to put his shoes back on. While he was doing that, Jerry strode to the corner of Third and I Streets, where he reached up to put his hands over the street sign. It was an enameled steel one, mounted on a galvanized iron pipe. That sign was unusual in that it wasn't as high as most of them are or Jerry couldn't have reached it.

He chinned himself on it half a dozen times. When he let go, he hallooed, "I bet you can't do that, Marvin."

"I'll show you what I can do," Jess roared, advancing upon the sign. He reached up and began to pull it down, in an incredible display of strength.

"Jesus, Jess, stop it," Jerry shouted at him. "What if the police show up?"

The headlights of approaching automobiles illuminated the scene as they came down I Street and went up onto the bridge.

"What if one of these cars coming down the street right now is a police car?" Jerry pleaded. "Think of the headlines, Jess. My God, you'll get the damnedest publicity any speaker of the Assembly ever got."

"We know you can do it," John Francis Foran yelled, and we all joined in, shouting the same thing like a Greek chorus. But the Speaker didn't cotton to having us humor him; he kept bending the sign further and further, grimacing horribly all the while.

Deliverance appeared in the form of a ragged, dirty, unshaven derelict in a patched gray overcoat and shoes with holes that had been worn through the uppers by his two grimy little toes. On his wrinkled, toothless old head he wore a dirty navy blue stocking cap.

He shambled up to us, taking no notice whatever of Jess pulling down the street sign. He pulled an old harmonica out of an overcoat pocket and mumbled, "I'll play you six songs for seventy-five cents."

"Hey, Jess," Jerry said in his most earnest voice, the one he used on the floor in debate and before juries, "we've got a musician here who'll play six songs for us for seventy-five cents."

"Too much," Jess grunted between his teeth, still straining mightily, bringing the sign lower and lower.

Jerry turned to the music man and said, "How about seven songs for eighty cents?"

The mouth organist shook his dirty old head slowly, as if there were something loose rattling around inside it. "No. I can't cut my price." He was speaking up as an artist should, making a declaration about the value of his artistry. I sympathized with him.

"How about six songs for seventy cents?" Jerry countered, with one eye on Jess's contorted face, hoping he'd take an interest.

"No," the old drunk said, with another slow shake of his head.

Jerry is one of the most humane men in the world. If he has ever thought back on his haggling with that poor fellow over pennies, I know he must have felt uneasy, even though he only did it to distract Jess before a cop arrived.

"Well," Jerry said, after a deliberative pause, "I think we might be able to go as high as seven songs for eighty-five cents."

The old man gazed around at all of us hesitantly, looking at Jess pulling at the sign as long, but no longer, than he looked at any of the rest of us.

Jess let go of the sign and stepped back to survey it; by then it was cocked over at a forty-five degree angle. He seemed aesthetically satisfied and turned to join the rest of us in observing the negotiations.

"Could you make it seven songs for eighty-seven cents?" the old man mumbled.

"I don't think I'm empowered by my clients to go that high." Here Jerry looked around at Jess, who was breathing heavily. "But I think I can offer eighty-six cents."

The poor old wreck pondered that offer briefly and said, "I accept." He started to raise his harmonica to his stubbly lips, but Jerry stopped him.

"Not here," he said; "follow me."

Jerry stepped off across I Street, after giving us the army hand signal to follow him.

As we walked across the street, I heard Jerry say to the musician, "I really like your coat."

"You want to buy it?"

"No, but I really like it."

I wondered where Jerry could be leading us. All I knew was that he was trying to get us away from that bent sign. He went across Third Street after he crossed I. Diagonally across the intersection from the Español was an even more ramshackle two-story brick building that leaned crazily in various directions. He led us up a narrow flight of creaking stairs, toward an afflatus of two-step music.

At the top of the rickety stairs we entered a dilapidated dance hall with a crowd of outcasts moping around the floor. Nobody seemed to be with anybody. There were some overpainted middle-aged women who were standing around, each of them looking professionally detached. There was a motley crew of men standing around, each looking as if he were thinking about engaging one of the overpainted women to perform one or more of her professional services. There were a few shop-worn old crones sitting around on wooden folding chairs, who looked as if they were held together mostly by their foundation garments. There were a couple of old geezers with them who looked as if there were nothing at all holding them together.

At the end of the room, on a battered platform, a three-piece band—a saxophone player, a pianist, and a drummer, a trio of threadbare old failures in shirt sleeves—were plugging through *Dancing in the Dark* as though they were playing in the dark.

Jerry took his harmonica player with him to the bandstand and said to the three old coots, "Here's five dollars if you'll knock off playing for a few minutes. I've got a guest artist here."

They stopped short, at the end of the musical phrase that accompanies the words: *Waltzing in the wonder of why we're here.*

Jerry turned to the hobo and said, "You're on."

The old boy nodded carefully and stepped up to the microphone and played *Old Folks at Home, Old Black Joe, My Old Kentucky Home,* and four other grand old racist songs. He played them very slowly, so he wouldn't have to move his head too quickly. He wasn't too bad, either. He mostly hit the right notes, though not always on the first try.

When he was done, our little company applauded and shouted, "Encore!" though no one else in the place did.

Jerry held out his hand to us and said, "We owe the musician eighty-six cents."

We all reached into our pockets and held out to him the change we found in them. Jerry took eighty-six cents from our outstretched hands and paid our obligation to the wandering minstrel. Then we all creaked down the stairs.

When we got back out onto the sidewalk again, I wandered off to my room and went to bed. It was just as well that I did because Jerry told me the next morning, "After you left, everything pretty well went to hell."

13

Unruh Triumphant

Good fortune is not known until it's lost.

Miguel de Cervantes

$\mathcal{A}$t the close of the legislative session of 1963, it seemed that the Speaker bestrode Sacramento as Caesar had surmounted the world on the morning of the ides of March. The Governor, his only rival for control of the political processes of the state and those of the Democratic Party, was seen by the news media, and therefore by the public, in its ovine wisdom, only as a bumbling foil for Unruh.

Jess was perceived by the press to have won every battle he had fought, including the one for the reelection of Pat Brown. Newsmen and women never gave poor old Pat much credit for defeating Richard Nixon, which, whenever he thought about it, made him emote like a wronged woman in a Verdi opera.

Jess had earlier embarrassed Pat in two direct confrontatons. The first was when Pat had tried to prevent him from becoming chairman of the Ways and Means Committee. The second was when Pat attempted to keep him from being elected speaker. And Unruh had made the Governor look a fool in 1960 by supporting Jack Kennedy for the Democratic presidential nomination while Pat dithered, blithered, and finally did nothing at all.

The press took pleasure in informing the public that President Kennedy thought Pat Brown was such a klutz that he always got in touch with the Speaker when he wanted to talk politics with somebody in California. That was, of course, the simple truth. JFK repeatedly asked Unruh to come to see him to discuss matters of great pith and moment, and he never invited Pat.

Newspaper columnists and other professional babblers floated rumors that Jess was being considered by the President for a cabinet post in his administration. Everyone believed he could have had one for the taking. However, whenever he was asked if he might be going to Washington soon, he always said he'd rather stay in Sacramento.

He told me over a glass of gin in his office once, "I've been frustrated ever since I got to Sacramento by governors I've had to get around or run over in order to get anything done. What I really want is to sit in the governor's chair. That's where I'll be able to make the things happen that I've been working so long for."

In respect to being elected governor, he had, of course, won a major victory. The C.D.C. was the enemy force he had to overcome in his campaign for the Democratic nomination, and he had deprived that army of the one effective weapon it had to use against him, by getting the bill passed that required the C.D.C. to identify its endorsements as the recommendations of an unofficial organization. The club people could have headed him off only if their endorsement of some other candidate had appeared to the average Democratic voter to be the official recommendation of the party itself.

It did not appear then that anything or anyone could keep him from gaining his new goal, even as he had achieved all his others in the past. If Pat Brown lived up to his promise not to run, there was no one on the political horizon who could challenge Jess as a candidate for the Democratic nomination for governor; and we who were his friends were so used to seeing him overmaster all opposition, we didn't doubt that, as the Democratic nominee for governor, he would win the general election. What he had in mind for himself after he had put in his time as governor, we didn't know; but, whatever it might be, we expected he'd achieve that, too.

In politics, as in all other warfare, victories breed victories and defeats breed defeats, and Jess had never known defeat.

14

How We Locked Up the Republicans

The evils of popular government appear greater than they are.

Ralph Waldo Emerson

*I*n 1981 the general diagnosticians who render their opinions on the editorial pages of California's newspapers began to examine all the potential candidates for the office of governor in the election campaign scheduled for the following year. The state treasurer, Jess Unruh, was one of those singled out for editorial dissection, which, in his case, took the form of a cooperative autopsy.

After a good deal of forensic knifework, they reached a unanimous conclusion, which is not an uncommon one among those who conduct autopsies. It was that the subject was dead.

His having served the state brilliantly as treasurer since 1974, they reported to their readers, would not erase from the public mind the memory of how grossly he had abused his powers as speaker of the Assembly when he'd locked all the Republican members in the chamber overnight in July of 1963 for refusing to follow his orders to vote for the budget bill. Nor could the people ever forget that he had compounded that grievous offense by punishing all of the Republican committee chairmen for that display of independence by relieving them of their chairmanships. And those political commentators were right; the people certainly would not forget—not so long as they were being reminded in the editorial pages of their daily newspapers that they wouldn't.

In those discourses no reference was made to any of his other victories or defeats, and in their conclusions the journalistic illuminati went on to prophesy that the people of California, recalling how Jess Unruh had been greatly corrupted by great power in the past, would be unwilling to give him even greater power in the future for fear that he would be even more greatly corrupted by it. Those commentaries were based on the assumption that the great lockup of 1963 was a textbook case of an autocrat trying to impose his will upon a dauntless little band of independent and highly principled idealists; yet, in actuality, that classic drama was the product of the workings of providence—and improvidence—like almost all political adventures and misadventures.

Neither the Democrats nor the Republicans had anticipated any excitement when the Assembly gathered in its pale green Corinthian oratorium at 10:30 on the morning of July 30. The business of the day was to adopt a supplement to the state budget. Everyone was in good spirits, and there was no hint that the chamber would darken into a modern political equivalent of the Black Hole of Calcutta by nightfall.

In those days the Constitution of California provided that the Legislature should meet in a regular session on the first Monday in January of every odd-numbered year and adjourn 120 days later, not counting Saturdays and Sundays. That meant we concluded our business and broke up during the third week in June. The Constitution also required that we adopt a budget for the state before we recessed.

A conference committee of three members from each house always met to resolve the differences between the Senate and the Assembly versions of the budget. In that June of 1963 the conference committee had not been able to work out a program of expenditures for all the money the state expected to come in. The trouble was that no one knew just how much was available because a major tax bill was hanging fire. In those days corporations in California did not have to pay taxes on their income as promptly as other categories of taxpayers did. Therefore, Nick Petris, a Periclean liberal from Oakland, was carrying an administration bill that would have made the corporations pay as quickly as everybody else. Nick's bill would have improved the cash flow into the state treasury and have provided some new money for school and other activities. The Republicans in the Senate had flown to the defense of the business community and had defeated the measure, with the help of some cow-county Democrats, during the last few days of the regular session. We had been working out all the details of the budget on the assumption that the Petris bill would pass. When it didn't, we had to knock together a stopgap bare-bones appropriations bill at the last minute. We passed it and went home on the day the

Constitution required that we must, having reached an understanding with the Governor that he would call us back in a special session in July to complete our work by hammering out and passing a supplemental budget and a school finance bill that together would expend a small surplus of money we had on hand.

Pat Brown called us back into session at the beginning of July, and by July 30 the budget supplement, Senate Bill 4, had been wrought into its final form by a new conference committee. It was to be in print and ready for a vote right after lunch. The school finance measure, Senate Bill 12, by Senator Joseph Rattigan of Santa Rosa, would not be in print for another two days. Another conference committee, of which I was the chairman of the Assembly contingent, was still working out the details of that bill.

The train of events that led to the lockup was set in motion just before that supplementary budget bill came up for a vote. Smiling Bill Bagley and three other light-hearted Republicans, Bob Monogan, Alan Pattee, and Jack Veneman, lived a block from Capitol Park at 1420 O Street in a three-story, gray-and-white-painted apartment building, the front of which was quadrisected into boxy porches, which gave the impression that the architect had gotten his inspiration from a stack of apple crates.

They were the sort of pragmatic hedonists who would never let business interfere unnecessarily with their pleasures. Since the vote on the budget wasn't to be taken until 1:30, they absented themselves from the floor just before noon and traipsed over to 1420 O Street to wrap themselves around some cold sandwiches and colder drinks, taking with them Victor V. Veysey, a narrow Republican colleague from the Imperial Valley. After they had eaten and drunk their lunches, they lounged around the apartment house swimming pool in their trunks, soaking up a little more of the hot soft sunshine and cold hard liquor. Then they showered and got dressed to return to the Capitol. As they sauntered through the east end of the park in the light green shade of the spreading maples, chestnuts, and elms, they were feeling as carefree as five sailors on leave.

Victor Veysey volunteered a chance thought. "It wouldn't be responsible to vote against the budget and defeat it, but we ought to do something to show everyone that Jess doesn't have total possession of our balls, and I have an idea. Why don't we get the Republican caucus to take the position that none of us will vote for the budget until we see the bill on school finance?"

Jack Veneman said, "That's a great idea." Bob Monagan said, "It sounds good to me," and Alan Pattee said, "I like it," as did Bill Bagley.

When they got back to the Capitol, the five of them asked for a meeting of the Republican caucus in the Assembly lounge to consider the idea. After a short discussion behind closed doors, the caucus agreed on it as an official position.

Upon their adjournment, Don Mulford, a jovial, hulking, red-headed, service-club-type Republican from Alameda County, who served as the G.O.P. caucus chairman, issued forth to proclaim the position taken. His broad ruddy face was radiating sincerity (which he had learned to project wonderfully well in the course of a long career of selling insurance) as he addressed himself to a platoon of reporters and television cameramen in the hall.

He announced, "The school bill is a big part of the whole budget picture. We can't understand any part of it until we see all of it. We don't know how the schools will be affected by what we spend in the budget bill until we see the school bill. Maybe there won't be enough left for us to do for the schools what we think we should do. The Republicans in the Assembly are not going to vote upon any part of the package until we've seen how the whole spending program affects the schools in all parts of the state."

The Republican floor leader, Charlie Conrad of Sherman Oaks, stood nodding in agreement. He was used to playing supporting roles. That's what he did for a living. I had seen him in dozens of movies and television shows, though he never had more than two or three lines in any of them.

Don Mulford's announcement raised the hope of a good story among the reporters who covered the Assembly. The California Constitution requires an aye vote of two-thirds of the entire membership of each house to pass any bill containing an appropriation, and since there are eighty members in the Assembly, it takes fifty-four votes to pass a budget. There were fifty-two Democrats in the lower house at the time, but Clayton Dills had decided that he wasn't going to let a little thing like a state budget stand in the way of his vacation, so we only had fifty-one Democrats on the Assembly floor, and we couldn't pass the bill unless we could line up three Republican votes. Therefore, it seemed that an interesting confrontation might be shaping up.

When word flurried among the Democrats about what Don Mulford, whom we always called "the Mulf," had said to the press, the more nervous ones came to ask me, as their caucus chairman, what was going on. I made my way up to the podium, where Jess was surveying the scene, to see if he had any word I could pass along to the troops.

He smiled benignly and said, "Tell them not to worry, Jimmy. Remind them that I never appoint anyone to a chairmanship who doesn't accept three conditions. The first is that they have to commit themselves to vote for me, in case anyone ever makes a move to try to dump me as speaker. The second is that they have to promise to vote against any motion to withdraw a bill from committee. If they want to be committee chairmen, they have to support the committee system. The third thing they have to do is to pledge themselves to vote for the budget. We've got four Republican committee chairmen, Alan Pattee, Miltie Marks, Frank Belotti, and Ike Britschgi. All of them promised me they'd do all three, and they're all men of their word." He grinned at me and said, "Hell, the only reason I give the Republicans those chairmanships is that we have to get fifty-four votes to pass the budget."

I went down from the dais to pass the word to the Democrats that the Republicans were just posing for the news media. Bob Crown took up the conference committee report that embodied the agreements the two-house committee had reached on new state spending. "This bill is a $126 million supplement to the bare-bones budget we passed during the regular session," Bob said, "and I hope we can limit our discussion to the provisions of this bill, which is all that is before us. There is nothing controversial about it. Most of the money in it goes to finance a five percent increase in the pay of state employees and for additional state support for public schools, which will be specifically allocated in a bill that will be before us in another day or two. I ask for an aye vote."

After Bob finished, Hugh Flournoy, the Republican spokesman on legislation relating to education, rose to his feet and spoke over our heads to the reporters around the edges of the room. He explained why the G.O.P. caucus had taken the position that none of its members would vote on the budget. By trade Hugh was a professor of political science. When he addressed the Assembly, he always sounded as if he were back at school lecturing to a dull lower-division class. He argued, "We don't have the information we need to cast an intelligent vote either for this bill or against this bill. We won't have it until we have seen the details of the whole spending package."

I looked up at Jess on the rostrum and saw that he was gazing down upon the Republicans as though they were wayward but engaging children.

In his rebuttal Bob Crown was logical and coolly pacific. "This budget is a reasonable bill, and no one can say that it isn't. There are no mysteries about it. Everyone knows how much money is left for additional financial aid for schools once this bill is passed. Unless the Republican members of this house are dissatisfied with the total amount available for education, they have no reason not to vote for this budget; and neither Mr. Flournoy nor anyone else has expressed any dissatisfaction with the total amount available for school aid.

"The particular provisions of the school bill, how the money is to be allocated to the various school districts, are separate issues that should be debated when the school bill comes up for a vote, but those are questions that have nothing to do with whether this is a good or a bad budget. As I said in my opening arguments, this is simply a measure that provides justifiable and needed cost-of-living increases for state employees and programs and sets aside a good deal of money to be used as additional state support for the public schools. Again I ask for an aye vote on the passage of this bill."

The Speaker announced, "The vote is on the urgency clause of Senate Bill 4. The clerk will open the roll."

The bell rang to indicate that the electronic roll call was open. The fifty-one Democrats present threw the voting switches on their desks to register aye votes, which showed fifty-one little green lights after their names on the tote boards on the front wall of the chamber. The twenty-seven Republicans on the floor had no little lights after their names, neither green to show they were voting aye nor red to show they were voting no.

After a portentous pause, the Speaker said slowly, "The clerk will close the roll and tally the vote."

Bob Crown rose to say, "Mr. Speaker, I move a call of the house."

The Speaker said, "Those in favor of the motion indicate by saying aye," and all of the Democrats voted aye. He said, "Those opposed, no," and all the Republicans voted no. Jess said, "The ayes have it, the Assembly is under a call. The sergeant-at-arms will lock the doors and bring in the absentees."

The hour was 1:40 P.M., and the great, dark carved walnut doors of the Assembly chambers were closed upon the world.

I should explain just what a call of the house is. It is a routine parliamentary motion ordinarily made by the author of a bill that doesn't have enough aye votes showing on the electronic tote boards for passage. The effect of the motion is to delay the announcement of the vote on the bill until the call is removed by a subsequent motion. The call provides the supporters of the bill under consideration time to try to round up the votes needed for its passage. It is the commonest of procedural motions. Seldom does a day go by on the floor without a call being applied. Hardly ever is a budget bill passed by either house on the first roll call.

In those days someone composed a little ditty that was sung by a musical few, more or less to the melody of "The Rambling Wreck from Georgia Tech" every time a call was imposed. It went:

> *The sergeant-at-arms will lock the doors*
> *and bring in the absentees,*
> *The sergeant-at-arms will lock the doors*
> *and bring in the absentees,*
> *He must bring in Dills and Mills,*
> *If we want to pass some bills,*
> *The sergeant-at-arms will lock the doors*
> *and bring in the absentees.*

A few Democrats and Republicans raised their voices in the refrain, and most of the rest of us laughed. No one among the Democratic majority was concerned at that point. Not one of us had any notion that we were stumbling into a Gargantuan pitfall.

For an hour or two I moseyed about on the floor visiting with various friends, watching while the Speaker made his rounds among his little brothers, the Republican committee chairmen. He was friendly and apparently in good spirits, and so were they. I didn't doubt he would soon have the votes for the budget.

No one could work a bill so effectively as he, which was why the rest of us were standing back and leaving it to him to round up the votes of the G.O.P. chairmen.

After going head to head for some time with each and every one of them, he came to talk to me at my desk.

I stood up and said, "How does it look?"

He reached up and tugged at his collar with two fingers and said, as if to himself, "I think we should have a meeting of the leadership in my office."

I made my way up to the podium and through the door behind

it into that quiet haven of rest where I settled into one of the big leather chairs, and Betty Coffey, without asking, fixed me a regulation glass of what I usually drank, Scotch and water. Jerry Waldie came into the room just as Betty handed me my drink.

Jerry smiled boyishly, bashfully at me, as he always did when greeting a friend.

"Gee," he said, "I really like your suit."

"Why, thank you."

"I always did like padded shoulders and wide lapels, and I hope they start making suits like that again some day."

"And I like your socks."

"You do?" He looked pleased.

"A lot of the guys here wouldn't have the guts to wear argyle socks with a charcoal Ivy League suit."

"I'm glad you like the effect," he said modestly, "and I wish I could take credit for it, but I can't. My wife is the person who really deserves it. She's got all of my other socks in the wash."

"Oh really? Do you have more than one pair?" I said. "I've been wondering about that."

Bob Crown, Tom Bane, and Jess filed in, sat down, and accepted drinks from Betty. It was a casually tense sort of gathering.

Jess stuck out his chin, undid the button of his shirt collar, and relaxed into relief. Taking a contemplative taste of his gin on the rocks, he said, "I can't budge any of the Republican committee chairmen. I don't understand it. Guys like Belotti and Pattee and Marks and Britschgi aren't the kind to go back on their word once they've given it."

"Maybe they don't see it that way," Jerry Waldie said, sounding tentative, probably because he knew Jess wouldn't like what he was saying. "Maybe they have every intention of living up to their commitments, but only after they see the school bill."

In a voice even deeper than usual Jess said, "What kind of a commitment do you call it—if it's subject to conditions or qualifications that one party decides to impose unilaterally after the other party has lived up to his part of the bargain?"

He frowned and sucked up an ounce of his drink.

To me Jerry said, "Jim, when will you have that school bill in shape to show them?"

"We won't have it in print," I could feel a little tightness in my throat as I said it, "for two days."

Bob Crown's brow wrinkled into a deep set of worry lines. "Can't you tell the Reeps what's going to be in it? You must be just working out the details by now."

"No," I said. "I can't say what's going to be in it."

Everyone looked dissatisfied, first at me, then at Jess, who said reluctantly, "Jimmy can't tell the Republicans what's going to be in it." He heaved a little less than half a sigh and explained why. "That bill is being put into a form that will allocate most of the additional money in it to the poor school districts. We can't let the cat out of the bag just yet. If those cowpunchers in the Senate get an advance look at that bill and have time to figure it out, they'll kill it."

The problem was that Senate seats in those days were still apportioned on the basis of area rather than population. Therefore, most of the senators came from rural counties and represented vast herds of cattle, which are subject to the property tax, and relatively few school children, who consume it. As long as state money was meted out to school districts only on the basis of enrollment of students, the taxes on cows remained low. However, if state school support came to be apportioned on the basis of the financial circumstances of the school districts, those districts that had lots of cows, orchards, and farmlands to tax would get less and would have to cover a larger percentage of the costs of their own schools out of their property taxes.

The buckaroos in the Senate always wanted to make sure that a pro rata share, based on enrollment, of all new school moneys would go to rural areas. If they could do that, the property taxes, which were much lower in the rural areas of California than they were in the urban areas, would always remain so.

"We can't even tell the Democrats the provisions of that bill," Jess said, and it worried me to hear him say what I already knew. "There are no secrets around here. Word would get back if we told either caucus. We have to make sure no one in the Senate knows how we're planning to divvy up that money except for the Senate conferees."

The Senate members of the conference committee were Joe Rattigan from Santa Rosa and two other liberals who agreed with us that we should provide more money to improve the education of the children in the poor urban districts and they were in on the plot to keep the bill under wraps.

Jess rumbled on, "I'm convinced that our only chance to get the bill through the Senate lies in keeping it a secret until we bring it to the floor for a vote."

"I wish we could tell Hugh Flournoy and Bill Bagley," Bob Crown said. "They would want to help us with a school finance bill like that, instead of throwing a monkey wrench in the machinery."

"It's too late for that now." Jess's eyebrows, barometric indicators of internal storms, were well below their normal positions. "I don't think they can get themselves clear of the caucus position unless the caucus as a whole is let in on the secret, because they are probably the deep thinkers who came up with the idea of screwing us around on this vote in the first place. I just wish to hell they'd talked to me before they did it."

Jess tossed off the remainder of his first gin on the rocks, planted his elbows on the leather panel in his desk top, folded his thick fingers together, and began to twiddle his thumbs, a sign that he was thinking hard. We all sat and thought with him.

He was the first to speak. "I guess we'll just have to wait them out. I think they're wrong if they expect the press to side with them on this. The rules require every member who is present to vote on every bill. They can't be defended for a conspiracy to violate the rules."

Everyone nodded.

Jess rumbled on, "And besides that, the law says that it's a felony for any member of the Legislature to condition a vote on a bill upon the action of any other member, and that's what they're doing when they say they won't vote for the budget bill unless we show them the school financing bill. They can't be defended for conspiring to commit a crime either." He looked around at us for a response."

"That's logical," Bob Crown said in a subdued voice.

Our in-house skeptic, Tom Bane, looked as worried as Jess, but that was the normal expression on his pale face. Tom ran to long bones and high shoulders, like Abraham Lincoln. Also, like Lincoln, he had a small head and large features and a small, thin, reedy, nasal, tenor speaking voice. It has always seemed incongruous to me that serious worriers like Abraham Lincoln and Tom Bane should have had such little voices.

He piped up, "We need to be careful about the way we present this thing to the press. Jess should say that we will only keep the

Reeps here until they comply with the rules and vote, and it doesn't make any difference how they vote. He should say that he is the speaker and is elected by the house to enforce the rules and that's all he's doing. If the Republicans will abide by the rules and vote either aye or no, we'll take the call off and announce the vote to go home. If they all vote no and defeat the budget bill, we'll declare our intention to ask for reconsideration tomorrow. What could be more reasonable than that?" He never shifted his eyes from Jess's heavy features as he made his case. "If we can just get them onto the roll call, those Republican committee chairmen will have to vote aye. They won't vote no after they've given their word to vote aye. We have got to get the Reeps to cast their votes, and they can't defend not doing it. We should leave the call on as a matter of normal procedure until the members vote, just as we would on any other bill."

After a pause Bob Crown said, "It seems to me that the one thing that no one around here can justify is a refusal to vote. An aye vote or a no vote can be defended on almost any bill, for one reason or another, but not a refusal to vote. And no one can blame us for keeping a call on till we get the members recorded as voting. We do that every day."

"I agree," I said.

Jerry Waldie, whose crew-cut head was the coolest in the Assembly, said pensively, "I think it's a defensible position."

That's how the decision was made. I have read in a hundred different places that Big Daddy, in a fit of petulance, ordered the plucky Republicans locked up because they wouldn't do as they were told and vote for the budget, even though his level-headed brain trust of Jerry Waldie, Bob Crown, Tom Bane, and Jim Mills tried in vain to convince him that it was the height of high-handed folly to do it.

The truth is that the lockup was begotten by all of us in concert. It was to be some hours before any of us would realize that our decision would develop into the damnedest state Capitol news story of the century.

15

How We Kept the Republicans Locked Up

> *Nine out of ten events that occur in the name of government are not the result of careful deliberation or conspiracy, but of accident, mistake, inadvertence.*
>
> Hodding Carter III

*H*aving decided that keeping the call on seemed to be the best course of action, we finished our drinks, rose up, and emerged into the Assembly chamber through the door from the Speaker's office.

The first thing I saw on the floor was Don Mulford posing like Joan of Arc before an audience of reporters at the back of the chamber. With face uplifted and eyes alight with sanctity, he was obviously making some heroic declaration. I went back to join the congregation listening to what he was saying. I got within earshot in time only to hear this closing remark: "The Republican members of this house will never be coerced into voting for the budget until they know just what effect it would have upon the education of the school children of California."

A few moments later, Jess issued forth from his office and descended into the boiling expectation on the floor, with his collar done up again in case some news photographer took his picture. The reporters who had been listening to the Mulf turned to him like a pack of wolves onto a bull buffalo that is showing signs of weakness.

"How can you justify locking up the Republicans until they vote for the budget?" the one with the loudest voice bawled over the clamor of the others.

"They can get out of here without voting for the budget." Jess tugged at his shirt collar with two fingers. "They can go home if they vote against it. What could be more reasonable than that?"

"They're calling you a dictator," another reporter yelled. "What is your response?"

"As speaker of the Assembly I have the responsibility for enforcing the rules of this house. The rules say they have to vote, and that's all I say. I'm not trying to tell anyone how to vote."

The faces of the reporters reflected their dissatisfaction with those answers, which they looked upon as legalistic quibbling. They had a great story shaping up, and they weren't going to let anybody mess it up with technical equivocations. They continued their cross-examination. All of their subsequent questions were restatements of their first two, and all of Jess's replies were also variations upon his first two.

The Republicans were exuberant about the way the situation was developing. When I wandered into the back hall, I saw most of them jubilantly waiting to get into the phone booths where they could call their local newspapers and television and radio stations to tell of their heroic refusal to cave in to Big Daddy and vote for the budget even if he kept them in all night. And I realized that the press, which always likes a simple story, was accepting their version of what was happening without any reservations.

It was clear right from the start that the Republicans felt we had them right where they wanted us to have them.

The afternoon wore away, and so did some members' concern about how the press might report what was happening. John Quimby, Alan Pattee, Paul Lunardi, and Lester McMillan withdrew into the Rules Committee hearing room to start a bipartisan game of poker that was to last, with interruptions only for Democratic and Republican caucuses, for almost twenty-four hours.

The floor was clotted with clumps of conversation, among which Jess was circulating, trying to get a few words with one or another of the G.O.P. committee chairmen, so he could persuade them to deliver on their commitments, but I saw other Republicans gather around whenever he began to talk to one of them, to keep the pressure on their colleague to stand firm. Even from Milton Marks, who was the most liberal and friendly of all of the Republicans—as befitted a man who looked so much like Hubert Humphrey—Jess couldn't get anything more satisfactory than,

"I'm really sorry, Jess, but I'm going to have to see the school bill before I can vote for the budget."

It was all very oblique. The Speaker couldn't ask them to live up to their solemn promises to vote for the budget when other Republicans were listening in. Any such colloquy would have been presented to the press as Big Daddy's trying to twist the arms of idealistic Republicans.

Most of the exchanges between the Speaker and the other three G.O.P. chairmen went pretty much like this one with Ike Britschgi.

Unruh: "The schools are getting a good deal out of the package. Nobody says we've set aside too little money for them."

Britschgi: "Why don't you show us the bill? Why all the secrecy?"

Unruh: "It isn't put together yet."

Britschgi: "That's bullshit, Jess, and you know it. You could show it to us if you wanted to, so we figure you must be hiding something."

Jess was looking more and more like a losing football coach as he continued to circulate, glumly giving Democrats comforting pats on the back, trying to keep up his players' spirits in the course of playing a losing game.

Once when he was on his way down to the floor from the rostrum after talking with Carlos Bee, who was presiding, his eyes fell upon a striking blonde secretary, as she was submittting something to the chief clerk.

He stopped and said, "You're new here, aren't you?"

She said, "Yes, I am."

He said, "I'm Jess Unruh."

She said, "I'm aware of that."

He said, "Who are you?"

She said, "I'm Helen Jones. I work for Mr. Donovan."

He said, "If I offered to buy you a drink tonight before you go home, just to welcome you aboard as an Assembly employee, would you accept it?"

She said, "I guess so."

After that solemn exchange, I walked with him into the back hall. He stuck his head into the Rules Committee room to see if there was someone in there he could talk to about the vote on the budget. On seeing the poker game under way and a bottle of whiskey and piles of money on the table, he said, "If any reporter looks into this room and sees you guys gambling and drinking at a time like this, the result will be some lousy publicity for the Assembly. You ought to fold up this game and do something else."

The four of them listened to him respectfully and stopped playing, until he left the room. As I walked out the door behind him, I heard Alan Pattee say to John Quimby, "I'll raise you fifty cents."

Suppertime came, and Jess asked the Democratic leadership to come to his office again. He said to us, "Some of our guys have asked me for passes to go out for dinner. Whenever we have a call on, I always let members have passes if they've voted and if they have a legitimate reason to leave, and if they promise to come back as soon as possible. That is how both houses have always been run, and I'm afraid that if I try to keep all of our guys in, we'll have trouble with them. What do you think?"

Jerry said, "I think you'll have to let them go."

The rest of us agreed, and Jess wrote passes for a dozen Democrats to go out to eat, telling each one, "We've got to have more Democrats on the floor than there are Republicans at all times or they'll take the call off. Come back as quick as you can so someone else can go."

Some of the reporters had a picnic with that; and, even to this day, stories written about the lockup by people who weren't there tell of how the Democrats trooped out of the chamber to Sacramento's best restaurants to eat, drink, and be merry for most of the evening, leaving the poor Republicans imprisoned in the Assembly chamber, a lonely but doughty little band of martyrs. Actually, the majority of the Democrats, like me, never left. There was never a time that I could go because we needed to let others go, the ones who might become troublesome if they were kept in.

The twenty-seven Republicans sent out for thirty-eight steaks and had a nice supper in the chamber. (The extra meals were for wives and secretaries who stayed to sympathize with them.) Their steaks certainly looked a lot better than the hamburger I was masticating at my desk on the floor.

Both Republicans and Democrats sent friends to fetch bottles of booze from office desks or liquor stores. Pretty soon almost everyone had had a few drinks, and the Republicans were beginning to act boisterous. Before they had finished their suppers, they were starting to make fun of us.

Bill Bagley said to me, "You should be eating something better than a hamburger, Jimmy, because we're going to be here for a long time."

I was in Jess's office for another rap session when John Quimby, the only paraplegic ever to serve as a member of the California Legislature, struggled in on his stainless steel sticks, having taken a break from the poker game in the Rules Committee room to impart a piece of unwelcome intelligence to us.

Offhandedly he said, "I thought you fellows ought to know that Alan Pattee called Bill Geyer to come to the Rules Committee room. [Bill worked for the Committee on Agriculture, of which Alan Pattee was chairman.] When Bill walked in, Alan looked up at him and said, 'Bill, I want you to take these keys, go to my room, bring me a shaver and a clean shirt, and, oh, yes, one more thing, you're fired.'"

Jess Unruh's face turned red and then livid.

John went on, "I thought you should know they really are planning to stay the night. I also thought you should know about Alan telling Bill Geyer he was fired. I guess that means he and the other Republican committee chairmen aren't planning to live up to their promises to vote for the budget, and they're expecting to lose their committee chairmanships."

Jess said, "Those double-crossing bastards."

John looked around at our long faces and said, "I guess I'll get back to the game," and he crutched himself out.

Jess's face metamorphosed into a mask of living fury. It had never really been at all believable to him that the Republican committee chairmen would give their word to him when it was to their advantage to do so and renege when he needed them. His word was sacred to him, and he thought theirs would be to them. He looked upon their breach of faith as a personal betrayal. He stormed out of his office and through the chaos in the chamber and out the great dark main doors into the mosaic-floored hall outside, where all of the television cameras had been moved on their tall tripods to do some interviews of members. As the cameramen focused their lenses upon him and started all of their gear whirring, the Speaker dumped all over the Republicans.

"They would lure us into committing a felony by trading one

bill for another." His voice was like summer thunder. "A number of Republicans have given me their solemn word that they would vote for the budget, and they have been blackjacked by the Republican caucus into breaking their word."

When Jess was done, Don Mulford took center stage before the battery of cameras, his broad red face glowing with an insurance man's rectitude. He said, "The problem is that the Speaker is power mad. Until Unruh went into orbit and accused the Republicans of suggesting a felony, an agreement on the budget could have been reached easily."

An aggressive young reporter asked Jess, "What do you have to say about that?"

He snapped, "That's bullshit."

The reporter said, "May I quote you?" but Jess had already turned on his heel and was stomping off into the chamber again.

I followed him in and saw Charlie Meyers moving about. Obviously uncomfortable with the feeling that his friends were angry with each other, he was offering everybody mints.

Thus far, both the Democratic and Republican leaders were acting in an intelligent fashion, based upon what they then knew, even though the Republicans' putting pressure on their committee chairmen to go back on their word was not honorable. In politics, as everyone knows, a lot of things that are intelligent are not honorable, and vice versa.

Certainly the Republicans felt they were being eminently rational. They couldn't imagine any good reason why we shouldn't tell them what was in the school bill. They were sure we could let them know if we wanted to and that we had simply decided to engage them in a conflict of wills. They felt Jess was being highhanded, stubborn, and dictatorial, and they weren't going to allow him to push them around. Naturally, the press sympathized with their position, not knowing any more than they did.

Jerry Waldie took George Zenovich to talk with Don Mulford. When they came back to report to Jess and the rest of us in the Speaker's office, Jerry looked downcast. He said, "We told the Mulf, 'If you want to know about the school bill, we'd probably be able to answer your questions. It's very likely that your concerns relate to parts of the bill that have been agreed upon, and we could tell you what you want to know.' The Mulf just looked at us with those big sincere eyes and said, 'We want to see the bill. What's so unreasonable about that?' And I said, 'Nothing, except we can't show it to you yet because it's not finalized.'"

"Man," George Zenovich said with a quizzical smile, as he said most things, "those cats don't really care what's in that bill; they're happy as hell screwing us around."

We were clearly at a dead end, and Jess's jaw was becoming more and more grimly set. He gnarled at us, "I've had more than enough of bad faith for one night," and he got Betty Coffey on the office intercom and said to her, "I want you to get hold of Helen Jones—she works for Dick Donovan—and ask her where I could find her to buy her the drink I promised her." Betty came in a few minutes later to report, "She says she'll see you at the downstairs bar at the Mirador Hotel."

He stalked out of the chamber to find her there.

John Parkhurst was a tall, handsome fellow who didn't look properly turned out in his Brooks Brothers suits. He always looked as if he should be wearing a varsity letterman's sweater. For many years he lobbied for Pacific Bell Telephone Company. Acting in that capacity, he took me to dinner one evening a couple of years ago at the Firehouse, and in the course of our conversation we got on the subject of the lockup.

He said, "You know, I was sitting in the lower bar of the Mirador having a drink that night when Jess Unruh came into the bar and sat down with Helen Jones, who was at the next table. I said, 'Can I buy you a little touch, Jess?'

"He said, 'A Beefeater's on the rocks.' He sounded, and looked, gloomy as hell. And from that time forward he settled down to get himself well and truly gassed."

"He sure did," I said, "and when I heard that was what he was doing, I couldn't believe it. He never drinks much when he has decisions to make."

"I've heard that."

"I guess what was different about him that night was that he was so mad at the Republicans he couldn't see straight."

"You're right," John said. "When I brought him his drink, he invited me, no, he *told* me, to sit down with Helen and him at their table, and I did. Helen and I tried to make small talk, but he wasn't interested. He just sat there looking gloomy. He didn't say anything until after he tossed off that first drink, and then he complained to Helen and me, 'They had no right to blindside me. If they were worried about the school bill, they should have talked to me about it. They don't really give a good goddamn about it or they would have.'"

"That's absolutely true," I said to John.

"Of course it is, Jim. The whole thing was directed at him, and he knew it. So he sat there brooding for a while. About halfway through his second Beefeater's on the rocks, he said, 'I've always gone out of my way to be fair to the Republicans. I've always given them a part of the action. I've always consulted them on the operations of the house. I've always kept my word with them.'

"By that time he was just a mouldering heap of resentment. I couldn't think of anything to say or do to cheer him up, and neither could Helen, so we just sat there and drank with him in silence. We hoped that would be taken by him as an expression of sympathy and support. Everyone else in the place could see what kind of a mood he was in, and no one came anywhere near.

"After a while he said, 'Goddamn it! It isn't any fun anymore. I'm going to quit as speaker.'

"He pulled a ballpoint pen out of his coat pocket and wrote on a red paper napkin that was on the table, 'I, Jesse Unruh, hereby resign as speaker of the Assembly,' and he signed it.

"'Here,' he said to me, 'you take custody of this.'

"I didn't want to touch it. I didn't know what I should do. Jess kept holding the resignation out for me to take, and I decided I'd better take it, so I did. The three of us just sat there until Bobby Crown came into the bar looking for Jess. He sat down at our table to talk to him.

"He said, 'Jess, you've got to get back over there. It looks bad for you to be here when we've got the Republicans locked up.'

"Jess didn't look up from his drink.

"Bob pleaded with him, 'Come back with me, Jess. The Reeps are bound to find out where you are, and, when they do, they'll tear you to pieces.'

"Jess said, 'They can go to hell.'

"I thought that discussion would go better without me, so I said, 'I think I'd better be getting along,' and I started to get up.

"But Jess said, 'Sit down. You're one of us now.'

"Bob Crown was beginning to look pretty desperate. He said, 'The press is going to crucify you, if you don't get back over to the Capitol.'

"Jess said, 'They can go to hell, too. I'm sick of all this bullshit and bad faith. I've got better things to do.'

"Bob said, 'My God, you can't just throw everything away you've worked so many years for.'

"'The hell I can't. John's got my resignation right there in his hand.'

"Bob looked at me and saw the red napkin I had in my hand. He grabbed it away from me and sat there clutching it in his fist.

"I was feeling pretty superfluous just then, so I got out a cigarette and started to light it. Bob stuck the napkin into the flame of my cigarette lighter and dropped it into the ashtray on the table where we all watched it burn up.

"Bob said to Jess, 'That's what I think of your resignation.'

"He tried to talk to Jess for twenty minutes or more, but Jess wouldn't answer him. Instead, he wrote out another resignation on another napkin. Finally, Bob's voice broke and he got up and stumbled out of the place wiping his eyes with his handkerchief.

"After ten minutes of silent drinking, I asked Jess, 'Would you like to have some dinner?'

"He said, 'Yeah, I would.'

"We got up and walked into the dining room, and Victor, the head waiter, showed us to one of the booths in one of the corners of the room."

John took a taste of the excellent claret he had chosen to go with our dinners and then went on with his story. "When the waiter showed up to take our orders, Jess said gloomily to Helen, 'How about a beefsteak à la Chateaubriand for two?'

"She said, 'Okay.'

"I ordered a New York cut, and the waiter said, 'Would any of you care for another drink?'

"And Jess held up his empty glass."

While Helen, Jess, and John were ordering their dinners, an enterprising G.O.P. staff man, who had been gumshoeing around downtown Sacramento looking for Unruh, came into the Grenada Room and found him there. The man sat down to have dinner at the next table to keep an eye on the Speaker and report everything that took place to the Republican leadership on the floor.

In the chamber Bill Bagley would rise periodically, ask to be recognized, and announce to the house and the attendant press,

"The Speaker has just been served another Beefeater's on the rocks," or "The Speaker has just ordered beefsteak a la Chateaubriand for himself and a blonde lady friend," or, "The Speaker has now ordered a 1957 Inglenook cabernet sauvignon to go with his and her dinner." The press duly noted every course, right through to when Bagley announced, "The Speaker and his friend are now having cherries jubilee for dessert."

Bob Crown, who had by then come despairingly back to the floor, said to me, "Oh, my god, Jim. This is absolutely going to ruin him. We've got to do something. Let's have another meeting with Jerry and Tom and George Zenovich."

In Jess's office we mooned about how bad things looked for twenty minutes. At last Tom said, "I think Jerry Waldie and George Zenovich should try to talk to Don Mulford again, to see if they could work out some sort of compromise. If we could just get some little concession that would save some face for everyone involved, we might be able to convince Jess to put an end to this fiasco before he's destroyed by it."

Jerry and George set out again on another diplomatic mission. Tom, Bob, and I remained in the Speaker's office and waited for them to return. They reported back after a long hour. George said, "That cat isn't willing to give an inch." And Jerry told us the Mulf had said, "I'm terribly concerned about the bad publicity the Assembly is getting."

Bob Crown said bitterly, "I'm glad to hear he's so concerned."

As detached, calm, and reasonable as ever, Jerry laid out a plan, "He has us over a barrel. We've got to put an end to this before it destroys Jess. The Mulf suggested as a compromise that we take the call off and go home and come back tomorrow and talk things over like gentlemen. Now, that isn't really a compromise at all, but I think we should pretend that it is and go along with it. I think the best thing we can do now is to let them go home now before the situation gets any worse than it is. It won't actually do any harm if we don't pass the budget bill for a couple of days. I think Bobby should go back and tell Jess. He's Jess's best friend. And he should take Pierce Young with him. Pierce is living with Jess this year and he likes him."

Bob hurried out to get Pierce Young off the floor and take him with him to the Mirador to plead with Jess in the Grenada Room.

After awhile Bob reappeared, distraught. He got Tom, Jerry, and me together on the floor to tell us, "That second resignation he wrote on a napkin, he gave it to Martha Gorman, who's sitting with them now. He told her that if she doesn't hang onto it, he'll have her fired, and she won't let anyone get it away from her. Tom, you go talk to him. He may listen to you."

Tom left. When he came back awhile later, he told us between tight lips, "He's as drunk as a skunk. I couldn't talk to him. He's just sitting over there holding Helen Jones's hand, moping and drinking. All he'd say was, 'I don't want to talk about it. You guys do whatever the hell you want.'"

Helen Jones told me much later, "After that, Jess just sat and gave no sign that he heard anything that any of his friends who had come over to talk to him were saying to him. For at least an hour they tried to convince him that it was time to take the call off and go home, and the only person he would talk to was the cocktail waitress. Finally, he turned to me, looking like he didn't have a friend in the world, and said, 'What do you think I should do?' And I told him, 'I think you should talk to somebody you trust. Who would you like to talk to?' He said, 'Jerry Waldie.' And I said, 'Will somebody call the Capitol and get word to Jerry Waldie to come over?' And someone did."

As soon as Jerry got the word that Jess wanted to talk to him, he left for the Mirador. He asked George Zenovich to accompany him because George had been with him when he had talked to Don Mulford.

After Jerry and George left, I started looking around for a place to collapse, but every couch in the lounge and the Speaker's office was occupied. I hadn't heard so much snoring since I got out of the army. Finally, I decided to go out onto the floor to visit with the Democrats who were awake because some of them were wondering where in hell their leadership was. Carlos Bee, who was in the chair, and I were all there were who passed for leadership in the chambers at that time.

George Deukmejian, the present governor of California, who was always a quiet, friendly, and nice man, came to me and said, "You guys should really try to get yourselves out of this situation, you know."

I appreciated his concern and sympathy, and I couldn't disagree with him because he was right. On the other hand, I couldn't agree with him either because that would have been a signal to the

Republicans that we were wavering in our resolve, which would strengthen theirs. So I told him about my vacation plans.

An age or two passed while I visited around on the floor. When Jerry Waldie and George Zenovich returned from the Mirador, a sergeant-at-arms came to tell me I was wanted in the Speaker's office. I went there.

Jerry, in a voice flat with exhaustion, told me what had passed between him and Jess.

"We went in and found Jess, Helen Jones, John Parkhurst, Martha Gorman, Bob Crown, and Pierce Young all sitting in one booth, and that was all it would hold. We took chairs from a table nearby, pulled them up to the end of the booth and sat down." Jerry paused and then continued, "I said to Jess, 'I want to talk to you.'

"Without looking at me, he said, 'Go ahead and talk,' and he waved to the cocktail waitress to bring him another drink." Jerry lowered his eyes from me as he went on. "I said, 'All of the guys you look upon as your friends have talked this situation over, and we think it's time to take the call off and let everyone go home for the night. We can come back in the morning, and maybe the Republicans will be ready to vote for the budget then. If they're not, we can pass it the day after, when Joe Rattigan and Jimmy will have the school bill on the floor.'

"Jess gave me a funny look and said, 'If you guys want to run the Assembly, you can run it without me.'" Jerry looked at me again and said, "'Nobody wants to run it without you,' I told him. 'It won't do any harm if we pass the budget two days from now instead of tonight, but it sure will do a hell of a lot of harm to keep this call on. Jess, the publicity is going to be terrible if we don't shut down.'

"The waiter brought Jess the drink he'd ordered, and he tossed off half of it. Everybody else in the booth was keeping pretty quiet. I guess they'd said everything they could think of to persuade Jess, and they seemed to be played out, so I went on. 'There isn't one of us who doesn't agree you're morally and legally right in keeping the call on. The Republicans have no right to withhold their votes on the budget. That's illegal, and it's also against the rules. And the Republican chairmen who promised to vote for the budget and then refused are a bunch of shit heels, okay? But that doesn't help you. That's not the way the press is handling it. As far as the reporters are concerned you've locked up the Republicans because they won't vote for the budget bill, and they're making you out to be a petty tyrant.' Jess didn't even look at me. He just tossed off the rest of his drink.

"I went into my closing arguments. 'What I'm trying to say is that what you're doing is morally right, but it's politically dumb, and nobody's ever known you to be politically dumb before.'

"Jess raised his eyes slowly from his drink to give me that funny look again. I couldn't tell if it was a look of anger or what it was," Jerry said softly in a monotone. "I waited for him to say something, but he just kept looking at me. I couldn't figure it out and couldn't think of anything better to do than to sum up, so I said, 'Jess, all of your friends agree that we should have Jimmy call the Democrats into a caucus and tell them that we've decided to take the call off and go home.'

"He kept on giving me that funny look. At last he said, 'Okay. Have Jimmy call the caucus.'

"So I came back to tell you to call a caucus so we can tell the troops we're going to call it a night and go home."

I said to Jerry, "Thank God he finally agreed to that."

Jerry looked wearier than I had ever seen him. He said, "Yes, thank God, he finally agreed to that, at least I think he did."

It was at 11:52 that I went out on the floor and announced, "There will be a meeting of the Democratic caucus in the Assembly lounge."

We rousted all of the sleeping Republicans out of the sofas in the lounge and made the Democrats sit up. We broke up the poker game in the Rules Committee room and another one that had started in the Speaker's office. We called in the Democrats who were collapsed in the coffee room and on the floor. When all of our troops were in the lounge, sitting in the low leather chairs and sofas that furnished the plain, square, blond-oak box of a room, I could see that most of the members were slack-jawed with fatigue and drinking. There was, after all, not much to do in the chamber that night except play cards and drink. (The Republicans were in the same condition as we, but they were enjoying it more.)

Banging on the top of the big television set with the flat of my hand, I called the caucus to order. I said, "The leadership of this caucus has reached some conclusions about our present situation and wants to make some recommendations to you. Jerry has been over talking to Jess, and I'm going to ask him, in his capacity as majority floor leader, to tell you what has been concluded."

Jerry stood up, looking worn and earnest. He said, "I think we've come to a point where it would be best if we just called it quits for the night. We're getting terrible publicity for locking up the Republicans. We're not getting through with our story that we're simply enforcing the rules the same way we do every other day we're in session. The Republicans are having a field day with the press, saying that we've locked them up until they vote for the budget, and the press is making Christian martyrs out of them."

At that point Jess gloomed into the room and stood against the wall, a human storm cloud against a blond wooden backdrop.

Jerry went on, "We might as well go home. We can bring up the budget for a vote in a couple of days when the school bill is ready to go. That is the best judgment of the leadership of the caucus, and I cleared it with the Speaker."

The caucus seemed confused but willing to go along. Bob Crown and Tom Bane offered a few words in support of what Jerry had said, while Jess looked on with the expression of a bulldog hanging onto a rope.

At last he put two fingers inside his shirt collar, took a tug at it, and said, "Aw, shit." He started to move across the floor to the front, passing among Democrats in their leather chairs and sofas like a battleship picking its way through a crowded anchorage. As he passed Tom Bane, I heard him say, "Don't leave me, Tom."

Turning to face the caucus, he planted his feet about fifteen inches apart. I thought I saw the light of battle in his eye. I hoped I was wrong. But I wasn't.

He roared, "Are we going to let those miserable bastards push us around?"

John Quimby, who was as drunk and belligerent as Jess, sounded the battle cry, "Attaboy, Jesse baby. Go get 'em. Don't take any shit from the bastards. Kick 'em in the ass, Jesse baby."

Animal sounds rose from the throats of dozens of drunken Democrats.

Terry yelled, "Let's keep the sons-of-bitches here till next year if that's what it takes."

There was a supporting roar of drunken bellicosity from the ranks. The majority were with the Speaker. Actually, the whole caucus was with him. Those who thought the call should be dispensed with were his friends. Our only concern was for him, and the only thing that would have made him look worse than keeping the call on would have been repudiating him by voting to take it off over his objections.

Jerry Waldie slumped on the leather sofa beside me, with his crew-cut black head in his hands. He raised his face to look bleakly at Jess for a moment, and I saw that there were tears on his cheeks. He had done his best to save his friend from himself and he had failed, just as Bobby Crown had earlier, and, like Bobby, he wept at the tragedy of his failure.

16

How We Passed the Budget
and Went Home

One night's drunkenness can defeat the labors of forty days well employed.

Samuel Johnson

*W*e broke up the caucus, united in our resolve to stand behind the Speaker as he bloodied his head on the adamantine wailing wall of Republican intransigence. When I walked out onto the floor, I saw that three of the four Republican committee chairmen looked as down in the mouth as if they'd been apprehended for some much too petty crime. The fourth, Alan Pattee, who was waiting for the poker game in the Rules Committee room to begin again, appeared more disgruntled than downcast, and the end of his nose was bright red.

That year my seatmate was Milton Marks. I said to him, "What happened to Alan's nose?"

Milton replied, "He's been drinking a lot tonight, and it's beginning to get to him, so while he was trying to light the stub of a dead cigar with that flame thrower he uses for a cigar lighter, he burned his nose."

He looked like Rudolph the red-nosed reindeer before Santa told him that he was finally going to get to go along with the other reindeer on his first Christmas Eve flight. Most of the Republicans were carrying on as if they were at a New Year's party, however.

Jerry Waldie said to me at one point, "I wonder when they're going to come out with the paper hats and noisemakers."

Recently, when I asked Hugh Flournoy his recollections of the lockup, his face lighted up and he said, "Jimmy, that was one of the greatest nights of my life. We spent it drinking, playing cards, and laughing at you guys."

My fellow San Diegan, Clair Burgener, later a Republican state senator and a congressman, was then a Republican assembly-man. He told me the last time I saw him, "My clearest recollection of that night was of Charlie Chapel sidling up to me and saying, 'Would you like to get out of here? I'm always glad to help out a Democratic friend. I'll show you how to get out of here.'

"Out of curiosity," Clair said, "I let him hustle me out into the hall and into the office of the chief clerk. 'See that door over there?' he said. 'It goes out into the main hall, and they never put a sergeant-at-arms to guard it because nobody knows it isn't locked when there's a call on.'

"I said, 'Gee, thanks, Charlie, but I'm a Republican.'

"Charlie scowled and said, 'If I'd known that I wouldn't have showed you the way out.'

"That was my first year in the Assembly, and Charlie hadn't noticed me in the Republican caucus meetings. Sometimes he didn't notice much." Clair chuckled, as everyone did when marveling about how much Charlie drank. "What Charlie had in mind was to get enough Democrats off the floor so the Republicans would have a majority in the chamber, and then we would have been able to take the call off by a majority vote and we could have gone home."

Charlie was never more full of beans than that night.

Don Allen, who had served in the marines with him, told me, "I haven't seen Charlie look so damned happy since he was hunting rebels in Nicaragua thirty years ago."

Charlie spent a lot of his time taking Democrats into the chief clerk's office to show them how to get out of the chamber without a pass.

Once he asked for recognition and gave a speech in what he said was Spanish, although the Spanish-speaking members said that it wasn't.

Finally, Charlie realized that none of the Democrats he had shown the door to freedom was leaving by it; so, after the Democratic caucus broke up, he went to Jess and told him, "I feel like hell, and I want a pass so I can go home and get some sleep."

Jess wrote the pass for him, as he did that night for every other Republican who said he didn't feel well, and Charlie marched off the floor as if he were leaving a parade ground after receiving a decoration.

Charles Garrigus, the chairman of the Education Committee,

stood up at about two o'clock and recited an ode he had composed about the heroic events of the night. He was practicing up to be poet laureate of California, which he is now.

There were coatless, tieless, rumpled men laid out wherever I looked, on every sofa and chair in the Assembly lounge, and in the Speaker's office, and in the chairs on the floor, and in the visitors' seats at the back. They were members, staff, newsmen, all dead to the drama still building around them.

Don Mulford was continuing to play his role of chief martyr. A few minutes after two, he rose on the floor to announce with great gravity, "Mr. Speaker, a few hours ago I telephoned the commanding general of the California National Guard and requested him to send army cots for the use of the members. Those cots have now been delivered to the basement. I rise to ask that the sergeant-at-arms be directed to bring them up to the chamber."

Carlos Bee, who had been presiding most of the time since the call of the house had been imposed, had taken a half hour off to sit in on a blackjack game in the Speaker's office, and John Williamson was in the chair temporarily. With a poker face he said, "We are not going to have any army cots on the floor of the Assembly."

Bringing those cots to the floor would have resulted in the most memorable news photographs in the history of the California State Legislature, shots pictorially publicizing the imprisonment of the hapless Republicans by the Speaker. The refusal of John Williamson to allow the cots to be brought to the floor was represented by the Republicans to the press as just one more manifestation of the despotism of Big Daddy, who could have taken the chair and reversed John's ruling, if he had seen fit to do so.

As for Jess, the gravity of the situation and a lot of black coffee were sobering him up. He was wandering about in a state of blinking exhaustion.

Decent, brilliant Joe Rattigan, the author of the school bill the Republicans said they wanted to see, came among us to try to help. He asked Don Mulford to call a Republican caucus in the lounge so he could tell them what was in the bill. After Joe came out of it, he reported to the Speaker's office, and on his dark Irish face was that amused look of wonder at the foibles of mankind that he often wore. With a rueful smile he said, "They don't have any objections to anything in the bill, but they still say they won't vote for the budget until they see the school bill in print."

Jess's face was lax with resignation; he said, "Thanks for trying to help, Joe."

Joe replied, "I hate to leave you fellows here to sweat this out, but I'm going to get some shut-eye."

He left us looking at each other gloomily.

Shortly after that, we went back out on the floor to see if anything was happening.

Exuding bonhomie from every pore, Don Mulford approached me and said, "As the Republican caucus chairman, I thought I should mention to you, as the Democratic caucus chairman, that I'm terribly concerned that this situation will result in terrible publicity for the Assembly."

"I'm glad to hear that," I said. "So am I. Why don't you release your guys from your caucus position and let them vote on the budget?"

"We will. As soon as we see the school bill."

"Joe Rattigan told you what's in it. Are you suggesting that Joe can't be trusted to tell the truth?"

Joe was perhaps the most universally respected man in either house of the Legislature, just as today he is perhaps the most universally respected appellate court justice in California.

"No, no, no, no," Don answered in the same gracious tone of horror he would have used if I had told him I thought he was trying to sell me a lousy life insurance policy. "We simply want to see the school bill before we vote on the budget. What is so unreasonable about that?"

"Is it possible to talk to you on this subject and ever get beyond that point?"

"No," he said. "It isn't."

I slumped into my old swivel chair on the floor, crossed my arms on my green leather desk top panel, and tried to get a little sleep.

I don't know how much time passed before an assistant sergeant-at-arms shook my shoulder gently to wake me and said, "Mr. Mills, the Speaker would like to see you in his office."

As I blinked drowsily, I saw that daybreak had begun to wash the dark sky outside through the tall, arched windows of the Assembly chamber with the faintest of tints, dimly outlining the black, multirectangular skyline of downtown Sacramento. I pulled myself together somewhat, struggled to my feet, and shambled off to the

Speaker's office, where I found the rest of the Democratic leadership, and some of the followership as well, sitting bleary-eyed, accepting strong drinks, as usual, from Betty Coffey, but this time the only choice she was offering was hot black coffee.

After I sank into a big leather chair, Jess led off gravely with, "I think we ought to give Joe Rattigan's approach another try." I was relieved that he was in command of himself and the situation again. "We might package it a little differently to make it appear to be a new offer on our part. We could put a summary of the school bill on paper and give it to them. Enough time has passed so it won't do much harm now."

"That's right," I said. "The final agreements on the bill have been in the hands of legislative counsel being drafted since yesterday morning and they'll be in print in a few hours anyway. It's too late for the farm bureau and the cattlemen's association to analyze the final form of the bill and stir up their membership about it before it comes to a vote in the Senate."

One of our brightest young freshmen, Leo Ryan, complained bitterly, "We all know that the Republicans' line about how they simply have to know all about the school bill before they can vote on the budget is pure bullshit. Joe Rattigan told them what was in it, and they know that he was telling them the truth. Why would they give a damn about having us tell them what Joe already has told them?"

"The way I see it," Jerry Waldie said, "they'll keep the call on until they've decided they've gotten everything they can out of it, and then they'll take it off the first time we give them an excuse to do it. Maybe they'll be ready to do that by the time we can get a written summary of the bill prepared."

Tom Bane said, "I don't see how it could do any harm to give it a try. We sure as hell don't want this to go on any longer than it has to."

George Zenovich said, "What have we got to lose, Jesse baby?"

Jess looked at me. "Will you take care of that, Jimmy?" he said.

"Okay," I said, and I got on the telephone to talk to the staff people who'd been working with us on the bill and to ask them to get out of bed and get down to the Capitol and get the summary put together as quickly as possible.

By midmorning the job was done. As soon as I had a typed copy in hand, I gave it to Don Mulford without comment. He rose at his desk with ponderous dignity to say, "Mr. Speaker, I rise to announce a Republican caucus in the lounge."

After a half hour of gritty-eyed suspense for the Democrats, the Capitol news corps, and the Assembly staff, the Republicans emerged from the lounge and took their seats at their desks on the floor. They still hadn't seen the school bill, and they didn't know any more about what was in it than they had learned the night before from Joe Rattigan, but they had apparently decided in caucus that they had indeed gotten everything they could out of being locked up, because Charlie Conrad, the Republican floor leader, stood up on the floor and declared in the official voice that he used on the bench when he played a judge in the Perry Mason television series, as he occasionally did, "Mr. Speaker, the minority party has seen a digest of the proposed conference committee report on the school bill. This fulfills the party's request. I move that further proceedings under the call as it pertains to Senate Bill 4 be dispensed with."

When the reading clerk called the names of those who hadn't voted, nine Republicans voted for the supplemental budget, eighteen voted against it, and the bill was granted final passage by a vote of sixty to eighteen.

After the vote was announced, the reading clerk said, "There is a resolution at the desk."

The Speaker said, "Read the resolution."

"Assembly Resolution 125 by Mr. Bane."

"Referred to the Committee on Rules," the Speaker said very emphatically.

Sensing something out of the ordinary, a couple of reporters closed in on Tom Bane and asked him, "What's that resolution all about?"

"Oh," said Tom lightly, "it's just a little resolution to amend a couple of rules of the Assembly to bring them into conformity with the rules of the Congress of the United States."

The reporters rushed to the Chief Clerk to request copies of the resolution. They read it with goggly eyes, and immediately the entire press corps and the Republican caucus went into a twisting turmoil. The rules in Congress provide that the Speaker be elected by the members of the majority party only rather than by the house as a whole, and they also require that all committee chairmen be members of the majority party. Tom's resolution was drafted to amend the Assembly rules to incorporate into them those provisions of the rules of Congress.

The idea had been proposed by one of the senior statesmen in the Assembly, Carley Porter, in the middle of the night. When our tempers were short after the Democratic caucus had adjourned, Carley had asked to talk to Jess and the rest of the Democratic leadership in the Speaker's office.

"What do we get for those chairmanships that you've given to the Republicans?" Carley demanded of us with a pale intensity. "Nothing. Nothing at all. All four of those Republican chairmen promised you they would vote for the budget, and now they're breaking their word. I say we ought to adopt the rules they have in Congress and give them nothing. Jess, you could help four of our guys to get themselves re-elected if you'd give them those chairmanships."

Bob Crown said the same thing, though he put it more lyrically. He said, "We should treat the bastards like ladies."

No one had to think twice to figure out what he meant by that.

Jess said nothing. He listened and twiddled his thumbs as we expressed ourselves one by one. Half of the caucus had crowded into the Speaker's office after Carley, and they all agreed with him.

At last Jess said, "If that's what you all want, I'll go along. Tom, you're the chairman of the Rules Committee. It's up to you to draft the resolution to change the rules."

The longest daily session since 1939 broke up, as did the poker game in the Assembly Rules Committee room, shortly after Tom introduced the resolution changing the rules, and we all went to our hotel rooms to shave, shower, and fall into our beds.

During the afternoon, while the rest of us were so engaged, the Committee on Rules met, considered Tom's resolution, and sent it to the floor with the recommendation that it be adopted, over the shouted objections of the Republicans on the committee. At four in the afternoon we were all back on the floor for that day's session.

After the resolution and a favorable Rules Committee recommendation upon it were read across the desk, Tom Bane rose and presented it.

"Mr. Speaker," he said, "we all agree that the United States Congress is a distinguished body. We look to it as a pattern for the protection of the liberties of the American people. Therefore, all of the state legislatures are modeled upon it, though on a more humble scale. We should try to make of the California Legislature a more true reflection of the House of Representatives, so Californians who take the time to learn about one will also understand the other. This modest little resolution simply brings the rules of this house into conformity with those of Congress with respect to the manner in which the speaker and committee chairmen are chosen. I ask for an aye vote."

The Mulf rose to wrathfully denounce the change. "It would mean," he cried, "one-man bossism in California." He went on to characterize the Speaker as "a man without humility... a very insecure man... an unhappy man."

All the members of the Republican caucus put on histrionic performances that afternoon. As had been the case the night before, the hall was filled with Republicans waiting in line to get into the eight telephone booths there to call all of the newspapers and radio and television stations in their districts to express their amazement, shock, and outrage at what the Democrats, under the leadership of Big Daddy, were doing to Republicans for standing up for their principles.

Of course it was all an act. They had always known what they might expect if they required the Republican committee chairmen to go along with a caucus position and break their promises to vote for the budget. Certainly Alan Pattee had been under no misapprehensions the night before when he told his committee consultant Bill Geyer, "You're fired." That statement showed that he clearly understood that he was, by his action, giving up his chairmanship and that the Republicans had it all figured out the night before and had concluded that it would work out to their advantage in terms of public relations, as it did.

The resolution was adopted on a straight party line vote—it required only a simple majority for passage—and after we adjourned once again, a pack of reporters gathered around Unruh at the front of the chamber.

"How can you possibly justify this retribution against the Republican committee chairmen?" one reporter shouted the question for all of them.

"It wasn't retribution," he said, eyeing them coldly. "It was self-defense. When someone is jabbing you in the eye, you blink or go blind."

That was the end of the legislative battle of the century. When the Legislature met again the next year, it was a memory, and we were all more friendly enemies again.

Jess would have been happy to give the Republicans back their chairmanships then, but he couldn't because that would have involved taking them away from the new Democratic chairmen, who didn't care much for the idea, naturally. He saw to the repeal of our rule change, though, the next time we met, and when the Assembly was reorganized in 1965, Milton Marks was committee chairman again. In 1967, at the beginning of his last term as speaker, Jess appointed eleven Republican committee chairmen. That was a greater number of chairmanships than anyone could remember going to the minority party in the Assembly.

In the final event, every consequence of the great lockup was transitory, except for its disastrous effect on the career of Jess Unruh.

The day after we passed the budget, the conference committee report on the school bill was finally ready to go. When I took it up on the floor, no one rose to argue against its passage. It was adopted by a bipartisan vote of sixty-seven to seven, and we adjourned that memorable special session once and for all.

That night a group of Democratic assemblymen trooped out to a barn of a Western-style steakhouse called Johnson's Del Prado to celebrate our delivery from the bondage of answering roll calls. Over our steaks and California claret we succumbed to the politician's propensity to indulge in postmortems.

Leroy Greene was an officious little white-haired freshman in that year of 1963. (He is today an officious little white-haired freshman in the Senate.) He pronounced what the majority accepted as the final judgment in these words: "I'll tell you one thing. This is the end of Jess Unruh."

The passing years have ratified Leroy's verdict. The press worked Jess over without mercy. *Time* and *Newsweek* made major national stories of the lockup, as did *Life Magazine*, which ran pages of photographs taken in the Capitol that night. It was *Life* that did Jess the most harm in an article that had for its lead illustration an unbelievable photograph, which had been taken by their cameraman on the floor of the Assembly. The photographer had used a wide-angle lens, and he had dropped down onto his knees to focus on Jess's huge belly from about two feet away to take the picture.

The Speaker's head looked like a pea on top of a hot-air balloon. I have never seen such an extreme editorial slant in a news photograph in my life, but it was no more pronounced than the editorial slant of the text of the article, which was entitled "Big Daddy of California."

It was not surprising that the national news magazines took that slant in covering the lockup. They did not know how and why we had blundered into the lockup, and we couldn't tell them without enraging the members of the Senate into implacable hostility. It was for the same reason that the newspaper editorials on the affair were just as critical of Unruh as the news magazines.

The *San Francisco Chronicle*, in all of its Republican dignity, said, "Unruh stands revealed for what he is—a crude political adventurer out to gain totalitarian control of the Assembly."

The *Sacramento Bee*, although it was ordinarily kinder to Democrats than the other major California dailies, was not on this occasion. It called the lockup "a glaring abuse of power."

Naturally, the Republicans of California made the most of the opportunity that fortune had presented to attack Jess. He was the Democrat upon whom they liked to concentrate their fire anyway because he was the most effective champion of Democratic positions and philosophy among California's policymakers.

Caspar Weinberger, otherwise known as Cap the Knife, a tight-lipped former assemblyman from San Francisco, was then doing a stint as chairman of the Republican State Central Committee. That was before he went on to glory in Washington as Secretary of Health, Education, and Welfare and Secretary of Defense, after being director of the Office of Management and the Budget and undersecretary of almost everything else.

In a long press release Cap declared that the actions of the Democrats in the Assembly, "raised the naked threat of a denial of all representative government in California. . . . These are the tactics Stalin, Hitler, and other dictators used until they could get rid of their legislators entirely."

Knifing away enthusiastically, Cap continued, "Nowhere in the United States has any man or any political party tried to stamp out, as Mr. Unruh has, the wise protection of the people's rights that has been built into the legislative process for over 1,000 years."

He announced that the Republicans would mount a crusade throughout the state against the changes in the Assembly rules, which he said were "subversive."

All of these statesmanlike comments, remember, pertained to the Assembly's adopting rules that had governed the Senate and House of Representatives in Washington for many generations and the British Parliament for ever so many more. I have always thought it regrettable that Cap, when he went to Washington, didn't let the leaders of both parties in the two houses know that they are subversive and that they are denying the people of the United States representative government and that they are employing tactics of Stalin and Hitler and other dictators. Anybody who is in possession of such a basic truth should feel some obligation to impart it where it would do the most good.

Certainly in 1963 Cap had no hesitation in expressing himself on such matters. He said, "The fact that all the Democratic assemblymen blindly followed the orders of an overgrown bully who wants to be governor makes it very clear that the only way Californians can restore representative government at Sacramento is to eliminate enough of our home-grown dictator's pawns so that the term representative will again mean something."

Many of California's daily papers printed Cap's diatribe in full and endorsed it in powerful editorials. No California politician was ever the subject of such frightful publicity as Jess Unruh was, and, as a result, the lockup became, and remains, the focal event of all his years in the Assembly. That is what the hard-boiled eggheads who write political commentary were telling the people of California in 1981 when they ruled him out as a candidate for governor in 1982, because the public could never forget how he had locked up the Republicans in the Assembly chamber on the night of July 30, 1963, and how he had subsequently punished the Republican committee chairmen by firing them. That is not entirely fair, of course, because those decisions were not made by him alone but by a number of us. Yet he did commit a great sin that night, and it is for that reason that he has been punished so severely. I refer to going over to the Mirador and getting drunk; if he hadn't done that, he wouldn't have become so truculent and he would have seen the political wisdom in letting the Republicans go home. Sober, he was much more intelligent than any other politician in California. Unfortunately, that was the one time that he ever had an important decision to make when he didn't stay sober, and it is for that lapse that he paid with his political career.

To put it in his own words, which I have at various times heard him repeat, "It has been all downhill for me since that night."

Although it is true that he became the Democratic nominee for governor in 1970, that was mostly because no one else really wanted that honor. Everyone thought that Ronald Reagan, who would be running for re-election that year, was unbeatable, and, when I say everyone, I include Jess. When he talked to me about making that race and I told him that it was political suicide, he confessed to me that he was doing it mostly because it was for him the most acceptable way to get himself out of the State Assembly, where he was no longer happy and hadn't been since the lockup, which was the first of many defeats.

I learned from Jess years later how it happened. He told me, "You know, Jimmy, Sig Arywitz, who was secretary-treasurer of the Central Labor Council of Los Angeles then, lost over a hundred pounds during the first half of 1963. He told me he'd done it by taking benzedrine, and he urged me to try it and gave me a bottle of pills. At the time of the lockup, I was popping three times what is now considered the maximum daily dosage. Cy Farber told me not long ago that the combination of those pills and alcohol is dangerous, and I'm lucky I lived through that night."

Cy Farber was his doctor, and mine, too. Cy told me later that it was clearly the stunning effect of the benzedrine and alcohol together that so clouded his judgment that it resulted in his drinking more than he ever drank when he had business to conduct.

It is of such ingredients that history is compounded.

17

How I Became a Casualty of War

What deep wounds ever closed without a scar?

Lord Byron

*D*on Allen once told me, "The most basic rule of politics is, 'Always kick a man when he's down.' That'll keep the bastard from getting up again."

It seemed to those of us who were close to Jess Unruh that Pat Brown subscribed to that creed. After the lockup, when the press was attacking the Speaker as the worst thing to hit Sacramento since the earthquake of 1896, Pat stepped up his campaign of attacks upon Unruh and his friends, and the internecine conflict among Democrats degenerated into guerrilla warfare.

Jess, when in public, never showed any signs that the frightful publicity he was receiving as an aftermath of the lockup was getting him down, although late at night, among his friends, he was sometimes pretty glum, and I assumed that was the cause. However, during the day he worked harder than ever to get good liberal legislation enacted.

As time passed, he also began to devote himself more and more to trying to nail down the Democratic nomination for governor in 1966. He knew that being locked in mortal combat with Pat Brown, who was popular among party people, wasn't easing his way toward that objective. On a number of occasions he went to see Pat to attempt to work out some sort of a truce with him. After every one of those peace conferences he said to me, with a sigh of relief, "I think I've finally buried the hatchet with the Old Man," and each time that happened, I looked forward to a more relaxed future, but the newspapers, which love to carry stories about conflicts, would in time print a commentary on the Governor's history of ineptitude in dealing with Jess's purposeful drive for control of the party, and Pat would respond by doing something to one of us to show the press and everyone else that he was not, by God, inept.

We went from day to day wondering when we'd be waylaid by the Governor and reading in the newspapers that the conflict between us was a war of aggression on the part of the Speaker, aggression born of heedless, grasping, blind ambition.

The news hawks who covered the Capitol were never conscious of the Governor's continual attacks on us, which were always designed to be unworthy of newsprint, and that was why they, in explaining our hostilities to the public, always represented us as the aggressors.

The best way for me to give an example of Pat's bushwhacking tactics would be to tell about one of my own journeys into ambush. It started at noon in the darkly lustrous seclusion of the men's grill in the U. S. Grant Hotel in San Diego. Harry Farb had invited me to have lunch with him there just after the primary elections in June of 1964.

Harry was a financial highflier who had fled from Russia at the beginning of World War I to avoid service in the Czar's army. He had come to this country to make his fortune, and he had done it.

Jess once said in his presence, "You know, Harry is a personification of the advantages of the free enterprise system. I have never heard of any young man fleeing from the United States to Russia and doing very well there."

Because he was a Jew, Harry had remained a Democrat, even after he had gotten to be a very rich man. Democratic gentiles who become wealthy usually also become Republicans, out of pure self-interest. Jews do not. They are not so prone as the rest of us to slough off old beliefs which have become inexpedient. That is what accounts for them still being Jews, I guess.

For me, an invitation from Harry to have lunch was a summons to a command performance. On such occasions Harry usually spent a lot of time telling me about all the money he had given to the Democratic Party, and I was living in hope that he would someday decide that he wanted to give a lot to me for one for my campaigns, but he never did.

To the eye, Harry was a well-tailored American eagle. He resembled our national emblem in beak and claw. His eye was as autocratic. His mien was as imperial. His head was as white. The rest of what could be seen of him was brown, like the rest of our national bird. Also like the American eagle, he had only one expression. He looked—and acted—proud and fierce all the time.

As I walked into the Grant Grill, I saw him sitting in his favorite booth, with a vodka and orange juice clutched in one talon hand, like a sheaf of arrows or an olive branch, though I wasn't sure which.

As soon as I had sat down and had ordered a Scotch and water from a waiter whom Harry had immediately summoned, he fixed me with his piercing eyes and announced, "The primary election is over. A new county committee has been elected. Next month the committee will meet to elect a chairman."

"You mean, re-elect Bill Moeser," I said.

"Listen, look, it's time to get rid of Bill Moeser."

I certainly hadn't expected that. I asked, "Why?"

"He's a bumbler. Like Pat Brown's supposed to be but isn't."

"Pat Brown is tougher than a mess hall steak, Harry, but that hasn't got anything to do with it. I think Bill has done a pretty good job as county chairman, and I think it would be ungrateful of us to reward him for all of his years of service to the party by dumping him."

I took a first taste of the Scotch and water the waiter had set before me, and Harry went at his screwdriver like an eagle drinking water.

Then I added my clincher. "Besides, who else is there?"

"You," Harry snapped, pointing an accusative finger at me over his vodka and orange juice in the manner of Uncle Sam on a recruiting poster.

I was in the act of taking my second sip of Scotch and water. I inhaled it, choked, and finally gasped, "Me. Why me?"

"Listen, look," he said, "the party needs you. There is no one else on the county committee who is anybody."

"Now wait a minute," I protested, "I don't want the chairmanship of the county committee. I've got enough problems now."

"Could you refuse a draft?"

Harry had his own savings and loan at that time, and his expression was the one that savings and loan executives use on people who default on their home loans.

"A draft?" I said, totally overcome with disbelief.

He repeated himself. "Could you refuse a draft?"

"Could I refuse a draft? Oh, come on, Harry, there's no such thing as a draft in politics, and you know it."

"Listen, look, if a majority of the members of the committee say they want you to be the chairman, and they put it in writing, you can't refuse it."

"They won't, thank God."

"They will." Harry was as sure about it as he was about everything.

"I can't be county chairman. The committee meets on Tuesday nights. I have to be in Sacramento from Monday through Thursday or Friday every week during the session."

"The committee will change its meeting night to Saturday."

"They will?"

"They will."

"I'll have to talk to Bill Moeser about it."

"So talk. You and Bill will both be free at noon next Wednesday. I've already checked with your secretaries. I've told Bill you want to have lunch with him here on Wednesday. I've made a reservation for you with the head waiter for this table. By then I'll have the petition for you signed by a majority of the members of the committee."

"I'll have to think it over," I said.

I pondered Harry's plan all afternoon, and it didn't improve any on reconsideration. My problem was that I simply didn't have time to do the job. I decided that I should ask Jess Unruh for his advice since he was smarter politically than anyone else I knew. I called him up the following morning and told him about my conversation with Harry.

His laughter rumbled through the line into my ear; he said, "You've surely got trouble."

"Right here in San Diego," I replied. "With a capital T, and that rhymes with P, and that stands for panic."

"You're between a rock and a hard place, Jimmy. You can't turn it down without alienating a lot of the members of the committee and a lot of other Democrats, too. It'll be a hell of a headache for you but, if Harry gets the signatures, I think you ought to go along with it. The biggest thing to worry about is losing; that would be a catastrophe for you."

"You mean as far as my standing in the party in San Diego is concerned."

"Of course. But as long as you make it clear that you won't consider it unless a majority of the committee put their names on the petition, you ought to be safe enough."

"But I don't have time for it."

"Don't worry about that. Anybody who's going to do a decent job as a county committee chairman has got to get other people to do all the work anyway."

On Wednesday morning Harry Farb delivered on his promise. A messenger brought that petition he had talked to me about, and it had been signed by a majority of the members of the county committee, much to my chagrin. The more I had thought about assuming the burden of party leadership, the less it appealed to me. My daughter Beatrice was three years old and Joanna was seven months pregnant, and I was seeing too little of them as it was.

I had lunch with Bill Moeser that day, in accordance with Harry's plan for us, at the Grant Grill. As little as I cared for Harry's idea, Bill liked it even less. He was a kindly old duffer, a human dumpling, both physically and psychologically. I was very fond of him. He had always been a good friend. He had helped me in all of my campaigns. Reluctantly I told him about my conversation with Harry and showed him the petition.

He said, "I've always tried to do what was best for the party, and if a majority of the members of the committee think it would be best for the party if you were the chairman, I guess I should go along."

He took out a fountain pen and added his signature to the bottom of the petition.

That settled it. I had been maneuvered by Harry Farb into accepting a job I did not want. However, it turned out that there was at least one other member of the county committee who wasn't crazy about the proposal. That was San Diego County's freshman Democratic congressman, Lionel Van Deerlin, who had decided that he was the leader of the party locally. Therefore, he thought that the county chairman should be his man.

He exhibited what I thought to be very bad form by not letting me know that he objected to my being county committee chairman. I found out when I heard from some of the committee members that he was urging them to renege on their commitments to me. He had his own candidate for chairman, a pale young lawyer with a querulous voice and big glasses.

When I called Harry to tell him, his laugh was staccato. So was his answer. "Listen, look, the committee wants you. The majority of them have asked you to take the job. They promised you they'd vote for you, and they put it in writing."

"Harry, it isn't a good thing for the party for me and Lionel Van Deerlin to get into a donnybrook."

"That kid he's running for county chairman is a nobody. Who ever heard of him? What has he ever done for the party? Nobody's going to go back on their promises to you and vote for him. Listen, look, it will be a good lesson to Van for him to lose, and it will serve him right for going behind your back to stick a knife into your ribs instead of talking to you like a man. Then, after you're county chairman, you can sit down with him and work things out."

I wasn't happy with Lionel Van Deerlin at that point, so I said, "Okay, Harry."

A few days later I drove up to Los Angeles to attend an Assembly committee hearing in the state building there. During the meeting a sergeant-at-arms brought me a note from Jess that asked me to come upstairs to his Los Angeles office when the committee adjourned. When I got that note, I presumed he wanted to talk with me about a major tax reform bill he was hammering out with Nick Petris, who was by then chairman of the Assembly Revenue and Taxation Committee. It was turning into a good bill, a simple, fair one, and I knew Jess was becoming preoccupied with getting it perfected.

When I finally went upstairs and saw him, I was impressed with how fit and strong he looked. I knew he'd been put on a diet by his doctor, Cy Farber, who is a great man and a noted authority on the inner workings of mankind. Even so, I was surprised he had lost so much weight.

"My God, Marvin, you look terrific," I said.

"I'm down to 250."

"Fantastic! Are you still on Cy Farber's diet?"

"I am."

"Is it still mostly lettuce, with a steak every other day?"

"It is." He looked sad but proud of his accomplishment, as well he should.

He really did look splendid. I'd always known he must be magnificently muscled because he was so strong, but his musculature had always been concealed by fat. Now he was starting to look heroic.

I shook my head in admiration and said, "You're a marvel. I've never known anybody to take off weight the way you have without using some kind of pills."

"Jimmy, after my experience with Siggie Arywitz's pills, I'll never take one of those damned things again."

"What did you want to see me about?"

"I wanted to be sure you knew Tom Bane has gone and got himself elected chairman of the Los Angeles County Central Committee."

"Why did he do that?"

"Tom likes to be in charge of things."

"I wish him happiness in his new career as a political boss."

"I thought you should know about it. It could have some repercussions in San Diego. By becoming my friend, you've become an enemy to my enemies, and they're likely to see all of this as an attempt on my part to take over the party in the state's two biggest counties."

"Nobody in San Diego who knows how I became a candidate will buy that."

"It isn't people in San Diego that you need to be concerned about."

"Maybe I should start looking for a graceful way out of running for county chairman."

"That's true. Maybe you should, but don't do it 'till you think you're in trouble. I'd hate to see that kid who's running against you get to be chairman. By opposing you, he's shown himself to be your enemy."

"He's Van Deerlin's man, and Van thinks that because he holds the highest office of any Democrat in San Diego County, he should be running the county committee."

"Did he ever talk to you before he got that guy to run against you?"

"Never once."

"That's damned hostile of him. Anyway, what I wanted to see you about was to tell you about Tom and to warn you to be on the alert."

"Thank you."

"If you pick up word of any defections of committee members who are committed to you, you should get to the bottom of it at once."

"I'll do it, and thanks."

However, I picked up no such word. I talked to any number of committee members who had signed the petition, and they all reaffirmed their wish for me to take the chairmanship of the committee.

The newly elected members of the county central committee met on the third Tuesday in July in a room in the county courthouse, as prescribed by law, to elect a chairman.

A minute after I had come into that room and had sat down, I was surprised to see my old nemesis, Hugo Fisher, enter the room with Lionel Van Deerlin. They were an oddly assorted pair. Hugo was a big, handsome man, virile and sensual-looking in an Eastern European way, with dark curly hair and full lips. Van was a wispy failure in politics, who had finally won his first election by running in a newly created congressional district no Democrat could lose, or so I thought till he lost it.

Hugo was being as gracious and condescending as the king of France to the lesser beings who greeted him, which didn't seem entirely appropriate. He had lost in his campaign for re-election to the State Senate in 1962. He should have won easily but had conducted himself as if he believed in the divine right of state senators. His opponent, Jack Schrade, overcame him only because Hugo had come down with a fatal case of self-esteem.

Hugo was by then living in Sacramento, having been appointed by the Governor to be one of his four cabinet secretaries. He must have made a special trip to San Diego to be at that meeting. His presence was significant, I knew, but I didn't know why. He sat down in the front row of folding chairs next to Van Deerlin. I sat in the back, beside Bill Moeser, and watched them whispering to each other. It was apparent when they had come in that they were conspiring and that they had been doing so before they had arrived.

The law said that the county clerk should conduct the election of a chairman. I was surprised again when Van moved that Hugo be elected temporary chairman to preside over the balloting for a permanent chairman. Nothing like that had ever been done before.

Always in the past the election of the permanent chairman had taken place under the gavel of the county clerk. It hadn't occurred to Harry Farb or me that anyone would propose to elect a temporary chairman. Harry wasn't present because he wasn't a member of the committee. I was at a loss because things were moving so quickly; I couldn't think of any argument to present against the motion; it was adopted without debate, and the county clerk left the room.

As soon as Hugo assumed the chair, he announced, "The election of the permanent chairman will be conducted in a democratic fashion by the use of a secret ballot." He had yellow paper ballots already prepared and ready to pass out. As he took them out of his briefcase, I knew that he and Van had set up his election as temporary chairman so that those members who had prevailed upon me to accept the chairmanship by committing themselves to vote for me could take refuge behind the secret balloting procedure to go back on their commitments.

"Don't worry," Bill Moeser said to me; "you have the majority of the votes committed to you."

I was nominated by Bill, who had asked me if he could do it and who made a nice speech. The pale, bespectacled young lawyer was nominated by Murray Goodrich, another fugitive from Russia, one even richer than Harry Farb. When the ballots were cast and counted, I came out second best. That was the only time in my political career that I was ever railroaded both ways—into something I didn't want and out of it again. I remained slumped in my folding chair, feeling stunned, unable to understand what had happened, hardly answering Bill Moeser and other friends on the committee who were offering their condolences. The effect of losing would, I knew, be politically devastating as far as my influence among Democrats in San Diego was concerned, as Jess had told me it would. As I sat there, I was vaguely aware of Hugo, Van, and the pale young lawyer congratulating one another with decorous enthusiasm in the front of the room.

When I gathered myself up and left, I wandered into a courthouse elevator where I found myself alone with a young civil engineer named Bob Coates, who was one of the county committee members who had pledged themselves in writing to support me. By his hangdog look, I knew that he was among those who had deserted me.

I asked him, "Bob, how could you do that to me?"

He replied sheepishly, "What else could I do when the Governor called me and asked me to vote for Paul as a personal favor to him?"

"The Governor? Do you mean to tell me that the Governor was calling members of the San Diego County Democratic Central

Committee to ask them to vote against me as a personal favor to him? Come on, Bob. You've got to be putting me on."

"You mean you didn't know?"

I shook my head. At first I couldn't believe it, but it was true. Van Deerlin had called Pat Brown and had done just what Jess had anticipated. He'd informed him of my impending election as county committee chairman and had told Pat it was part of a plan of Big Daddy's to take over the party machinery in the two largest counties in the state.

In light of what had just happened in Los Angeles County, it isn't surprising that Pat accepted at face value what Van had told him. He had promptly got on the telephone to talk to most of the thirty-odd members of the committee to appeal to them to vote against me, and he had persisted until he had prevailed upon enough of those flaming idealists to go back on their signed pledges to vote for me.

The next time I saw Pat was at a Democratic fundraiser in Los Angeles. He was his old back-slapping, hand-shaking, amiably owlish self.

"How are you, Jim?" he hailed me in his gravelly voice. He put an arm around my shoulders.

"You should know," I said.

"Oh, that!" he growled jovially. "There was nothing personal in that, you know. I was really sorry I had to do it, but I don't think that anyone who holds public office should also hold an office in the party."

Removing his hand from my shoulder, I said, "You mean like Stanley Mosk?" Stanley was the Attorney General of California at that time and had recently been elected national committeeman as Pat's candidate for the job.

Pat looked hurt.

"Look," I said, "there is no excuse for what you did to me, and you know it. If you didn't want me to be the county chairman in San Diego, you should have called *me* up. Instead of that you blind-sided me by calling up all those other people and keeping me in the dark about it. If you'd told me you didn't want me to be county chairman, I wouldn't have run. You knew that, didn't you? But you decided you wanted to defeat me instead."

He didn't answer that. He just looked hurt for a couple of seconds more.

I said, "I've always thought that it's wrong for people to go back on their commitments; and I think it's just as wrong to push them into doing it, don't you?"

He looked yet more gravely wounded, and then he changed the subject, as he always did at such times. "How's Joanna and that cute little girl of yours?"

"They're mad at you, too," I said, and he turned with a glad cry to greet someone else.

Right after my defeat, when I called Jess and told him what had happened, he shared my suspicion that the reason Pat hadn't called me was that he did indeed know I would have withdrawn from the race for county chairman if he had done so. I would have known he could beat me by making his wishes known to the members of the committee. However, withdrawing from the race would have been a graceful way out. We felt confirmed in the belief that he wanted to inflict defeats upon us whenever and wherever possible, so the press would stop saying how inept he was. As a result, things between Jess and Pat went from bad to worse to much worse.

18

The Civilized Art of Conversation

Good company and good discourse are the very sinews of virtue.

Izaak Walton

*A*fter the legislative day's work was done on an eve-
ning that was like any other, I repaired to the Speaker's office to join
in the usual twilight symposium upon the affairs of state and of
statesmen. Jess, who had lost another twenty pounds by continuing
to adhere to the diet Cy Farber had laid out for him, was enthroned
behind his walnut flying wing of a desk with an unsipped glassful of
gin and ice enveloped in one thick hand. He bassooned, "Hello,
Jimmy," and Bob Crown, who was fashionably composed in one of
the leather armchairs, greeted me gaily with, "Who was the only
actor to win two academy awards in a row?"

"Spencer Tracy. What are the real names of Robert Taylor
and Cary Grant?"

"Spangler Arlington Brugh and Archibald Leach."

"No shit," said a San Francisco liberal who came sauntering in
behind me. Almost as tall, dark, and handsome as Archibald Leach
or Spangler Arlington Brugh, he appeared to have been turned out
by his maker and his haberdasher to stroll the boulevards of Paris,
leaving behind him a trail of broken hearts and depleted bank
accounts.

When I turned to him, I saw that his brow was uncharacteristi-
cally furrowed with care. He grumbled, "That goddamned Cy
Farber! He's screwing up my life."

I referred to Cy Farber in the last chapter; he was one of the
deans of Instruction at the University of California Medical School
in San Francisco. He is a bear of a man, a teddy bear in both mind
and spirit, though he is physically more on the scale of a California

153

grizzly. He still practiced medicine on a limited scale, to keep his hand in, though only caring for patients he liked. Luckily for us, he loved politics and politicians, especially Democrats. All of us in Jess's office that evening were among his patients. And, as I've mentioned, it was he who was supervising Jess's diet program.

"How in the hell can Cy Farber be screwing up your life?" The question, which had occurred to me, rumbled forth from Jess Unruh. "He's the greatest doctor I ever met. Every time I see him he tells me I should be getting more sex. He says it's better exercise than jogging. He says that a man burns up 1,200 calories every time he does it, so it helps keep your weight down. He says it helps prevent hypertrophy of the prostate. He says it's terrific for the heart and it's good for the soul. What more could any man want from a doctor?"

"He always says the same things to me," Jerry Waldie added, with a look of amused approval, "and he also tells women that it will keep their complexions clear."

Bob Crown nodded. "Cy Farber is a great man. Why, he even takes the indignity out of a rectal examination, the way he waves his middle finger at you with a grin and says, 'You know, I've probably had my finger up the rear ends of more politicians than any other man in the world.'"

"How in the hell can Cy Farber be screwing up *your* life?" Jess repeated the question with a quizzical grin.

The young liberal grimaced. "Why, he's been telling me for a year that I should give up smoking, and the other day, when I saw him for my annual checkup, he told me I should never go down on any woman I don't know. He says a guy can catch a lot of grungy things that way."

He made a face and so did Bob Crown, who commented, "I've always lived by the rule that there's nothing wrong with oral sex as long as it's done in good taste."

With one of his terribly sincere looks Jerry Waldie asked the young lib, "Are you going to follow his advice?"

Draping himself over a leather armchair in an elegant and casual pose, he lit a cigarette, inhaling the smoke deeply as he did so.

"Oh, hell," he sighed, breathing forth smoke and words together, "I guess I shouldn't ignore him completely. After all, he is my doctor." He held up his cigarette to contemplate it dolefully and mused, "Maybe I'll give up smoking."

"That's a wise choice," Jess said, and I realized then that I hadn't seen him with a cigar in his mouth for months.

"Bobby," Jerry said, "that woman you were having dinner with last night at Fat's was built like a world-class belly dancer."

The young liberal added, "She sure was. Did you get screwed?"

"No," Bob replied, "but I did this morning."

"By who?" Jess always took a friendly interest in his friends' affairs of the heart.

"By the Governor."

"Oh," Jess said, "what happened?"

"You've heard me talk about Mark Lewis."

Jess looked rueful. "The way you talk about him always makes me jealous."

Bob didn't smile at that. "He decided he wanted to be a judge. Old Judge MacDowell died last month, and Mark asked me to try to get Pat to appoint him to the vacancy."

"After all the times you've taken the heat for Pat as chairman of Ways and Means by killing bills he doesn't want to see on his desk, you should be able to talk to him about judgeships in your own county," Jess said, with the look of a bereaved bulldog, "but he accepts the protection we give him as a matter of divine right."

Bob appeared frostbitten as he went on. "Mark told me he'd like to see the Governor. I knew it wouldn't do any good, but I requested an appointment to talk to Pat. When I saw the old man, I asked him, as a favor to me, to let me bring Mark in for a personal interview, and he agreed to do it. I appreciated his doing that, even though I knew that Mark wasn't likely to accomplish anything by seeing the Governor; but what the hell, at least he would know I'd done all I could do for him. So today he took the day off and drove up to Sacramento in the morning."

Bob was talking only to Jess.

"When he came into my office at ten o'clock, he was as happy as a sailor in a whorehouse, and he was even happier when I told him that I was going to take him down to introduce him to the old man personally. We went down to the Governor's office and sat on the sofa in the anteroom and talked to Jackie while we waited to see Pat."

"I think I'm in love with Jackie," the young liberal said, and Jerry Waldie replied, "Who isn't? But what happened to Mark?"

Bob continued with his story. "The poor son-of-a-bitch told me he'd never forget what I'd done for him. Then he picked up an

Oakland Tribune that someone had left on the coffee table in front of us to find out what had happened yesterday in the old hometown. His face went white as a sheet, and I looked to see what he was reading. It was an article that said Governor Brown had appointed some guy I've never heard of to the vacancy on the superior court bench in Alameda County."

Bob Crown's own face went white as he told us that.

"I never really expected that Pat was going to help me by giving Mark that appointment and making me look good in my district, but I didn't expect that he would hurt me either, but he sure as hell did. If he wasn't out to hurt me, he would have waited for a couple of days before he announced the appointment. He made me look like a goddamned fool to Mark and to all of the people Mark told about what a great buddy I was, lining him up to have an interview with the Governor."

In telling the story, Bob was biting off his words grimly. "I said to Mark, 'Let's get out of here,' and that nice Jackie said, 'Don't go, Mr. Crown; I'm sure the Governor will be available to talk with you in a few minutes.'

"'There isn't anything to talk to him about,' I said, and we left.

"Mark went home madder than hell, but he wasn't as mad as I am."

Bob paused and then squared the story off with, "I suppose that's not the kind of thing that would bother a really big man, but I'm not a really big man."

Jess sipped a little gin for the first time since I'd come into the room and said, "Well, Bobby, you know how it is. Pat wants to make sure all the other Democrats know what the price is for being my friend, so he makes you and Jimmy pay it."

"You know something?" Bob looked as if he were taking an oath. "It's worth the price."

At that point Tom Bane came in, and our circle was complete. He said, "We're going to have a hell of a time trying to spring Byron Rumford's fair housing bill out of the Senate committee, now that all of those wild-and-woollies are lying around in the rotunda on their mattresses making threats to stay there till it's passed."

"Yeah," Jess said. "I thought we were going to get that bill out of that committee without too much trouble before those damned longhairs moved in."

"You can't blame the senators for getting their backs up," Tom said. "They figure that if they approve the bill now, every bunch of jerks that wants anything out of the Legislature will come up here to camp in the halls till they get it."

"They're right," Jess said, "but black people in this state have always been treated like dirt whenever they go to buy a house or rent an apartment, and it's long past time that somebody did something about it."

So it was that the conversation turned from the affairs of statesmen to the affairs of state, and we got down to the kind of business we'd all gone to Sacramento to do.

19

The Decline and Fall of the C.D.C., Stanley, Alan, and Plucky Pierre

At the extremes of the political spectrum one encounters people who are moved chiefly to find an outlet for the venom within them.

D. Sutten

By coming into existence and by endorsing good Democratic candidates, and thereby securing for them the nominations of the party, the C.D.C. transformed California politics. No longer did the leadership on our side of the political fence have to look on helplessly while Republicans spent their way to victory in the primary elections of both parties. And once the Democratic Party was able to gain control over its own destinies, it was able to provide effective opposition to the Republicans and, in 1958, to wrest from their grasp the governor's office and control of both houses of the Legislature for the first time in this century.

After doing so much for the party, it's not surprising that the C.D.C. took credit for its accomplishments. It soon perceived itself, with a good deal of justification, as the backbone of the party, and by the early 1960's most of the sixty thousand members considered that the club movement had, in fact, become the Democratic Party in California. At its annual conventions the C.D.C. began to pass resolutions on every conceivable subject, enacting them as political dogmas for Democrats to accept.

However, while the club movement was claiming more and more doctrinal authority for itself as the official curia of the Democratic Party, it was becoming less and less representative of the views of most Democrats. The greatest danger to any political organization is, of course, the accumulation of too many radicals

within it. Both parties had that problem in spades—and clubs—by
1964. That year saw the right-wing evangelicals take over the
G.O.P. and nominate Barry Goldwater, rallying beatifically to his
battle cry, "Extremism in the defense of liberty is no vice." The
signs we saw delegates flourishing on the convention floor, as we
watched on our living room television sets, read, "Get the U.N. out
of the U.S. and the U.S. out of the U.N." We witnessed their
howling rapture as they endorsed the abolition of the graduated
income tax and such other socialistic fetters to the enterprise of the
people of this great republic. Democrats felt like voyeurs as we
watched their transports of ecstasy during that mass orgy.

In California the woolly fringe at the other end, the left end, of
the political tapestry was soon attached to the C.D.C. We became
conscious of that development as the rapidly increasing contingent
of leftist club members began to employ on us the standard tactics of
radicals everywhere. They would raise all kinds of interminable hell
over obscure points of order and technicalities of parliamentary
procedure in all of the meetings at the C.D.C. conventions. Their
goal was to wear out those of us who held more moderate opinions,
to bore us, to exasperate us, to exhaust our patience, to outlast us.
In the committee meetings, which took place on Saturday nights,
they would harangue the majority on trivial matters, yelling like
maniacs hour after hour. Usually by three in the morning enough
moderates would have given up in disgust and gone off to bed so that
they would be in the majority, and then they'd start to vote on all
the motions and resolutions. Those who did it were the leather-
lunged veterans of radical attempts to take over California's labor
unions by the same means in the 1930's and 1940's. Obnoxiousness
was their weapon, and they had learned to wield it with telling
effect.

When I talked about them to Republican friends, I learned
that the right-wingers were conducting themselves in the same way
at every G.O.P. convention.

Jess infuriated himself to our radicals by saying, "The biggest
difference between the zealots on the left and those on the right is
that the ones on the right smell better."

Our militants employed the same tactics on Sundays during
the general meetings of the convention. They knew that most of us
lived in the San Francisco Bay Area and in Southern California and
that we'd have to pack up, get into our cars, and start on our long
journeys home from Fresno by midafternon if we wanted to get to

bed before midnight and be in shape to make it to work on Monday morning. Therefore, they would again drag out the proceedings with endless ranting over parliamentary questions until enough moderates had gone home to put them in control. Then, as in the committee meetings, they would get all of their wild and woolly resolutions adopted. We would tune in to the news on our car radios on the long drive home and listen unhappily to breathless announcers telling about the extreme positions the California Democratic Council had taken at its annual convention—all of which had been adopted after our departures.

The woollies were especially committed to passing resolutions calling for the United States to divest itself unilaterally of nuclear armaments. That put the C.D.C. in the position of condemning the policies of President Kennedy. Jess Unruh was the President's closest friend and ally in California, and it fell to him to defend the national administration. The Speaker made speeches tearing into the C.D.C. for passing such resolutions, which, he said, were based on the assumption that the Soviet Union is governed by a council of philosopher-princes who stand ready to give up all their atomic weapons as soon as the United States makes it clear to them that we are no longer a threat to Russia and the other peace-loving nations of the earth. Jess was really right about that, as he was when he pointed out that all of the left wing's nightmares about a nuclear holocaust involved an American military loony, like General Jack D. Ripper in the moving picture *Doctor Strangelove*, setting it off. Such insanity, he said, was not feared by them on the part of Russian military leaders, who were, in their eyes, responsible men or they wouldn't have been selected to hold their high positions by the statesmen who guide the Soviet Union on its enlightened way.

Those comments made the leather-lunged set in the C.D.C. absolutely livid, as nothing but the truth could have done.

As the months kept on passing, the Governor and the Speaker kept on fighting. As in George Orwell's *1984*, the warfare never ceased, and no one expected it to anymore.

Mostly the battles were over party organization. Jess would have preferred to avoid them, but he couldn't.

Whenever Pat and Hale Champion began to cast about for people to support for high positions in the party, they looked for somebody who was an enemy of Unruh's. Naturally, Jess opposed such candidates.

After the grave wounds Jess had suffered as a result of the lockup, he lost every one of those battles, and every one of them gave Pat a new opportunity to get into print with another attack on the Speaker for his disloyalty to Pat as the leader of the party.

Sometimes those decisions of Pat's relative to party leadership could be pretty funny. He promised to support Carmen Warschaw for Democratic National Committeewoman. She certainly deserved his support. She had been a great financial supporter of the party and a hard worker. However, she was also a friend of the Speaker's. Pat had second thoughts and decided to back someone else, someone who didn't like Jess. The fight that ensued was particularly bitter. Jess supported Carmen, of course, but she lost, in one more of his string of post-lockup defeats by Pat.

At one point Carmen cornered the Governor and gave him hell for going back on his word to support her.

Pat replied to her, "You didn't get it in writing."

"He'll regret that," Jess said to me.

Carmen wasn't a person you'd want for an enemy. (She was generally referred to among California Democrats as the Dragon Lady.) At the Democratic National Convention in Atlantic City in 1964, she had people in every hotel lobby giving out pens that had printed upon them, "Get it in writing, Carmen." She also hired skywriters to blazon the same words across the heavens in white smoke. As a result, the 1964 convention didn't turn out any better for Pat than the 1960 one in Los Angeles did. All of the delegates, alternates, and newspeople in Atlantic City asked one another what it was all about, and by word of mouth they learned, and Pat was the laughing stock of that convention too.

At our next meeting in Jess's office Jerry Waldie said, "The pity of it is, Jess, that Pat isn't cutting you and your friends up out of malice. As far as his motives are concerned, he's like us. He just wants to make California a better place for the average citizen, and he thinks any threat to his influence is a threat to his power to accomplish his goals."

"I know that," Jess replied, "but his being so damned paranoid doesn't help him or us or the party."

In that year of 1964 every friend of the Speaker's was secretly spoiling for a no-holds-barred fight. We wanted to show the world who was the stud duck in the Democratic Party in California. We were all sick and tired of the years of sneak attacks; but we never expressed any such desire for general hostilities, not even to each other, and it seemed there was no prospect of open war. It seemed that the guerrilla poltroonery would drag on and on and on into the indefinite future. But we were wrong. The unexpected happened. The newspapers announced that the junior United States senator for California, Clair Engle, had undergone cranial surgery. The press hadn't been able to get a word out of him about what the operation had been for. That made it hard for him to line up support for re-election; but he was a feisty little rooster; he declared that he was in the race to stay, and he asked Tom Carrell to head up his campaign effort.

Alan Cranston, then the state controller, had always had a hankering to be a United States senator, and he thought his time had come. He knew he could get the C.D.C. endorsement if he ran because he was revered by the majority of the members as the founder of the organization. In addition, he had assiduously kept in touch with everyone active in the Democratic clubs. He and his chief aide, a brilliant political junky named Irwin Nebron, spent a hundred evenings every year addressing and writing personal messages to individual members of C.D.C. clubs on picture postcards bearing scenes of Washington, D.C. Once each year they would take a flying trip to Washington to talk to California politicians there, and they would lug along boxes full of the thousands of postcards they had written in the course of the year, and while there, they would mail them. That kind of personal attention made ardent disciples out of the ordinary club people.

Cranston announced that he was a candidate for the Senate, and Pat Brown declared his support for him because he knew which way his faithful followers were going to go, and he wanted to make haste to get out in front of them, to keep them behind him.

The fireworks began when Stanley Mosk, the attorney general, announced that he, too, was a candidate for Clair Engle's seat.

The following afternoon, over drinks in the Speaker's Sacramento office, Jess told his inner circle, "I've got to support Stanley. He's always been a friend and Alan never has."

Bob Crown said, "Absolutely. And, if we beat Alan, we'll be sticking it to the C.D.C., which says it's going to keep you from getting the nomination for governor in 1966."

"It's a great way to cut off their balls," Tom Bane said.

So it was that the unanticipated, but not unwelcome, war

broke out, and at the start, the winds of that war seemed to be blowing our way.

Jess was elated when he reported to Bob Crown, Tom Bane, and me that the earliest polls showed that Mosk had better and more favorable name identification statewide than Cranston.

Bob Crown said, "He also has a lot more hair and a nicer smile than Alan."

Those are vital considerations in this electronic era when the voters get their impressions of candidates through the medium of television.

"And Stanley's Jewish," Tom said; "he'll attract most of the contributions from the rich Jewish Democrats in the state who like to see a nice Jewish boy make good."

We signed up all of Jess's friends as Mosk supporters, even though we felt awful about deserting Clair Engle. That feeling deepened when we became aware of the macabre campaign Pat Brown was conducting to get Clair out of the race.

I learned of it one day when I was in Pat's office, trying to talk him into appointing a friend of mine to the board of the San Diego County Fair. Instead of telling me yes or no, he rasped confidentially, "Say, isn't it terrible about poor Clair Engle. He's got cancer of the brain, you know. That's what his operation was for, but they couldn't get it all, and he's only got a few months to live."

When I mentioned that to Jess that afternoon, he told me the Governor had said the same thing to other members when they'd gone to talk with him about something else.

Jess also said, "I guess Clair's doctor hasn't told him the bad news, but Pat has somehow gotten wind of it and is telling it to everyone he knows."

Clair would deny that he was dying whenever reporters told him that Pat said he was; but he kept losing weight and growing weaker, and the doctor finally decided it was time to tell him the truth. When he heard it, he forlornly announced that he was dropping out of the race.

Clair Engle spent the last few months of his life bravely carrying on, doing his duty as the representative of the people of California in the Senate while he wasted away. It was heartrending to read about him insisting on being taken to the floor in a wheelchair to attend the sessions and, when there was so little left of him

164

that his voice could no longer be heard, putting himself among the ayes or noes by feebly pointing with one finger toward a burning eye or his nose.

With one of Cranston's opponents out of the way, the Governor went to work on eliminating the other. One of Alan's supporters had gotten word of a jaunt Stanley Mosk had allegedly taken to Mexico with a pretty blonde, and had, in fact, obtained photographs of the two of them there. Rumors around the Capitol had it that the Cranston campaign had sent a photographer to Mexico to take the pictures, which may or may not have been true. In any case, the somebody who possessed the photos made Pat Brown party to the secret, and Pat promptly began to spread it.

"Gee, isn't it too bad about Stanley," he called to me one morning when I saw him getting out of his limousine in the basement, just as I was debarking from the blue Oldsmobile I was driving then.

"What's too bad?" I said as I walked over to him on the assumption that, whatever it was, it probably would be better if it wasn't said loudly enough for the garage attendants to overhear.

Then, in the same sincere rasp he had used to convey his grief to me about Clair Engle, he said, "Oh, I thought you knew."

"Knew what?"

"I never would have mentioned it if I'd thought you hadn't heard." He seemed overwhelmed with contrition. "But I guess I might as well tell you now. You'll hear about it anyway. Stanley got himself involved with some blonde and took her to Mexico with him, and a photographer got some very interesting pictures of them there." Pat made it sound as if the photographer had caught them on the glassy-eyed edge of a joint orgasm.

Then, with owlish eyes softening in a fine display of sympathy, he added, "It's really a shame. Stanley is such a nice fellow, and this will ruin his political career."

That was how I first heard about the pictures. I was naturally inclined to agree with Pat that they would destroy Stanley, until I talked with Bob Crown about it.

Bob had a great distaste for injustice, and it was in his mouth as he told me, "I hear those pictures are just some shots of them by a hotel swimming pool, but that's not what Pat's making them out to be. Our governor can do some pretty crummy things sometimes."

A few days later Jess said to me, "Pat's been calling newspaper editors all over the state, to keep in touch, he tells them. In the course of every call he mentions how terrible he feels about poor Stanley. Since none of them knows what he's talking about, he tells them about the pictures in the same way he told you."

If Pat hadn't taken the story in hand, Cranston would have had a devil of a time getting it out effectively. As it was, Pat used the lady in the pictures to edge Stanley out of the race, although some thought it was another blonde in Stanley's life, his wife Edna, who really was his biggest problem just then.

The Speaker told me he was having to talk to Stanley every day to keep him in the race. I was in Jess's office, as was Bob Crown, one afternoon when he picked up the telephone on his swept wing desk in answer to a ring on his office intercom.

"It's Stanley on line one," he said, as he pressed the telephone button to take the call.

"Hello, Stanley," he rumbled cordially, but Stanley's reply made his face fall. "You're making a hell of a mistake," he said. "You'll win if you hang in there."

After a heavy silence while he listened to Mosk again, he said, "Can't you put off making a final decision for a day or two? At least let me and a few of your other friends talk to you before you burn your bridges."

After another minute of listening morosely, he sighed, "Okay, Stanley, but I still think you're making a hell of a mistake."

He hung up the phone and grimaced as if he had a charley horse in his leg. "He's quitting," he said.

Bob Crown said, "Why?"

Jess shrugged. "He's cagey about his reasons, but I guess it's those pictures."

Bob replied, "How can Cranston use those pictures? The newspapers aren't going to publish any photographs of a man and a woman talking to each other by a swimming pool. They might have met there by chance. What kind of a news item is a picture like that?"

"It isn't one," Jess said.

"Cranston can't get those pictures out to the public," Bob fumed. "He can't put them in his campaign literature. What can he do with them?"

"Not a thing," Jess replied.

Bob was a picture of dynamic tension, as if he were flexing all his muscles simultaneously. "If anybody asks Stanley about them, he can say that he intends to campaign on the issues that concern the people of California and that he refuses to dignify character assassination like that with any response."

Jess took a sip from the glass of gin in front of him. From the look on his face, it might have been kerosene. "You're right," he said.

Bob's face reflected Unruh's look. He said, "It doesn't make any sense for him to drop out."

Jess pulled his face together and replied, "It doesn't make any political sense, but I don't think Stanley's problem is a political problem."

"What is it then, for God's sake?"

"I think that his hang-up is that Edna, who is a very tough lady, is probably raising hell with him to keep him from running because she doesn't want Pat and Cranston's people spreading that story. She probably thinks it's a reflection on her."

"You know something?" Bob said. "She could be just a little bit right."

The next day Jess told me he'd heard a rumor that Pat had promised Stanley the next appointment to the State Supreme Court if he would drop out. We never knew if that was true, but Stanley did get the next appointment, and he has been on the Supreme Court ever since.

At that point it seemed that the Brown-Cranston-C.D.C. coalition was triumphant and that the Speaker and his friends had been outmaneuvered into defeat before they could do anything at all. However, that proved not to be the case. Organized labor had worked with the C.D.C. throughout the 1950's to elect Democrats and defeat Republicans, but by 1964, a lot of California labor leaders were beginning to feel uneasy about that alliance because of the increasing influence of leftists in the Democratic club movement. I had heard any number of war stories from labor skates about their battles for control of their own organizations with the same raving bedlamites who were shoving the radical resolutions through at the C.D.C. conventions. California's labor leaders feared the ascendancy in the Democratic Party of some of the same extremists they had had to fight for their own survival in times past. Consequently, they were waiting for an opportunity to take them down a peg.

In addition, the friends of Clair Engle and Stanley Mosk were all choked up with resentment about the way Pat Brown and Alan Cranston had diddled their heroes, and all of us around Jess were spoiling for a fight. A powerful anti-Brown, anti-Cranston, anti-C.D.C. coalition had come into existence. All that was lacking to set it in motion was a candidate for the United States Senate.

For a few weeks none of us heard anything from Stanley Mosk, who was nursing his wrath in the attorney general's office like Macduff in exile.

We were feeling as if we didn't want anything to do with him either. We were pretty glum.

It surprised me that Jess seemed cheerful one evening when we gathered in his office after the day's work was done. He leaned his mighty bulk forward in his chair, as he did when he had something important to tell us, and began to speak in slow measures.

"Stanley called me today and suggested that Pierre Salinger should run for the Senate."

The idea struck us momentarily dumb. Salinger had been John Kennedy's press secretary, of course, and was still working in the White House for Lyndon Johnson when this conversation took place four months after JFK's death.

"How can he?" Tom Bane trebled. "He hasn't lived in California for years."

Pushing the splayed fingers of his heavy hands together, Unruh rumbled on, "I said the same thing to Stanley. 'Pierre's lived in Washington for years now, and you have to be a resident of California to run. And Stanley said to me, 'He can run. He's in the same position as a congressman who's lived in Washington for years. No matter how long he's worked for Jack Kennedy and Lyndon Johnson, he's still a legal resident of California if he says he always considered California to be his permanent home and says he always intended to return here after he was done working in Washington.'"

Every face dawned with the joy of battle as Jess went on. "I called Pierre at the White House and told him what Stanley said. He couldn't believe it at first, but I pointed out to him that Stanley is the attorney general. He's the one who makes the rulings on all such questions. What he says goes. Pierre told me he's got to talk to the President before he makes a decision, but he really wants to run, and I can't think of any reason Johnson would say no to him."

Bob Crown looked as cheerfully expectant as if he had been

told about a beautiful secretary who had just broken up with her boyfriend. "When are you going to start putting his campaign together?"

"Right now. Will you all be willing to help?"

We all said we would.

"We'll win this one," Jess said solemnly; "we've got an appealing candidate."

And so it seemed. For three years Pierre had been a favorite with the press corps in Washington because wisecracks spouted from him like wine from a goatskin, and some of them were funny. White House reporters made him quite famous by quoting the good ones. They called him Plucky Pierre and treated him as the mascot of the Kennedy administration. He was a good political prospect because he was associated in the public mind with Jack Kennedy, whose tragic death was fresh in the hearts of Democrats.

The Speaker was grimly brilliant in the conduct of Pierre's campaign, and with our help he brought Salinger through the primary before anyone got to know him very well, in spite of all that Pat Brown and the club people could do on Cranston's behalf. Salinger's victory demonstrated to the world that Jess Unruh was a more effective political leader than Pat Brown. It also shattered the myth of C.D.C. invincibility in Democratic primary elections, making it clear that the endorsements of the California Democratic Council, now that they had to be qualified as the recommendations of an unofficial organization, were no longer worth a bucket of warm spit, to use John Nance Garner's favorite figure of speech.

We rejoiced that Jess Unruh had won a decisive victory over Pat Brown in that hotly contested primary, but it soon became apparent that it was just one more defeat. In politics, as in any other kind of warfare, a weaker force seldom can triumph over a stronger foe. And after the lockup, Jess was in a decline, from which he never recovered.

Pierre Salinger was approached by the Governor as soon as the primary election was over. Pat laid on Pierre the idea that his being Big Daddy's protégé would be used against him by the Republicans in the general election campaign, whereas being Pat's adherent would not lay him open to such attacks. Pat offered to help Pierre raise money and line up Cranston's supporters for him. At that point Pierre showed his class by turning his back on the Speaker and sucking up to the Governor.

By so doing, Pierre turned Jess's victory into a terribly disappointing defeat. Then he turned Pat's victory, and his own, into defeats for both of them.

He seemed a sure thing for election to the Senate. He was already the incumbent. Clair Engle had wasted away to nothing but a burning spirit, and one day that fine flame went out. A few days later Pat Brown had appointed Pierre to take his place.

Best of all, Salinger's Republican opponent in the general election was a washed-up old movie actor named George Murphy. Everyone knew then that no washed-up old movie actor would ever be able to get the American electorate, in its ineffable wisdom, to take him seriously as a candidate for high office.

However, in September, when Jess's inner circle met in his office, Bob Crown said, "It looks like Pierre may yet snatch defeat from the jaws of victory."

Jerry Waldie said, "He's getting bad advice from somebody."

Jess heaved a sigh. "He's getting it from the people who lost the primary for Alan Cranston."

We were talking about his too-vocal opposition to Proposition 14, an initiative measure that had been put on the ballot by the California Real Estate Association to repeal the Rumford Fair Housing Act, which had been adopted by the Legislature and signed into law by the Governor in 1963. Every poll that was taken showed that the proposition was going to be approved by the voters by a tremendous margin. When asked, the average Californian made it clear that he wasn't prejudiced against blacks; he just didn't want one living next door.

It should have been sufficient for Salinger to say that he was against the measure whenever anyone asked him. It was not, after all, a federal issue, and he should have left it to Jess and the rest of us who had been involved in the passage of the fair housing act to defend it. We were all doing what we could in that losing cause, as was Pat Brown. There wasn't anything Salinger could do that would help minorities as much as winning his election would. However, he insisted on making his opposition to Proposition 14 the theme of most of the speeches he made. He gave it much more attention than the national and international affairs that are the business of a United States senator, even though everyone was advising him to campaign on federal issues and to stay away from that political death trap.

He topped off any number of other boners with a masterpiece. Ever since the primary election, George Murphy had been challenging him to a debate, and everyone in the higher echelons of the Democratic Party had warned him against accepting. Murphy was a perfect charmer, an Irish song-and-dance man by trade. His smile, his blue eyes, his toes, everything about him twinkled. Pierre Salinger, on the other hand, was dark, fat, and mean-looking, with narrow eyes. Every time he opened his mouth to speak, he curled his upper lip into a sneer the likes of which I had only seen on the visages of gangsters in low-budget moving pictures. When he talked, the words came out in a rapid, monotonous staccato, as if they were being typed. Worst of all, he insisted on keeping a big black cigar in the corner of his sneer even while he spoke. The effect of those mannerisms, which he's relinquished since then, I'm happy to add, was sinister.

Even though Jess, too, telephoned Pierre and warned him not to, he accepted Murphy's challenge to debate.

"He's sure he can overwhelm the old boy with his scintillating wit," Jess told me after that call.

The debate was a catastrophe for Pierre. He made a lot of sarcastic remarks that weren't funny. It became clear to me, as I watched the fiasco on television at home with Joanna that night, that the White House press corps had given him a reputation for being a humorous fellow by quoting only the things that he said that were funny and that had involved ignoring ninety percent of his one-liners. And even those of his jibes at George Murphy that might have looked clever in print, when sneered, gave Pierre the air of a particularly obnoxious villain of Batman being flippant in the presence of virtue, which was being represented that night by twinkling George. If he hadn't already lost the election, he put it on ice for Murphy then and there.

The producers of the Batman series must have watched the debate and have had the same reaction to it as everyone else, since they starred him in an episode in 1967 as an archvillain named Lucky Pierre. In it he just played himself. He sneered, wisecracked, talked around his big cigar, and acted overbearing, just as he had done in his television debate with George Murphy. He was one of the most repellent blackguards ever to be confounded by the dynamic duo of Batman and Robin.

Seeing Pierre overplaying that role with such flair made me wince. On programs like Batman, anyone who fleered at nice old gentlemen like George Murphy was bound to be as rotten as a buzzard's lunch. The people of California had been conditioned by their evening entertainment to think that the big house Pierre Salinger would look right in wasn't the United States Senate.

Pierre's appearance on the Batman show as a jeering, leering caricature of evil was for me a bizarre reminder of that 1964 campaign when he, Stanley Mosk, Alan Cranston, and the California Democratic Council all met their Waterloos, although Cranston, unlike those others, was wafted back from the St. Helena of defeat by the winds of fortune to fight again. But that was much later.

As for Pat and Jess, they both had been continuing to shove each other in the direction of a like political exile all year; and it looked to a lot of Democrats as if one or the other might soon be joining Pierre, Alan, and Stanley in oblivion if they both didn't stop what they were doing to each other.

20

McCarthyism of the Very Worst Kind

Injustice is relatively easy to bear; it is justice that hurts.

H. L. Mencken

*I*nk blackened the slick pages of the *Saturday Evening Post* with my doings only once. It wasn't a favorable mention, and I'd much rather forget about it, but those who remember the conflicts between Pat Brown and Jess Unruh would say I'd left out the bitterest battle of them all, so I'm afraid I'll have to tell the story.

In his editorial column for the issue of May 8, 1965, Stewart Alsop wrote of me: "A chief Unruh lieutenant accused the Brown administration of apparent crime, though there was no real evidence to support the charge. Unruh refused to disavow his man. Brown's people accused him of being reckless, a renegade, a wrecker, and an apostle of rule or ruin."

Although Alsop did not actually mention my name, anybody who had been reading the California newspapers knew to whom he was referring. I had been all over the front pages like an axe murderer caught red-handed at the close of a swinging evening.

Quite apparently somebody close to Pat Brown had talked to Alsop and got him to declare the Brown administration wrongfully accused in the column that he wrote about me, and in reporting that Jess had refused to disavow me, Alsop crafted a clever solecism. He implied that Jess had refused to disavow what I had done, which was untrue. He had already done so and had publicly (and privately) asked me to withdraw my charges. Pat Brown, however, had demanded that he disavow me personally as a friend and an associate by firing me as chairman of the Assembly Rules Committee, which was a nag of a different color entirely, and it was that, and only that, that the Speaker had refused to do.

Alsop's editorial was simply a written transcription of Pat Brown's shrill vocalizing on the subject. My name was left out of it because, according to Pat, I was merely a tool the Speaker had employed to do his dirty work. If Jess hadn't put me up to it, Pat screech-owled, he would not have hesitated to disavow me.

Yet there was not a scintilla of truth to what Pat was yowling and getting the papers to print. I had not breathed a word of what I had in mind to anyone but Ken Cory, my chief aide at the time, before I committed my colossal boner. Only after I had done it did I discuss it with the Speaker, when he came to my office to talk to me upon getting word of what had happened.

At this point I should go back and describe some of the events that led up to my making criminal charges against the Brown administration.

I have already told the story of how Pat appealed to members of the San Diego Central Committee to vote against me when I ran for the chairmanship of that inconsequential body. On another occasion he had taken the time to telephone most of the leading Democrats in San Diego County to ask them not to contribute to my campaign unless I would renounce my friendship with the Speaker. That was pretty small of Pat, and I thought ill of him for it, although I held Hale Champion more to blame than Pat, because I knew the Governor discussed all such things with him, and I thought of Hale as the dominant member of that partnership, as did everyone else in Sacramento.

In time the two of them stuck a sharp political instrument named Bernard Teitelbaum into San Diego, nominally as an employee and functionary of the California State Democratic Committee.

At the time Bernard first came to San Diego, Pat invited all of the prominent Democrats in the county to join him in an upstairs suite in the U.S. Grant Hotel. A special invitation was extended to me. The Governor was anxious that I should be there, one of the Governor's aides called to tell me. Hoping for a thaw in our relations, I went.

At the meeting Pat stood up in front of all of San Diego's leading Democrats with his arm around Teitelbaum, whose face and haircut gave him the look of an urban Li'l Abner. He said, "This is my man in San Diego. I'd personally appreciate it if you'd contribute to keeping him here when he asks you, and whenever you want anything from me, ask him."

My old friend Bill Moeser, who wanted to be helpful, bumbled, "Governor, shouldn't we talk to Jim Mills about judicial appointments and things like that?"

With me sitting there aghast, Pat repeated what he had just said. "This is my man in San Diego. Whenever you want anything from me, ask him."

After the Governor had delivered that sockdolager the second time, every eye in the room, including his own and Bernard's, turned to look at me. I felt my face turning red, then white. It was a chilling affront.

As I look back, I suppose Pat may actually have intended the special invitation to me to attend that affair to be taken as a friendly gesture. If so, it was pretty empty-headed of him, considering what he'd come to say. At that time I was getting to be fairly paranoid about him (just as he was about me), and I assumed he had wanted me to show up in order for him to offer that gratuitous personal offense to me, and I was instantly furious.

My first suspicions were soon reinforced. Right from the start, Bernard Teitelbaum acted as if his primary responsibility was to make sure any attempts I made in my home county to build up my own position politically were thwarted, and I assumed he had been so instructed. I could not imagine that he had embarked upon such a program without authority.

Since I was the only Democratic member of either house of the Legislature from San Diego County at that time, it was up to me to try to put together party efforts aimed at winning another seat or two; but everything I did along those lines was frustrated by Bernard calling upon Democrats as the representative of the Governor and asking them not to cooperate. And every time Pat hit town, he would meet again with the leading Democrats and stand again with his arm around Bernard and say again, "This is my man in San Diego. If you ever want anything from me, talk to him."

Bernard's efforts to undermine me and gather control of the local party into his own hands on behalf of the Governor may have arisen simply from Pat's unwillingness to give up the initiative in his war with Unruh for control of the party. He was never known to let up on anyone who challenged him in any way except on his own terms, which were always unconditional surrender. However, the renewed offensive against me, which was similar to what he was doing to Jess's allies elsewhere, only made political sense if the

Governor were planning to live up to his commitment to Jess not to run again. If Pat had decided instead to stand for re-election in 1966, no prominent regular Democrat would oppose him. He didn't need to have the control of the party in San Diego in his hands under those circumstances. It automatically would support him with all of its resources. However, he had to put somebody like Bernard into San Diego County to take over the machinery of the Democratic Party there if he wanted to deliver it to a political heir; and when Democrats talked of whom the Governor had in mind as his successor, only one name was mentioned, that of Hale Champion. I was convinced that Hale was both the architect of, and the intended beneficiary of, the campaign to diminish me among Democratic Party people in my own county.

Word of Bernard's activities aggravated me day by day, week by week, month by month, and year by year. I came to a point where I was spending every night simmering about the destructiveness of the campaign being waged against me.

When it was pointed out to me by Ken Cory that Hale Champion had apparently been involved in a conspiracy to commit a felony, I felt that God was delivering him into my hands, and I thought it was decent of God to do that. I didn't really think that Hale, as the Governor's right-hand man, would be punished for the commission of a crime as an ordinary citizen would. Such things don't happen. But I did think he'd be at least as embarrassed as I had been on various occasions as a result of his machinations. I believed that the migraines Pat gave me were the brainchildren of Hale, and I still do believe that.

Hale had committed his apparent crime in the course of trying to get some favorable publicity for himself and for Pat. He had adopted and perfected an ingenious idea that had occurred to one Jack Halpin, a bright young man who was one of Hale's political tuft-hunters. Halpin's thought was that, for the sake of the Governor's public relations, the state of California should enter into four separate contracts with four different aerospace firms to study and make recommendations as to how the state might go about solving problems in the fields of transportation, waste management, preservation of documents, and treatment of inmates in state mental and penal institutions. Each of the four contracts was for $100,000.

With a blaze of fanfare, Pat announced the new program as a way to revivify the then-ailing aerospace industry in California. It would, he proclaimed, help relieve the problem of unemployment among the workers at Hughes, Lockheed, Douglas, Aerojet General, and Convair.

The plan was a sound one only to the degree that it did achieve its intended purpose of getting publicity for Governor Brown and Hale Champion as godfathers of California's aerospace firms. It attracted a good deal of national attention. When Pat was interviewed about it by *U.S. News & World Report*, he was full of schmaltzy lines that Hale, or someone else who was clever with words, had fed to him. One that *U.S. News & World Report* liked and used was, "Brains that are going to put a man on the moon can probably get a man to work a little more quickly."

The idea of asking people who build airplanes and rockets to devise answers to problems of traffic management, waste disposal, document preservation, and inmate control was ludicrous on the face of it. If the state wanted to pay for advice in those areas of concern, it should have contracted with organizations that had some expertise in each of those fields; and, of course, the suggestion that the expenditure of a total of $400,000 on such contracts would have any effect upon unemployment among workers in the aerospace industry was even more ridiculous.

Under the glaring eyes of television cameras, the contracts were signed. The beneficiary companies were happy enough to pick up the money, and most of the state's major newspapers lauded the plan, as Jack Halpin, Hale Champion, and Pat Brown had anticipated they would.

As might have been expected, no benefit whatever accrued to the people of California. The four volumes of recommendations the aerospace firms produced were expensively bound and made up of a hodgepodge of ideas plagiarized from papers that had been published in times past by people who had some standing and competence in each field.

One morning Ken Cory brought it to my attention that the whole humbuggery spoof was illegal. Ken had taken up golf, and he is one of those people who insist on doing everything well. He had, therefore, acquired a brand new thing to play with, the top twelve inches of the handle of a golf stick. Never did I understand why it was better than a whole club, of which he had plenty; however, it was apparently considered the proper equipment for office golf, and Ken always had to have the right gear for whatever he did. He broached the subject of the fund transfer as he was addressing an imaginary golf ball in the middle of my worn green office carpeting, preparatory to teeing off and driving it down a long fairway of the mind.

"Did it ever occur to you that no money was ever appropriated to pay for those studies the aerospace firms are doing?" he said, as he swung his half of a golf club and then followed the incorporeal ball with his eyes through half a dozen walls and then across a couple of hundred yards of Capitol Park and downtown Sacramento to somewhere in the front of the Catholic cathedral.

"By God, you're right," I said. "It's funny nobody has thought of that. Where did they get the money?"

He turned from staring off into that undisclosed distance where his phantom ball had landed. Looking at me with cool satisfaction, he said, "Hale Champion ordered various departments to cut back on the budgets of various programs that were funded by the Legislature, and he's using that money to pay for those $100,000 scrapbooks."

I froze in disbelief.

Ken added another whiz-bang. "It's illegal to spend state funds on any program unless and until the Legislature has appropriated the money for it."

"If it isn't illegal, it sure as hell should be."

"It is. I've checked out what the Legislative Counsel has said on the subject," Ken said with his accustomed casual elegance. "He's always said it was illegal."

"Do you have any idea what programs he took the money from?"

"I've checked that out, too. The waste management study contract that was awarded to Aerojet General was funded by a cutback in a program for the care and treatment of crippled children."

"Jesus Christ!" I said.

"One of the others was funded by a cutback in the budget of a clinic for the treatment of alcoholism in San Francisco." Ken sank a putt between my feet and continued. "What is more, the Auditor General has just issued an official finding that there were false reports made by the Department of Public Health as to how some of that money was spent, and he says that those false reports were prepared by order of the Department of Finance."

"Good God!" I said. "That would never have been done without the approval of Hale Champion himself."

Ken nodded without looking at me and sank another phantom ball in the imaginary hole in the carpet between my feet. He looked up at me. "There is also a statute that requires public officials in California to report any misuse, misappropriation, or misreporting where public funds are involved."

I found myself unworthily pleased with the idea that I was required by the laws of the state to blow the whistle on the Governor and Hale. Revenge, although one of the least commendable of motives, is certainly one of the most satisfying.

However, before I made my final decision to do anything drastic, I wanted to make sure there was no mistake about the illegality of the fund transfers. For that reason I went to talk to the Legislative Counsel, whose name was George Murphy, like that actor fellow. I really had no doubt about the impropriety of the false reporting of expenditures, but I wanted an official counsel's opinion on that, too.

George Murphy is a little chap, neat in his appearance and orderly in his thinking. Like Telemachus, he was centered in the sphere of common duties, decent not to fail in paying due adoration to his household gods. As he listened to my question about the propriety of unauthorized fund transfers, he seemed a bit jumpy.

He answered hurriedly, "I've been expecting someone to come in and ask about the legality of those transfers of funds ever since I saw the first news stories about the aerospace contracts. Naturally I've been thinking about the whole question, and I've come to a conclusion. I am prepared to rule that such reallocations of budgeted funds are legal."

"What?" I said. "Your office has always ruled in the past that such transfers were illegal."

"I know," he said with a quick, nervous, little smile, "but I've concluded that we were wrong in the past."

"How could you possibly change your mind about a question as basic as that?"

Looking as shifty-eyed as a transvestite in a ladies' room, he said, "The executive branch unquestionably has the power to spend less than was budgeted for any program, if the full amount isn't needed. Being able to spend some of the money to expand another program where an increased need arises is a proper exercise of executive authority. The executive branch must be able to respond to unforeseen emergency situations."

"But, George, this wasn't a case of spending a little more

money on a program that had been authorized. The legislature never approved those contracts or anything even remotely related to them. It never appropriated any money at all for any such purpose."

"That's really not important. If an emergency arises, the hands of the executive must not be tied. It must have discretion to deal with it."

"For God's sake! There wasn't any emergency. If the administration wanted money for these contracts, it should have asked the Legislature for an appropriation."

"I agree that it would have been more in accord with customary procedures if that had been done, but I will opine, if asked, that the administration was only exercising powers that inherently reside with the executive branch of government when it made those transfers."

"I can't believe it," I said. "My God! Why do we go through the process every year of agonizing over all those appropriations the administration asks us for? Why do we spend thousands of hours hearing testimony about them and debating them before approving them or disapproving them? Why do we wear ourselves out to put a budget bill together and get it passed? Is the whole process a meaningless waste of time?"

"Oh, you shouldn't consider it a waste of time."

Talking to him on the subject of the fund transfers was like trying to pin a custard pie to the wall. I gave up on it and went on to the other question I had to ask him.

"I want to request an opinion on another matter."

"What is it?" he said, taking a notebook out of a desk drawer to write down my request. He looked and sounded terribly anxious to please me, to make up for failing to do so up to that point.

"If any person made false reports as to how money was expended by any department of the state government, would that be illegal?"

"The law is very explicit on the point. It is clearly a crime to make any such false report."

"Would you prepare a written opinion for me on that subject? I'd like to have it by next week."

"I'll have it for you by then," George said eagerly.

I went from Murphy's office to Jess's. I wanted to fill him in on my plans to make a state park of Old Town in San Diego. I wanted to preserve and restore the only California town that is at all like it was when Mexico ruled the Golden State because I felt Californians should know more about that aspect of their heritage.

I didn't mention anything about the aerospace contracts. I was certain that Jess would be more tolerant of Pat and Hale's transgression than he should be and that he'd manage to talk me out of doing what I should do.

At the beginning of the next Ways and Means Committee meeting, as I took my place in a high-backed swivel chair, I saw at the gumwood lectern, from which witnesses addressed the committee, the portly form of the director of the Department of Finance. In his face and figure Hale Champion looked so much like Gert Frobe playing Goldfinger in the James Bond picture of that name that a lot of us had by then begun calling him Goldfinger.

He stood before us emanating an aura of superiority to the common run of mankind, which included me specifically; at least that's how I always felt in his presence.

Bob Crown, the chairman, said, "Will the committee please come to order. Mr. Champion, will you take up your first item, please?"

Hale spoke, as he always did, in the manner of a child prodigy, with self-confident precision. "I am here to ask this committee for a supplementary appropriation of $30,000 to keep the state alcoholic clinic in San Francisco from having to close its doors. There isn't enough money to operate it till the end of the year if this sum isn't provided. That clinic is doing excellent work, and I don't think anyone wants to see it shut down."

Alan Post, our saintly looking, white-haired legislative analyst, said, "I agree that the appropriation should be approved so the work of the clinic can be carried on. It is a desirable program. However, I do feel constrained to point out that there would be no need for this appropriation if the administration had not taken $30,000 from this program to help fund one of the aerospace contracts."

I was laying for Hale, and Alan's remarks gave me my opening. "This is ridiculous," I said. "Here we are being asked by Mr. Champion to fund for a second time a program we've already funded once upon his request. He wants us to give him the money again because he decided to raid the program to finance a gold-plated publicity ploy."

"You have a lot of unemployment in San Diego," Hale responded loftily. "Most of the people who are out of work in your district are aircraft workers. You should be grateful to us when we try to help your constituents instead of sniping at us."

"Who are you trying to kid?" I said, resenting his condescension even more than usual. "Spending $100,000 on a study with Convair will have no effect whatever upon unemployment among aircraft workers and you know it."

Ignoring my challenge, he looked at Bob Crown as if to ask how long he would have to put up with my impertinence.

That made me angrier. Raising my voice more than I should have, I said, "If you want to come before us to ask for supplemental appropriations, you should be requesting them for the boondoggles you dream up, not for programs we've already funded."

Ostentatiously resigning himself to answering me, since it seemed he wouldn't be able to get on with the serious business of the day if he didn't, he said coolly, "Mr. Mills, you may look upon the solution of some of California's most serious problems as boondoggles, but I don't, and Governor Brown doesn't." He looked back at Bob Crown and said, "Mr. Chairman, it seems that Mr. Mills thinks there was something improper about the fund transfers that took place. I'd like to assure you and the committee that there was nothing improper about any aspect of it. It was perfectly legal."

"Mr. Chairman," I said at Bob, "I'd like to know why Mr. Champion is here before us today. Is he just trying to humor us? He says that it's legal and proper to transfer funds without approval. Why doesn't he just go down to his office and transfer some to this alcoholic clinic? Why is he here wasting our time?"

Champion didn't say anything.

I broke the silence with, "What assurance do we have that Mr. Champion won't transfer this second appropriation for the alcoholic clinic to some other publicity scam he or one of the Governor's other flaks come up with?"

Bob thought the situation was getting out of hand, so he interrupted to say, "It has been moved by Mr. Bane and seconded by Mr. Kennick that the supplemental appropriation be approved," although it hadn't been. "Those in favor say aye, those opposed no. The ayes have it. The motion is adopted."

We went on to other things.

Before the committee met again, I had received the opinion George Murphy had promised me. It held that false reporting of expenditures of state funds was a crime and that there was no other way to read the law, just as he had told me it would.

I therefore told Ken to deliver a copy of George's opinion to the District Attorney of Sacramento County. No one but the District Attorney himself, Ken Cory, and I knew that I had done it when I showed up at the next meeting of the Ways and Means Committee.

Hale Champion stood up at the lectern again. He apparently was going to ask for a restoration of some other appropriation he'd raided for the contracts because he led off with, "I want to reassure this committee that there is nothing at all to Mr. Mills's suggestion that I or anyone in the Department of Finance did anything illegal or improper in connection with the funding of the aerospace contracts."

I asked him, "Are you trying to tell us that the falsification of official reports of state spending is legal and proper?"

He looked at me with undisguised contempt.

"Mr. Chairman," I said, "I have here an offiical finding by the Auditor General that the Department of Public Health falsely reported upon its expenditures, having been directed to do so by the Department of Finance. Attached to it is an opinion of the Legislative Counsel that any such false reporting constitutes a criminal act. I have copies for you and Mr. Champion, and it's only fair to add that I had additional copies made and I have put them in the hands of the District Attorney."

The members of the committee, the reporters in the hearing room, the legislative staff, the lobbyists in the audience, and the general public among them began to whisper like leaves in a flurry of wind.

I went on. "I'd like to have Mr. Champion tell us about the legality of false reporting of expenditures."

Hale was frigid, supercilious, haughty, and nonresponsive in his reply, which was, "I am not used to assemblymen of either party behaving like Joe McCarthy."

Over the pandemonium among the press, public, and committee members, Bob Crown said, "Mr. Champion, I want to apologize as the chairman of this committee for the unforgivable attack made upon you by one of its members."

I thought that was unworthy of Bob, so I got up and walked out. Later I understood that he had immediately foreseen the potential for trouble for the Speaker in what I had done. Everyone knew how close he was to Jess; by disassociating himself from me at that point, he hoped to make clear that my attack was not part of any plan that had been developed by the Speaker and those around him.

After I got back to my office, Jess came to talk to me.

"Well, Jimmy," he bassoed with a rueful smile as he settled his now athletic shape on the thin, dull green cushions of one of the regulation-issue stainless steel chairs, "I heard you really nailed Hale Champion's piles to the seat."

"He had it coming."

"I know how exasperated you are with Pat and Hale, and I can understand why you did it, but I wish you hadn't. I wish you'd talked to me about it beforehand. I would have tried to talk you out of it."

"I thought you would," I replied, feeling a little guilty, "but I thought it was the thing to do and that I should do it. I thought it would be better if you didn't know anything about it, so no one could hold what I did against you."

He smiled faintly. In reflecting upon it, I realize now that it must have been at my naïveté. He said, "Be prepared for Pat to dump all over you like a garbage truck."

"He's been doing it for years."

"I know he has." He paused, and the bereaved bulldog look that I knew to be a sign that he was deeply troubled furrowed his face. "Do you respect my political judgment?"

"Does Marilyn Monroe respect Jack Kennedy's?"

He managed only a fleeting smile at that. He said, "I think you made a hell of a serious mistake, and the best thing would be for you to admit it."

"It won't do much good to withdraw the charges now. The Sacramento District Attorney is on notice that Hale Champion was party to a crime. That can't be undone."

"No," Jess said, "but it would still be better for all concerned if you say you are withdrawing your charges."

"But a crime was committed. Would you like to see the documentation?"

"Jimmy, do you remember the night of the lockup, when you and all of my other friends were telling me that what I was doing was morally right but politically wrong?"

"Yes."

"Well, that's what I'm telling you now."

"You didn't listen to me that night, so you owe me one."

The conversation went on and on until well after six o'clock, and he had to go have dinner with a few of California's business

leaders to get their support for a major constitutional reform package that I was carrying that year. It was the one that made being a
member of the Legislature a full-time job. It required approval by
the voters, and Jess had taken the lead in drumming up support for
it.

As he heaved himself to his feet to go out, he said, "Let's talk
about it in the morning."

It was soon apparent that Pat had lost his temper, but not his
head. He and Hale realized how vulnerable my faux pas had made
their archenemy, Jess Unruh. The opportunity to work him over
was the best they'd ever had. I saw the Governor on the television
news that night, his jowls quivering with righteous indignation. He
growled as fiercely as any mother bear protecting her cub when he
said, "I demand a full investigation by the District Attorney of
Sacramento in order to clear Hale Champion, who is one of the
finest young men in government today."

Even more fiercely he said, "Jim Mills is the Speaker's right-
hand man, and Jesse Unruh must be held responsible for his
actions."

Pat had no trouble at all selling the press on the idea that I had
merely been Jess's hit man in an attack so cowardly and despicable
that he didn't want to be publicly associated with it himself.

I'm sure Pat believed that, even though it didn't make sense. If
Jess had wanted someone to do what I had done without his
appearing to be associated with it, I was the last person in the world
that he would have chosen. A much better strategy would have
been to suggest the idea to Alan Pattee, or some other Republican
friend, any number of whom would have been more than happy to
shoot up the Brown administration and do the Speaker a favor at
the same time. Choosing me to waylay Hale Champion would have
been an incredibly stupid thing for Jess to do, and the one thing
nobody ever accused him of was stupidity.

I kept on repeating my denials that the Speaker had any
knowledge of my attack on Champion before it was made, but the
fact that the reporters who heard me didn't believe me was obvious
even to the most casual readers of their stories. Newsmen are, after
all, cynics by profession.

Pat was able to enlist the aid of the press in painting Jess with a
whole potful of guilt by association, the specialty of the late Senator
Joe McCarthy, with whom Hale had compared me. The Governor

irately yodeled that as chairman of the Rules Committee, I was the assemblyman closest to the Speaker in the running of the State Assembly. Then he made his demand that Jess repudiate me personally by firing me from my chairmanship. In the press conference he called the day after the event, he picked up the McCarthy pitch from Champion. He said, "Mills is guilty of McCarthyism of the very worst kind."

When I saw my Republican friend Senator Jack Schrade in the hall the next morning, he said, "A reporter for the *Long Beach Press-Telegram* told me the Governor said you're guilty of McCarthyism of the very worst kind."

I boiled over. "Pat's the one who's guilty of McCarthyism of the very worst kind, Charlie McCarthyism. And Hale Champion is guilty of Edgar Bergenism."

Jack drifted away in a freshet of chuckles. When he got to his office, he put out a release giving those lines to the world. That didn't help the situation any.

Since his outraged innocence act was playing so well on television and in the newspapers, Pat kept it up. Every day he heightened the effect by appearing more righteously aggrieved by the Speaker's continued refusal to accede to his repeated demands that he repudiate me by removing me from my chairmanship. And every day the press would play it up again as if he had never said it before. By that time the reporters were referring to me in those stories as "Unruh's number one lieutenant." By the way, I wasn't. Jess's inner circle was essentially a society of equals, but the press liked Pat's version of what had happened. It made a better story.

To help him get even with the Speaker, Pat called upon Roger Kent of Kentfield, a hoary old aristocrat who was a perennial chairman of the Democratic State Central Committee. Roger put out a release, one that I presume had been prepared in the Governor's office, saying that Unruh and his associates were trying to embarrass the state's Democratic administration. The release said that the evidence of Unruh's responsibility for my action was overwhelming. There was no reference to what the evidence was because there wasn't any such evidence, and that really was McCarthyism of the very worst kind.

Jess tried to make the best of a bad situation. He repeatedly disavowed my accusations. He said to the press, "I had no knowledge of what Jim Mills had in mind before he did it. If I had known, I would have tried to talk him out of it. I think he should withdraw his charges, and I have told him so. I still hope that he will."

Whenever he was asked by reporters if he was going to dump me, he would say, "If I were to fire every chairman who criticized the Governor, I wouldn't have any chairmen left."

That answer reinforced the cynicism of the reporters relative to my statements that he was innocent of any complicity in my transgression.

By that time almost all of the Speaker's friends were urging him to fire me. Whether he went to the Mirador Bar for a Beefeater's on the rocks, or to Frank Fat's for some chow mein, or to the gym at the Elks' Club to lift weights, there would be someone there offering him that advice, which was unquestionably sound. He would have been far better off if he had followed it, but he never once said a word to me in the course of that sad affair which suggested that anything about it was as important to him as its consequences for me. Like Harry Truman, he was always more concerned for his friends than for himself, and like Truman he suffered as a result.

The consequences of my blundering attack on Hale Champion were all highly distasteful to me. Pat Brown convinced a lot of people that Jess Unruh was, in the words echoed by Stuart Alsop, "a renegade, a wrecker, an apostle of rule or ruin." By so doing, Pat was able to reinforce the idea that he himself was a long-suffering good guy who had to put up with all manner of offenses on the part of that renegade apostle of rule or ruin.

No one ever really cared that a crime had been committed. Steward Alsop was as wrong as he could be when he parroted the Brown line that there was no real evidence to support the charge. What had really been the case was that everyone responsible for the interpretation and enforcement of the law had scattered like chickens before the Governor in his wrath. George Murphy, the Legislative Counsel, when I had asked him whether the money juggling was legal, reversed the position his office had always taken in the past. (By the way, every legislative counsel's opinion that has been issued since that time on the subject has declared, like all of those issued before the fund transfers of 1965, that any such transfers would constitute criminal conduct.) George Murphy stayed out of trouble with that interim opinion, but I had caught him in a corner he couldn't get out of when I asked him about the legality of falsifying reports of expenditures. However, the Sacramento District Attorney, an elected official in a Democratic county, understandably wanted nothing to do with the prosecution of the director of finance of a Democratic governor, so he somewhat sheepishly concluded that no falsification of reporting had taken place. He did so by ignoring the official conclusions that had been published by the Auditor General. Since the Auditor General is not a prosecutor, that was the legal end to the affair.

The Governor naturally hailed the action of the district attorney as a complete exoneration of Hale, and he kept up his attack on Jess as an unscrupulous, ruthless renegade. And he continued to score with it.

Hale Champion and the Governor profited greatly from the affair because the outcome of it gave them an opportunity to discredit Jess Unruh, which they exploited effectively. For some months after, Hale's aides kidded him by calling him a Hale-felon-well-met, which always made him laugh. He certainly had no reason not to laugh.

I, who had acted so foolishly in trying to call such a powerful personage as Hale Champion to account for breaking the law, was universally condemned for it by the press and the leadership of the Democratic Party of California.

That was the only result of the affair that any of the actors in it deserved. My failure to anticipate the outcome merited the censure I got and more.

21

How the Amiable Owl Fell on
His Tail for the Last Time

Man can climb to the highest summit, but he cannot dwell there long.

George Bernard Shaw

*I*n the academic groves of Berkeley, a wildfire of emotions burst into flame with the autumn leaves of 1964. That ideological conflagration began as a demonstration against a century-old University of California rule prohibiting political activities on campus. It had begun peacefully, but on October first all hell broke loose. That day a police car had howled onto the grounds to carry away one of the leaders of the protest, who had been arrested for disorderly conduct. Thousands of student and nonstudent demonstrators had closed around the car. They held it captive with their bodies for thirty hours, with the cops and their prisoner inside it.

During those thirty hours, one long-haired firebrand after another climbed on top of the car to stir the blazing sea of passions around it with hot winds of oratory. (At least that is how the affair appeared to most citizens who were writing to Sacramento about it.) On the network news that frenzied scene was the most compelling television drama that I could remember. The nation was aghast. Americans at that time had never seen a domestic insurrection.

As the months passed, the chaos that enveloped the University of California became kaleidoscopic. In early December student demonstrators riotously occupied Sproul Hall, the university's administration building, and set up housekeeping in it. Acting on orders from Pat Brown, the police moved in and arrested 814 of them and bussed them to the Alameda County Jail at Santa Rita.

The initial outcome of the affair was that the university

administration capitulated and rescinded its ancient rule against political activities on campus, but that victory did not mollify the demonstrators. The uproar raged on all through the following year, 1965, over one thing and another. Nor was there any let-up in 1966.

By then Californians had even more alarming developments to watch before going to bed and to think about before going to sleep, if they could go to sleep while thinking about such things. In August of 1965 much of the black community of Watts in Los Angeles County was looted and put to the torch by what seemed to the general public to be an army of vandals.

Night after night Californians shrank from the full-color nightmares on the television network news programs. They felt like the Romans of a millennium and a half ago seeing the thin veneer of their civilization crackling and curling up in holocausts kindled by rampaging barbarians.

Like other liberal Democrats in California, I saw my bright hopes for a better future being obscured by the spreading smoke and tear gas. The wild men who were bringing their world down around their own and their neighbors' ears were blacks and students, members of groups identified by the average voter as the pets of Democratic liberals like Pat Brown, Jess Unruh, and me.

Doing all it could to goad everybody who was rioting to new excesses was the usual corps of leather-lunged Marxists. In every democracy the radical left has pursued as one of its basic aims the discrediting of liberals in order to put reactionaries in control of government. Their theory is that the reactionaries will make a mess of things and will create a favorable climate for the left to take control of the state.

The same ultra-cunning red strategy of raising hell in the streets to embarrass moderates in power helped give the world Adolf Hitler and Benito Mussolini and a sorry company of Latin American facsimiles. Since it had worked so well for leftists elsewhere, they were trying it again in California to see if they could once again deliver control of a state into the hands of hard-line conservatives. They succeeded, of course, and it turned out about as well for them as it has everywhere else in the Western world.

As is commonly the case, the liberals, while in office, were doing more than anyone else to contribute to their own overthrow by quarreling among themselves. I had added fuel to the flaming animosity the Governor and the Speaker were banking up in their hearts for each other when I had questioned the legality of taking money appropriated for programs to help crippled children in order to give it to Aerojet General Corporation so it wouldn't miss paying its usual dividend to its stockholders; but they had been snorting fire at each other even without that.

In March of 1965, Alan Cranston informed the press that Pat Brown had told him he had decided he would run for re-election the following year. When reporters asked the Governor to confirm or deny Cranston's report, he was evasive. He said he would have a reply for them by the time the first snows flew in the Sierras. When winter swept over the Alpine slopes and meadows of the Sierra Nevadas, trailing its white veils, they asked him again, and he said he'd answer the question soon.

Unruh said to me wryly, "Maybe he'll tell us when the swallows come back to Capistrano."

It became obvious to everyone that Cranston had been telling the truth, that the Governor was going to run, and that he was just stringing the reporters along to milk a little more publicity out of his decision than he would get by simply announcing it.

The Speaker had been working hard to put together his campaign for governor, mostly to get himself out of the Assembly, I believe, though I don't think he recognized that as his underlying motivation then as he did in 1970. He began to get more than a little irked about the game the Governor was playing. Pat's being so very cute and transparent about his intentions was to Jess as painfully graceless as his having gone back on his promise not to run for re-election in 1966.

Bob Crown loved Unruh dearly, and he was feeling even more deeply aggrieved and offended than Jess was. Bob was close to Ed Saltzman, a bright young reporter for the Oakland Tribune, so he told him how Pat had given his solemn word to Jess and Bob in 1962, with his right hand raised in the air, that he wouldn't run for a third term.

Naturally, Saltzman wrote an article based on Bob's story. The Governor was asked a question about it at his next press conference. He quivered with wrath and indignation, shaking very much like the tower of jelly that Time Mazazine had once said he was. From his color, as he appeared on television, the jelly was raspberry.

"I never committed myself at any time to support Jess Unruh for governor," he swore. "One of my closest friends wanted to run, and I never would have done anything like that."

Hale Champion has often denied that he had any such high ambition, but I have never heard anyone suggest that he was not the close friend Pat was referring to. I have never even heard anyone waste any time speculating as to whether Pat might have had anybody else in mind when he said that.

Pat's denial that he had agreed to support Jess was presented by the press to the public as a contradiction of the statements Bob and Jess had made about what Pat had said to them in 1962. And that infuriated them both. Neither of them had ever said that Pat had pledged himself to support Unruh in 1966. They had only said that he had promised that he wouldn't run for re-election. Pat had handled a tough question by following a basic rule of the clever politician: "If somebody asks you a question you don't want to answer, answer some other question."

By that time the Governor and the Speaker were taking no pains to conceal their mutual hostility from the public. In the issue of *Newsweek* for April 6, 1965, Pat was quoted in an apparent reference to my, by then, nationally infamous attack on Hale Champion. Pat said, "The Speaker has let his personal ambitions interfere with his good judgment."

The same story quoted Jess as firing back, in a reaction to Pat's apparent decision to run again, "There's been damned little evidence of good faith."

With Watts burning against the night sky like London during the Battle of Britain and with Berkeley doing so ideologically, who should come galloping into view, riding out of the sanguine glow — which was very much the color of the sunsets into which he had disappeared in so many cowboy movies — but Ronald Reagan. A hip-shooting personification of the Western hero, he glittered with charisma like the sugarplum fairy, and he moved about with the same airy grace. His socks were never down around his ankles, like Pat's were. Not a single hair of his lacquered head was either gray or out of place. He looked as athletic and appealing in the year of 1966 as we all remembered him in the part of the Gipper in the picture *Knute Rockne, All American*. Yet it was hard for professional politicians to take him seriously. His campaign didn't seem to be anything like real-life politics, all blood, sweat, and fears. He acted as though he were just playing the lead in a B picture to be entitled *Mr. Reagan Goes to Sacramento*. When he delivered such stock lines as, "We must preserve law and order," and "Let's take politics out of government," he made the conduct of government sound as black and white and simpleminded as most of the other melodramas in which he had previously starred.

His opponent in the Republican primary was George Christopher, the progressive mayor of San Francisco. As the wavy-haired hero of the Greek community in the state, he enjoyed a substantial base of support. If all those lusty Greeks could be motivated to do precinct work and pass out campaign literature, they would be a great political organization.

In addition, Christopher had compiled a solid record of accomplishments as a public official and another one, equally impressive, as a businessman, both of which were qualifications for office that Ronald Reagan lacked. The Mayor's business experience was expected to have a great deal of appeal to Republicans, who are so fond of saying, when they are out of power, that things would be much better if the government were being run by businessmen.

In the spring of 1966 Pat Brown didn't seem to be unduly concerned about the re-election campaign, although in April he asked Jess Unruh, Bob Crown, and me over to the old governor's mansion, and we presumed he wanted to talk to us about it.

Late in the afternoon we drove there together in Jess's black Lincoln. We mounted the steps of the mansion, a Victorian carpenter's three-story daydream of white-painted gingerbread. Bob rang the doorbell. A gray-haired maid in a black dress with a white lace collar and cuffs opened the front door. She asked us in and showed us down the hall over a long avenue of Oriental rugs, through a carved wooden archway into the dining room. The dining table and chairs were gone for some reason. I supposed they had been sent out to be refinished. Jess looked about like a man interested in moving into the place, as indeed he was. He raised his eyes to the stylized floral designs in the white plasterwork of the high ceiling. It was a bas relief complement to the equally stylized floral designs in magenta, tan, and blue of the Persian carpet on the hardwood floor.

I then looked about me, as I always did there, to admire the white-painted wainscoting. Each panel had a carved fish, duck, bunch of grapes, or ear of corn in the center, appropriate embellishments for the dining room of the governor of California, for they were all representations of California food products.

There was no furniture at all in the room except for four antique chairs, each one a composition of needlepoint cushions framed in sculptured rosewood curlicues. They were arranged in a semicircle around the fireplace, which was six feet high and six feet wide, a massive piece of Palladian architecture that had been carved and polished out of a huge block of purple Italian marble. Its salient features were two Doric columns, one on either side of a Roman archway into a cold blackness, for there was no fire in it. It seemed to me symbolic of the warmth of our relationship with Pat that the chairs were arranged around a fireplace that had no fire in it.

We sat down in three of the ancient chairs, leaving the one on the left end for Pat. Jess soon started to twiddle his thumbs.

Bob Crown glumly ventured a thought. "I wonder if he's going to raise his right hand and give us his solemn word that he won't run for re-election in 1970."

At that moment the Governor came bustling in. After greeting each of us with a hearty handshake and a jovial, "Hi, how are you?" he seated himself authoritatively in the chair at the end.

"Let's get down to brass tacks," he said. "Jesse, you and I have had our differences in the past, but I know you don't want to see the Republicans elect a governor. You'll never get any of your bills to increase funds for public education signed into law then."

Jess replied, "You don't have to tell me that."

I said, "You didn't call us here to convince us that we don't want a Republican governor, did you?"

"Oh, I just wondered if any of you might have any ideas as to how to keep George Christopher from getting the Republican nomination for governor."

"Governor, I think you've got this situation figured out all wrong." Jess was singing in the low range of his basso profundo, as he ordinarily did at the beginning of conversations. "In my opinion Ronald Reagan will be a lot harder to beat than George Christopher."

Jess spoke diffidently, knowing that Pat would question his motives as a matter of course.

Narrowing his eyes, which made him look like an owl in the presence of crows, Pat said, "Nobody's going to want a washed-up cowboy actor as governor of this great big state."

"Nobody should," Jess softly bassoed, "but a lot of people do. The polls all show him way ahead of Christopher."

"I hope that doesn't change," Pat rasped. "Those polls only show how the Republican voters feel. There are still an awful lot more Democrats in California than there are Republicans. Reagan is so far to the right, and he knows so little about government, the only people who'll vote for him in the general election will be the right-wingers who voted for him in the primary. They might be a majority of the Republicans, but they sure aren't a majority of the people."

"I think you're wrong," Jess answered him with increasing emphasis. "Ronald Reagan is clever. He's figured out just what the people want to hear, and he's saying it. He says that if he's elected, he'll cut the fat out of government and lower taxes. Now that's pure bullshit and everybody knows it but the voters. He says that if he's elected, he'll take the politics out of government. That's bullshit, too, but the people are eating it up."

Pat broke in, "More has been done for the people of this state during my administration than during the administration of any other governor in history. We enacted the Master Plan for Higher Education and we provided water for Southern California with the Water Plan after the Republicans had promised to do it and had failed time after time. We set up the best program of medical care for poor folks and senior citizens in the whole country. We found jobs for all of the people who've been coming into California in the biggest migration in the history of the world. I can campaign on my accomplishments. The people won't repudiate a record like that, especially not to elect a cowboy actor who has no record of ever doing anything useful in his life."

Bob Crown had been sitting looking into the empty blackness of the cold fireplace, evincing by his silence how he felt about the Governor, both for going back on his word not to run and for inferring that Bob and Jess had lied about it. When he finally looked up from the empty fireplace at Pat, it didn't seem that he was turning his face to him as much as he was setting it against him. Spitting out his words like hangnails, he said, "I agree with Jess."

Pat shook his head in disbelief and asked, "Why?"

Bob didn't reply. After a couple of seconds Jess said to Pat, "H. L. Mencken was right when he said that nobody ever went broke by underestimating the American people. That's as true in politics as it is in business, and Ronald Reagan understands that better than any American politician since Huey Long. He's the one you should be worried about."

Pat said to me, "What do you think?"

I replied, "Governor, I agree that the people should re-elect you on the basis of what's been done during your eight years in office. It's a great record. But I agree with Jess and Bob. George Christopher is campaigning against you on the legitimate issues, and you won't be in any real trouble with him. But Ronald Reagan is running a razzle-dazzle campaign against those kids who have been raising hell in Berkeley, and he says he'll crack down on them if he's elected governor, and that's what the average voter wants to hear."

"But that's just what I did," Pat protested. "I was the one who finally ordered the arrests there when things got out of hand."

"He's saying you should have done it long before you did, before things got out of hand."

Pat said, "Hmmph," putting as much disdain into that "Hmmph" as I've ever heard put into one syllable.

"I agree that you did the right thing," I said, "but the average voter wanted to see some heads broken right at the start, when those kids imprisoned the cops in their car."

Jess nodded in grave disapproval of, yet in agreement with, what I had said.

I continued, "And he's running against the blacks who went out of their minds in Watts."

"What did I have to do with that?" Pat said. "That's the phoniest campaign issue I ever heard of."

I added, "And he's running against the families who have been on welfare for three generations."

Pat retorted, "There are so few of them that they don't even show up on statistical samplings of welfare recipients."

"You know that," Jess said, "and I know it, but Reagan is making people believe that they're the reason our taxes are as high as they are. He says he'll make them get off their cans and go to work. If he does find jobs for them, they'll be happier about it than anyone else, but he won't, of course. He's running against fair housing, and he's picking up a lot of support from the racists."

With an impatient gesture, Pat brushed all that aside scornfully. "That's terrible demagoguery."

"Of course it's demagoguery," Jess said, "but it's going over big with the rednecks in the blue-collar jobs."

The conversation went on for an hour, and it was an hour wasted. Bob was saying nothing, and I finally shut up, too, though Jess kept trying to convince the Governor, but nothing he said made any impression whatever on Pat.

Pat concluded the discussion on the same note he had sounded at the beginning. "I can't believe that the majority of the people of California will want a washed-up cowboy actor to be the governor of this great big state."

The consequence of our failure to convince Pat was that he committed a horrendous political gaffe. Even though all of the public opinion polls showed Reagan was building up a big lead over Christopher, Pat wanted to take no chances that the Republican voters might come to their senses on election day, so he played a dirty trick on George Christopher.

At one point in his career as president of the Christopher Milk Company, the Mayor had been arrested for putting water in the milk. Apparently the charge wasn't well founded because it was dropped. However, the usual mug shots were taken when he was booked. A big, burly, heavy-featured, black-haired man, he invariably looked as if he needed to shave again by the time he had finished his breakfast, and the mug shots were taken a long time after breakfast. In addition, he seemed to be pretty grumpy about being arrested. With the license plate across his chest, he appeared to be the kind of character Lucky Luciano would hire to deal with his business competitors.

Pat's campaign manager, Don Bradley, obtained some prints of the police photographs of the Mayor and arranged for copies to be made and distributed to the press. Initially, everyone suspected that somebody connected with the Reagan campaign was responsible, which is undoubtedly what Brown and Don Bradley had counted upon. One of the reporters who received a print did some detective work and found out where it had really come from.

The damage to Pat was severe. If he'd ever had any chance of beating Reagan, it lay in making a successful appeal to the moderates in the Republican Party. Ronald Reagan was then, as he still is now, capable of scaring the liver out of people with inflammatory ad-libs. A perfect example was his comment relative to the student militants at Berkeley, "If it takes a bloodbath [to deal with them], let's get it over with."

The day the newspapers informed the public that Pat and his friends had put out the picture of Christopher, I joined the Speaker at Frank Fat's restaurant for some chow mein.

Jess mourned, "Well, Pat's blown whatever chance he may have had to win over any of the people who are supporting Christopher."

I agreed. "It's too bad he thought you were trying to screw him around when you told him to lay off the Mayor."

Jess looked frustrated. "And he's also kicked away the votes of a lot of Greeks who might otherwise have voted for him as a human reaction against Reagan for beating the first Greek who ever had a chance to be elected governor of California."

"True," I said.

"Probably the best thing Pat Brown had going for him with the people of California during his glory years was his nice-guy image," Jess said, "but now everybody sees him the way we do."

The Brown campaign, which had commenced with such a fanfare of sour notes, kept producing more and more of them. It became apparent that the advice and counsel of the smartest politician in the state were sorely needed, but the Speaker left the state in the fall and was soaking up sunshine and a modest daily ration of daiquiris on various warm Caribbean islands.

Gladwin Hill, a reporter for the *New York Times*, wrote a book about California politics that covered those years. Appropriately entitled *The Dancing Bear*, it provides a good overview. Yet there was one thing that Hill got wrong, as did everyone else who wrote about the defeat of Pat Brown in 1966. He accepted at face value the charge made by Brown and his friends that Jess Unruh sat out the election in the Caribbean because he was mad at the Governor, whereas the real reason the Speaker didn't play a major part in the gubernatorial campaign was that Pat wouldn't let him.

I heard about the problem from Jess himself one Thursday noon over lunch in the Sky Room of the Mirador Hotel. He looked glum as he consumed his lettuce salad, which was all he had for lunch.

I said, "Is there anything wrong?"

Looking out over the green clouds of treetops in Capitol Park, he said gloomily, "Yes, there is. Pat won't give me a position of any importance in his campaign. I asked him if I could be the statewide chairman and he said no. I asked if I could be the chairman for Southern California, like I was in 1962, and he said no to that. He and Hale have decided to make me serve as a private in the rear ranks of this campaign. They want to make the party people think I'm not important. I want to help them beat Reagan, God knows, but I can't bring myself to let them put me down that way."

"But you've got to help, no matter where they put you. If you sit this one out, you'll be playing into their hands. That's obviously what they're hoping you'll do. The whole idea is to make you look bad."

His face was heavy with frustration, as I knew his heart was. He said, "They've got me in a position where I'll look like hell no matter what I do. I think I'll take a trip somewhere. At least I'll enjoy myself a little, which I won't if I stay in California."

That was the most serious error Pat made, placing a higher priority on keeping Jess Unruh out of the governor's mansion in 1970 than on keeping Ronald Reagan out of it in 1966.

Even though he was so far away, Unruh was the dominant figure in the 1966 campaign. That is, his absence was crucial. Most of the Speaker's friends felt that, if the Governor had involved him, most of Pat's other grievous mistakes would not have been made.

One of Pat's worst boners came after he made a visit to an elementary school in the course of a day of person-to-person campaigning. Pat called out to a little black boy, "Just remember that it was an actor who killed Lincoln."

A television cameraman had been following the Governor and had filmed the sequence. Brown thought it was very amusing, so did Don Bradley so they used the footage in an "Edmund G. Brown for Governor" television commercial. They spent a lot of money to have it shown in every television market in California.

Joanna and I first saw it one night at home in San Diego just after supper.

I said, "Jesus Christ!"

She said, "Oh, my God."

The following morning I telephoned the local Brown headquarters and said to the man in charge, "For God's sake, get hold of Don Bradley and tell him to kill that ad about it being an actor who killed Lincoln. It's the worst thing I've ever seen."

"Yeah, I saw it, too," the man said sourly. "We've already had a couple of dozen calls to give us hell about it."

The following day I called the man again to find out how Bradley had responded.

He told me, "Don says that he and the Governor think that sequence is very funny. They think all the telephone complaints are coming from Republicans who want to get it off the air because it's so good, because it shows Pat to be warm and human and funny."

I said, "God help us," and I tried to get hold of Pat, but he was too busy to call me back.

In a few more days the outcry from the public and the press had mounted into such a howl that Bradley had to withdraw all further showings of the commercial; but once the last straw has broken a camel's back, it's too late to take it off, and that ad was the last straw for a lot of decent people who had only with reluctance forgiven the Governor for peddling the mug shot of Christopher in the spring.

There wasn't much of a campaign for Pat in 1966. Jess, who could have put it together, had been denied a position of leadership because Pat and Hale wanted to show they didn't need him to help them gain the victory they at first so confidently expected over the washed-up cowboy actor.

It transpired that nobody around Pat actually knew how to run a campaign, and the C.D.C., which had been doing most of the Democratic precinct work over the last ten years, was so demoralized by Alan Cranston's loss to Salinger, among other things, that it accomplished very little, and Pat lost to Reagan by almost a million votes.

Pat Brown stands in history as a good illustration of the truth of the old political adage, "Incumbents are not defeated by their opponents; they defeat themselves."

I suppose it is only appropriate in a democracy that it should be so, that those who govern should be subject to the same laws as those who are governed. Most people are, after all, the authors of their own humiliations, even as Jess was in 1963, when we locked up the Republicans for too long, and in 1966, when he let Pat Brown and Hale Champion psych him out of helping the Democrats win the general elections.

And that, in case you ever wondered about it, is how Ronald Reagan got his start in politics.

22

The Old Ordure Changeth

The old order changeth, yielding
place to new;
And God fulfills himself in
many ways.

Alfred, Lord Tennyson

*T*he story I've told about Jess Unruh is not simply one that took place in and around the neoclassical State Capitol of California in the early 1960's. The reaction of Pat Brown to Jess Unruh represents a laboratory example of the normal response of a head of state to a subordinate who is abler than himself and doesn't take pains to conceal it from the world at large. That has always been looked upon as unforgivable bad taste by the rulers of men. Human nature has not changed since David served King Saul far better than he could serve himself, and that fact became apparent to the children of Israel.

For the student of political science the career of Jess Unruh is also a case study of how casually history is often made. His projected rise into a high orbit was aborted by a chance thought that flashed upon the befuddled mind of Victor V. Veysey on a carefree walk back to the Capitol after a too-liquid lunch. Unruh's career illustrates the great truth promulgated by Hodding Carter: "Nine out of ten events that occur in the name of government are not the result of careful deliberation or conspiracy, but of accident, mistake, or inadvertence."

With the flight of the amiable owl south from Sacramento in the winter of 1966, a dark age of lowered expectations descended upon the state. However, Pat Brown's own personal expectations were not lowered. Getting beaten was the best thing that had ever happened to him, from a monetary standpoint. He went to live in Los Angeles and practice law there. Since he is shrewd, tough, charming, capable, and famous, he has made a fortune in the years since he relinquished the reins of California's government to the greatest cowboy actor in the history of politics.

I am delighted whenever I see Pat now. He is full of good humor and high spirits, and he enjoys reminiscing about our historic joint accomplishments during his years as governor.

As to Jess Unruh, his situation was altered as profoundly as Pat Brown's by the election of 1966. Pat's loss was really more of a downer for Jess than it was for Pat. It gave California a glossy new governor, one who loved to veto the kind of legislation that Jess lived to pass, so that his remarkable ability to get bills through the Legislature no longer counted for much with anyone, including himself. He was diminished also by the scattering of his little band of merry men. Jerry Waldie and Tom Bane had both run for Congress. Jerry had won and Tom had lost, but neither of them could run for Congress and re-election at the same time, so the Speaker lost two of his closest friends in the Assembly. And 1966 was the year Bob Visnick and the press destroyed Charlie Meyers.

At the same time Bob Crown had drifted away from Jess. That was an indirect consequence of the Speaker's having announced he was giving some thought to running for the State Senate in one of the new Los Angeles County districts created by the court-ordered reapportionment of 1966. After 1963 he yearned for a graceful way to get out of the Assembly, but what he told us was that he felt he was getting too badly battle-scarred as the speaker of the Assembly to hope for election to higher office. As the favorite target of the Republicans, the conservative press, and what was left of the C.D.C., he was getting more bad publicity, day in and day out, than any other public official in the state, and he said he thought he needed a respite to recover from it.

When he'd first publicly speculated that he might run for one of the open seats in the newly reapportioned Senate, Carlos Bee resurrected his own hopes of being speaker. Carlos started to call on the members in their offices to ask them to vote for him for speaker, if Jess decided to leave the Assembly. Bob wanted the job, too, and appealed to Jess to help him get it. Without Unruh's intervention, Carlos would surely have won. For years Carlos Bee had spent every night he was in Sacramento eating, drinking, and gambling with members of the Assembly, while Bob Crown was eating, drinking, and gamboling with their secretaries.

Jess looked inconsolably glum on the day when Bob asked him for his help. Carlos, ever since he had stepped aside in favor of Jess in the speakership fight of 1961, had been totally loyal in every crisis and in every conflict. Jess reported to me sadly on the floor after his conversation with Bob, "I had to tell Bobby that I don't see how I can reward Carlos for his loyalty by taking sides against him." Bob was crushed by that reply politically and emotionally.

In the final event, Jess decided to remain as speaker, partly, I think, because he couldn't stand the thought of watching Bobby go down to defeat; but by that time Bob had withdrawn from all of us like Achilles to his tent, to brood over his grievances. It was a terrible thing to witness. Theirs had been a Homeric friendship.

Bob Crown never let himself be close to anybody in the Assembly again. He served until 1972, when he was run down and killed by a drunk driver while he was jogging one evening in his hometown of Alameda.

I, too, left that charmed fraternity that had gathered around the Speaker. When the court ordered that the State Senate be reapportioned on the basis of population in time for the 1966 elections, a new Democratic seat was created in San Diego County. Everyone expected me to run for it, but I really didn't want to. In the Assembly I was the senior committee chairman and one of a small group of friends who ran the house. In the Senate I would be a freshman without any influence on the leadership, which was a closed circle of a few old cronies. It never occurred to me that I would be the leader of the Senate in just four years, at the beginning of my second term. The main reason I ran was that I was told that if I didn't, my old nemesis, Hugo Fisher, would. We had been locked in conflict during all of the time Hugo was in the Senate before. I shuddered at the thought of going through a never-ending ordeal by combat again. So I ran for the Senate, as did Nick Petris, Tom Carrell, Byron Rumford, and a dozen other assemblymen, including George Deukmejian, on his way to the governor's mansion.

The Kennedy White House, in the mythology of the time, became a new Camelot, a magic lantern show of chivalry on the banks of the Potomac. It seemed to me there was a like Arthurian mirage on the banks of the Sacramento at the same time. In the glistening white palace where the rulers of California occupied their various thrones, the most heroic of them all had a trusty band of companions who loved to join him in doing battle with the forces of darkness and in coming to the aid of the friendless and the afflicted, just as they loved to join him in eating and drinking at tables round, oval, square, oblong, and every other shape.

In Camelot and in Washington, the wounds suffered by the prince were physically mortal, while in Sacramento they were only politically so, but in all three cases the roistering brotherhood of romantic heroes that had gathered around him was dispersed beyond recall.

Oh, it's true that Jess Unruh held on for another two years as speaker of the Assembly, and he surrounded himself with a new and younger circle of paladins; but it was as if King Arthur had recovered somewhat from his wounds and had recruited a troop of fresh-faced, unscarred youths to take the place of his old band of battered but lusty companions.

As I look back on those years, I find that, like Pat Brown, I take pleasure in my memories of them. I know our best battles were not fought in vain. Remembering that Jess, with our help, made the California Legislature the best in the United States still fills me with pride. And I like to recall that we helped him improve the school systems of the state and that we helped Jerry Waldie make life more enjoyable and more rewarding for mentally retarded children, and that we extended some basic rights to a lot of Americans who didn't happen to be born white. Such things are much more worthwhile than anything most people ever get to do.

Having left Jess in the Assembly when I went to the Senate in 1966, I can't tell any more of his story from the point of view of one in daily contact with him, but I can add that his loss to Ronald Reagan in 1970 as the Democratic nominee for governor was like King Arthur's last battle. Tired of warfare, sore with old injuries, and weary of pride, he decided to go down fighting, and so to put an end to his dream, which had become impossible.

Appendix

*T*he California Democratic Council was estab-
lished in 1953 at a meeting called by Alan Cranston, who is now the
senior U.S. senator from California. He invited representatives of
the Adlai Stevenson Club movement, which had been organized by
Democrats throughout California as a component in the presidential campaign of 1952, to convene at Asilomar on the Monterey
Peninsula.

He got them together to suggest to them that a statewide
organization of Democrats should not be allowed to expire. The
Republican Party had a volunteer auxiliary called the Republican
Associates, which was doing the G.O.P. a valuable service by
endorsing candidates in the primary elections. The Democrats
sorely needed such an endorsing body, Alan said. With that
thought he rang more bells than the hunchback of Notre Dame.

In his campaign for re-election the previous year, William
Knowland, the archconservative Republican floor leader in the
U.S. Senate, had won the Democratic nomination as well as that of
the G.O.P. Big Bill Knowland, as the Democratic nominee for the
U.S. Senate, had been for active Democrats a large and bitter pill to
swallow.

That had been possible because in those days cross-filing was
allowed under California law. That is, anyone who wanted to run
for office could file to run for the nomination of both parties in the
primary elections. And there was not even a requirement that a
candidate indicate his or her own party affiliation on the ballot.

Under cross-filing, money decided who the nominees of both parties should be because the official party organizations had been forbidden to support any candidate until he or she won the nomination of the party. The Republicans always had a lot more money to spend than we did, and they were often able to buy the Democratic nominations for the Republican nominees through media campaigns. They even garnered the Democratic nomination for governor for the Republican incumbent on occasion.

The official Democratic party could do nothing about the problem. However, there was a loophole in the law. It had never occurred to the Republicans who had begotten that system to get a bill enacted prohibiting political volunteers from supporting candidates. The Republican Associates had established a precedent by stepping into the power vacuum on the Republican side and endorsing candidates in primary elections. The California Democratic Council came into being at Asilomar as a Democratic counterpart of the Republican Associates for the purpose of putting a semiofficial seal of approval on candidates in the Democratic primary elections. Before each primary, the C.D.C. sent every registered Democrat in the state a mailer that listed the names of the candidates in each race who had been endorsed by the C.D.C.

Receiving the C.D.C. endorsement soon became tantamount to winning the Democratic nomination for any office, and once we were able to nominate Democrats, we were able to elect them in the more Democratic districts. We began to move slowly toward control of the state for the first time since the Civil War.

I was a typical product of the C.D.C., a volunteer in politics, an idealist of the purest ray serene, a political amateur among political amateurs. That was how I came to be endorsed by the C.D.C., nominated, and elected.

Epilogue

*O*ver the course of the last ten years I have been assembling this book from my own memories and those of others who took part in the events described. Naturally, I hoped Jess Unruh would see it in its final form; but just as it was going to press he died of cancer, after having served the people of California as state treasurer since 1975.

No one now questions the fact that he was the most notable member of the California Legislature in the history of our state. Similarly, no one questions the fact that he made much more of the office of state treasurer—and accomplished far more that was in the public interest while he occupied it—than anyone else who ever held that title. In whatever role he appeared, there was a Shakespearean dimension to him.

I hope I have contributed, through this book, to his being remembered for what he was: a heroic figure in an age when heroism has become uncommon.

Index